Reader's Digest Paperbacks

Informative..... Entertaining..... Essential.....

Berkley, one of America's leading paperback publishers, is proud to present this special series of the best-loved articles, stories and features from America's most trusted magazine. Each is a one-volume library on a popular and important subject. And each is selected, edited and endorsed by the Editors of Reader's Digest themselves!

Berkley/Reader's Digest books

THE AMERICAN SPIRIT
THE ART OF LIVING
DRAMA IN REAL LIFE®
"I AM JOE'S BODY"
KEEPING FIT
THE LIVING WORLD OF NATURE
LOVE AND MARRIAGE
RAISING KIDS
SECRETS OF THE PAST
TESTS AND TEASERS
UNFORGETTABLE CHARACTERS
WORD POWER

THE AMERICAN SPIRIT

THE EDITORS OF

Reader's Digest®

A BERKLEY/READER'S DIGEST BOOK
published by
BERKLEY BOOKS, NEW YORK

THE AMERICAN SPIRIT
A Berkley/Reader's Digest Book, published by arrangement with
Reader's Digest Press

PRINTING HISTORY
Berkley/Reader's Digest edition/May 1981

All rights reserved.
Copyright © 1981 by the Reader's Digest Association, Inc.
Copyright © 1936, 1939, 1942, 1943, 1947, 1950, 1951, 1952, 1955,
1957, 1958, 1960, 1961, 1962, 1963, 1965, 1966, 1967, 1968, 1969,
1972, 1973, 1974, 1975, 1976, 1977, 1978, 1979 by the Reader's
Digest Association, Inc.
Cover design by Sam Salant.
This book may not be reproduced in whole or in part, by mimeograph
or any other means, without permission.
For information address: Berkley Publishing Corporation, 200 Madison
Avenue, New York, New York 10016.

ISBN: 0-425-05016-5

A BERKLEY BOOK ® TM 757,375
PRINTED IN THE UNITED STATES OF AMERICA

Grateful acknowledgment is made to the following organizations and individuals for permission to reprint material from the indicated sources:

The *Saturday Review* for "The Man in the White Marble Toga" by Marshall Fishwick, copyright © 1960 by the Saturday Review. All Rights reserved; The *Journal of the American Medical Association* (July 12, 1958) for "The Spivacks Beat the Odds" by John Steinbeck, copyright © 1958 by the American Medical Association; *Kiwanis* Magazine for "My Name is Ilya" by William Sambrot, copyright © 1951 by Kiwanis International; *Texas Monthly* for "Moonstruck" by Al Reinert, copyright © 1979 by Texas Monthly; Jim Irwin quotations from "To Rule the Night: The Discovery Voyage of Astronaut Jim Irwin" copyright © 1973 by Jim Irwin and William A. Emerson Jr., Published by A.J. Holman Co.; Michael Collins, quotations from "Carrying the Fire: An Astronaut's Journey," copyright © 1974 by Michael Collins, published by Farrar, Straus and Giroux, Inc.; The Yale University Press for "The Source of All Our Strength" by Dr. A.W. Griswold, copyright © 1954 by Yale University Press. This article appeared in the volume ESSAYS ON EDUCATION by Dr. A. Whitney Griswold; Mr. Gay Talese for "Offbeat Wonders of New York" by Gay Talese, copyright © 1960 by Gay Talese; *Holiday* Magazine for "The Glorious Great Lakes" copyright © 1968 by The Curtis Publishing Co.; American Legion for "The Life and Death of Casey Jones" by Tom Mahoney, copyright © 1966 by the *American Legion Magazine*, stanzas from "Casey Jones," copyright © 1909 by Newton and Siebert, copyright renewed and assigned to Shapiro, Bernstein and Co., Inc.; Curtis Brown Ltd., for "Suburbia: Of Thee I Sing" by Phyllis McGinley, originally published in *Good Housekeeping*, copyright © 1953 by Phyllis McGinley; The Travelers Insurance Companies for "Old Ben Franklin and His Miserable Maxims" by Mark Twain, from *Protection* Magazine (March 1965) published by the Travelers Insurance Co., Hartford, Conn; *The New York Times* for the following: "The Night John Alden Spoke for Himself" by Russell Baker, copyright © 1966 by the New York Times Co., "Genesis Passes Congress" by Russell Baker, copyright © 1978 by the New York Times Co., "All Quiet on the Western Front" by Jerry Klein, copyright © 1976 by the New York Times Co. and "Thanksgiving USA" by Janina

Atkins, copyright © 1978 by the New York Times Co.; The Stephen Green Press for "Wit and Wisdom from Vermont" condensed from WHAT THE OLD-TIMER SAID by Allen R. Foley, copyright © 1971 by Allen Foley; Harper & Row Inc. for "Our Town's Only Republican" condensed from MY LIFE AND TIMES by Turner Catledge, copyright © 1971 by Turner Catledge; Mr. Art Buchwald for "Last of the Big Time Spenders" by Art Buchwald, copyright © 1978 by Art Buchwald; Harper & Row for "Dark Yesterdays, Bright Tomorrows" condensed from STRENGTH TO LOVE by Martin Luther King Jr., copyright © 1963 by Martin Luther King Jr.; The Estate of Donald C. Peattie and agent, James Brown Associates, Inc. for "Your Bill of Rights" by Donald Peattie, originally appeared in *Reader's Digest* June, 1947; Mr. Henry Lee for "Our Lives, Our Fortune and Our Sacred Honor" originally appeared in *Collier's Magazine* May 1955; *Redbook* Magazine for "The Night the Martians Landed" by Edwin H. James, copyright © 1950 by the Redbook Publishing Co.; Simon & Schuster for "Baseball Stories for a Rainy Afternoon" condensed from FIVE SEASONS by Roger Angell, copyright © 1972, 1973, 1974, 1975, 1976, 1977, by Roger Angell; Doubleday & Co. Inc. for "My Search for My Roots" condensed from Alex Haley's ROOTS, copyright © 1976 by Alex Haley published by Doubleday & Co.; Brandt & Brandt for "Our Newest American" by Albert Q. Maisel originally appeared in *Reader's Digest* January, 1957; "The Epic Story of Gettysburg" from THE HALLOWED GROUND by Bruce Catton, copyright © 1955, 1956 by Bruce Catton, reprinted by permission of Doubleday & Co. Inc.; *Army Times* for "I Died a Soldier" by Hiram D. Strickland, copyright © 1967 by Army Times Publishing Co. Wash. D.C.; "A Walk with Robert Frost" from THE POETRY OF ROBERT FROST edited by Edward Connery Lathem, copyright © 1923 © 1969 by Holt, Rinehart and Winston, copyright 1936, 1951 © 1958, 1962 by Robert Frost, copyright © 1964 by Lesley Frost Ballantine, reprinted by permission of Holt, Rinehart and Winston, Publishers. The William Morris Agency for "An Old-Time Iowa Christmas" by Paul Engle, copyright © 1958 Paul Engle; Curtis Brown Ltd. for "Small Town Parade, Decoration Day" by Phyllis McGinley, originally published in *Good Housekeeping* May 1953, copyright © 1953 by Phyllis McGinley; Charles Scribner's Sons for "American October" condensed from OF TIME AND THE RIVER by Thomas Wolfe, copyright © 1935 by Charles Scribner's Sons; 1001 AFTERNOONS IN NEW YORK by Ben Hecht, copyright 1941 by The Viking Press, Inc., © renewed 1969 by Rose Hecht. Condensed by permission of Viking Penguin Inc.

Contents

THE FREE AND THE BRAVE
The Man in the White Marble Toga 3
Unforgettable "Bull" Halsey 7
Kosciuszko: Hero of Two Worlds 13
Our Legacy from Mr. Jefferson 18

NEW WORLD
Who Really Discovered America? 25
Homage to the Vanishing Prairie 30
"Free Land!" The Saga of the Homesteaders 34

BOLD DREAMS
The Spivacks Beat the Odds 41
"My Name Is Ilya!" 43
Moonstruck 46
The Source of All Our Strength 52
Xerox—The Invention That Hit the Jackpot 56
Unforgettable John Wayne 60

LAND AND PEOPLE
Country of My Heart 69
Offbeat Wonders of New York 74
Along California's Golden Coast 77
The Glorious Great Lakes 82
The Life and Death of Casey Jones 87

THE WAY WE LIVE NOW
Name-Changing—It's the Custom! **95**
On the Road With Charles Kuralt **98**
Suburbia: Of Thee I Sing **102**
Crack! Roar! It's World Series Time **107**
Comeback of the Small Town **112**

NATIVE WITS
Old Ben Franklin and His Miserable Maxims **119**
The Night John Alden Spoke for Himself **121**
Wit and Wisdom From Vermont **123**
Our Town's Only Republican **127**
Genesis Passes Congress **130**
Last of the Big Spenders **132**

HERITAGE OF FREEDOM
Dark Yesterdays, Bright Tomorrows **137**
The Right to Speak Out **141**
What America Means to Me **147**
Your Bill of Rights **149**
"... Our Lives, Our Fortunes and Our Sacred Honor" **153**

ONLY YESTERDAY
The Night the Martians Landed **161**
Campaign Buttons U.S.A. **166**
Baseball Stories for a Rainy Afternoon **168**
Thanks, Hazel **173**

MELTING POT
My Search for Roots **181**
The Happiest Man **186**
Our Newest Americans **191**
"I Give You Mr. Charley American!" **196**

FIGHTING FOR FREEDOM
The British Are Coming! 203
All Quiet on the Western Front 208
"Not Far From God" 210
The Epic Story of Gettysburg 214
"I Died a Soldier" 221

AMERICAN VOICES
Listen to the Sound of America! 225
A Walk With Robert Frost 228
Walt Whitman's Song of Democracy 231
The Wizard Who Created Oz 238

AMERICA CELEBRATES
An Old-Time Iowa Christmas 245
Small-Town Parade, Decoration Day 249
American October 251
Thanksgiving U.S.A.—The Privilege 253
New York Snowstorm Reverie 255
When Summer Bursts 257

The Free and the Brave

The Man in the White Marble Toga

by Marshall Fishwick

HE IS STILL first in everything. His aloof alabaster face stares at us from monuments, paintings, coins, postage stamps. Towns named after him are everywhere. Beds he slept in are relics, stones he stepped on are sacred, battles he lost are victories. But who among us really loves him? George Washington is the Man in the White Marble Toga.

Let the super-salesmen of the happiness cult in our times take note. The Father of Our Country did not have the quick smile and neat phrase which we are all urged to cultivate. He kept his distance, and few men called him George. We visit his tomb today not so much to pay our respects to a man as to visit a shrine. His body may be at Mount Vernon, but his spirit looks down from Mount Olympus.

This seems all the more incredible when we piece together what is known of the living Washington. There were fire and venom and drama enough in him. He was the soldier who wanted news "on the spur of speed, for I am all impatience"; the man who cursed his troops when they ran "like the wild bears of the mountains." He was the young buck who once danced for three hours without a pause, and the country boy whose stories about jackasses were decidedly Rabelaisian. There was hotter blood in Washington's veins than the dames of the D.A.R. dream of.

Yet, even during his life people referred to Washington as a "demigod." In 1800 a Pennsylvania farmer wrote *Washington's Ankunft in Elisium* [Washington's Arrival in Heaven], depicting the General strolling around heaven, chatting with Brutus, Alexander and Columbus. When the Russian diplomat Paul Svinin visited America a few years later, he wrote in his diary, "Every American considers it his sacred duty to have a likeness of Washington in his home, just as we have images of God's saints."

The worship of Washington jumped oceans with ease.

Translations of the Farewell Address girdled the world. In France, Napoleon Bonaparte ordered ten days of national mourning when Washington died. The modest squire of Mount Vernon became world-famous, and his legend supported a structure international in design and craftsmanship.

Many historic factors help explain this phenomenon. Washington was capable, aristocratic, commanding; he had the look of greatness. He lived at a time, and participated in events which aroused the heroic. His incredible patience and tenacity personified the colonies' noble but difficult task. He refused to usurp military or civilian power. When the times that tried men's souls were past, he returned to the land.

Washington's aloofness preserves his reputation, but it also minimizes his warm-blooded, human side. Think of Washington in Newburgh, N.Y., in 1783 when confronted by the impetuous document of his officers who felt mistreated by the Continental Congress. "Gentlemen, you will permit me to put on my spectacles, for I have not only grown gray, but almost blind in the service of my country," he said. Not a man felt, after that simple statement, that he should complain.

Recall the directions Washington's step-grandson gave a visitor at Mount Vernon. "You will meet with an old gentleman riding alone, in plain, drab clothes, a broad-brimmed white hat, a hickory switch in his hand, and carrying an umbrella with a long staff, which is attached to his saddle bow. That is General Washington."

By his own efforts, George Washington won his place as father of his country. But it was not he who added the toga. That was the work of many who admired him, but who never called him George. History, biography, oratory, journalism, poetry, art and fiction played their part.

Some of the legends about Washington can be attributed to specific sources. We know that Parson Weems, an 18th-century preacher, bookseller and poor man's Plutarch, invented the cherry-tree story and the tale about a Quaker named Potts finding Washington praying fervently in the snow-covered woods near Valley Forge. But all the scholars put together cannot erase the legend.

To no single source, however, can be attributed the notions that Washington was a man apart, with no real friends and too heavy a burden to smile; that he concealed a deep,

The Man in the White Marble Toga

unrequited passion for a haughty colonial beauty.

More elaborate are stories of Washington's miraculous escapes from danger. One has an Indian chief turning to his men during the Braddock rout and saying, "Mark yon tall and daring warrior? He is not of the redcoat tribe. He hath an Indian's wisdom, and his warriors fight as we do—himself alone is exposed. Quick, let your aim be certain, and he will die!" But no Indian bullet can find him. "It is in vain," concludes the chief. "The Great Spirit protects that man and guides his life."

In all the tales about him, Washington epitomizes the traits of which young America was fondest: virtue, idealism and piety. His flaws seem pale when held up against this central proposition: he was willing to stake his life and fortune on his high principles, to take up without question a task others could not perform.

The South was particularly proud of this Virginia aristocrat, who became the model for the antebellum planter class. "How much more delightful to an undebauched mind," Washington wrote to a friend in 1788, "is the task of making improvements on the earth than all the vain glories which can be acquired from ravaging it." Even the Republicans, out of sympathy with Federalist policies, were in accord with Washington's agrarian sympathies. Jefferson opposed him, but never stopped respecting him. "Washington was indeed, in every way," he wrote in 1814, "a wise, a good, and a great man."

The blue cloth fades, and the white marble remains. In one of his more puckish moments, Nathaniel Hawthorne asked if anyone had ever seen Washington nude. "It is inconceivable," Hawthorne concluded. "He has no nakedness, but was born with his clothes on, and his hair powdered, and made a stately bow on his first appearance in the world."

Men in gray flannel suits may learn a lot from the story of the man in the white marble toga. It is not by bending to every whim and request that we achieve real popularity, or by following every popular cause that we become great. There are times to smile, and times to scowl; to confuse the occasions is an act of cowardice. Washington lacked many of the attributes of some heads of chambers of commerce and multi-echelon organizations. The one thing he never lacked, even when he was in error or defeat, was *integrity*. Washington never looked to see which way opportunism pointed. That is why he became father of his country.

That same country, and the men who guide its destiny today, might well ponder this story.

Unforgettable "Bull" Halsey

by Admiral Arleigh Burke, USN (Ret.)

THE FIRST time I came face to face with Bull Halsey, I was literally shaking in my boots. He was the most famous admiral in the world, and I was in deep trouble. He sat behind his desk, the three stars of a vice admiral on his collar, shoulders squared, piercing eyes stabbing through me. For all the heat outside, the room grew very cold.

These were the desperate days of 1942, when the Japanese controlled both air and sea throughout the South Pacific. U.S. Marines had landed on Guadalcanal in August, but were holding on by their fingernails against an enemy who wanted this key to the Solomon Islands as a staging point for the conquest of Australia. If the U.S. Navy had owned a fleet of battleships and carriers, it would have sent them to help. Instead, it sent Vice Adm. William F. Halsey, Jr.

I joined Halsey down there as a commander in charge of Destroyer Division 43. My ships had been fighting some tough battles without major maintenance, and were in rough shape; just about everything that could go wrong with them already had. For weeks, I had bombarded Halsey's office with letters, raising hell because we weren't getting what we needed. I didn't know it then, but Halsey had no choice in the matter. He had nothing to give anybody, and was only too aware that one thin line of gray ships was all that stood between our boys on Guadalcanal and disaster.

Every night we were out fighting the Japanese as they came "down the slot," through the Solomons toward Guadalcanal. Our ships took severe damage and became less and less effective. Morale suffered, and to make matters worse, our battle-weary men had no beer, no whiskey, no recreation. In desperation, I drew up orders sending the destroyers to Sydney for repairs, and radioed Halsey that they were leaving. Back came the reply: "Keep them in the Solomons." It happened once. It happened again.

8 The Free and the Brave

One boiler of the destroyer *Saufley* was in such bad shape that I finally decided to send her to Sydney without telling Halsey. We scraped together every cent in the squadron and gave it to *Saufley's* captain. While the ship's boiler was being repaired, he would buy beer and whiskey for us. Only when *Saufley* was on her way did I tell Halsey what I had done.

I expected a kickback and, sure enough, a message soon arrived, asking me to drop in on Halsey next time I happened to be around Nouméa, New Caledonia, where the command ship *Argonne* was anchored. I knew what *that* meant, and immediately set out.

When I marched into Halsey's office, I found him seated with his back to the door, staring at the bulkhead. After what seemed an eternity, he turned around and glanced at me. "Oh, Burke," he said. He looked down at some scribbled notes on his desk. *"Saufley,"* he muttered. Suddenly he sat bolt upright and peered at me.

"Why in God's name did you take it in your own hands to send *Saufley* to Sydney?"

My heart sank into my freshly shined shoes. I knew that my whole career was in that room with us.

"Sir," I began. "My boys haven't had any beer or whiskey for months...."

"You mean," Halsey interrupted, shaking his head as if he could not believe it, "... you mean you sent that ship down there for *booze?*"

I was about to tell my sad tale about *Saufley's* boiler, but something—it must have been the look on the admiral's face—held me back.

"Yes, sir, the captain did pick up a lot of liquor," I began again. "But..."

Halsey's face relaxed. "All right, Burke," he said. "You win. Your boys have been doing a great job, and I can't condemn you for going out on a limb for them. But don't do it again." He leveled a gnarled brown finger at me. "If you had told me that you sent *Saufley* for *repairs*, I'd have had your hide."

That's when I knew I would follow Admiral William Halsey anywhere in this world, or beyond. And so would thousands of other sailors, from the lowliest apprentice right on up the line. After the Japanese bombed and torpedoed Pearl Harbor, Halsey had led a task force to attack the Gilbert and

Marshall islands and carry Jimmy Doolittle's Tokyo Raiders on their historic mission to bomb the Japanese capital. Months later, a pair of sailors were on the second deck of Halsey's flagship one day, speculating on where Halsey might be taking them this time. "I don't care where we're going," one said. "I'd go to hell for that old s.o.b."

Someone rapped the bluejacket on the shoulder. The sailor turned to see Halsey himself standing there. "Not so old, son," said the admiral, a big grin on his bulldog face. "Not so old."

During the attack against the Marshalls, Halsey saucily took the carrier *Enterprise* in just offshore so his boys in the fighters and bombers would have plenty of gas to attack and get back to the ship. Suddenly, out of nowhere, a Japanese plane swung toward the *Enterprise*. On the bridge, everybody flattened to the deck, with several men flinging themselves across the admiral to protect him. The plane missed, and Halsey sat up, struggling to recover his balance and decorum. He saw one laughing face: a yeoman had watched the undignified descent of his superiors and was now unsuccessfully trying to control his mirth.

"Who's that man?" Shouted Halsey at the duty officer.

"That's Bowman, admiral. Yeoman Ira Bowman."

"*Chief* Yeoman Ira Bowman, you mean," said Halsey. "Anybody who can laugh when my knees are shaking is somebody who deserves to be promoted."

When Halsey came to Guadalcanal that grim October of 1942, the Marines were as close to being beaten as they had ever been. Yet from the very first his orders were: "Attack repeat ATTACK," and he paid no attention to complaints that his men did not have the planes and ships to do so. Suddenly, the tide in the Solomons began to change.

"It was as if they had handed us two carriers," said one grimy leatherneck on Guadalcanal.

"No," corrected his companion. "Two carriers and a battleship."

When I say that Halsey was loved, I do not mean that he was soft in any way; on the contrary, he was tough as hardtack. His nickname—"Bull"—was coined by a war correspondent in honor of his charge-ahead spirit. The crucial naval battle for Guadalcanal came one night in November, when the Japanese sent their strongest force, led by the battleship *Hiei*, to shell the island's airfield and pave the way for a new landing. All Halsey could throw into the breach was a force of cruisers and destroyers—obviously no match for the enemy. But throw them in he did, muttering, "You can't make omelets without breaking eggs."

Halsey sat in the loneliness of his office that long night, pretending to read a magazine as he waited for word. The first news was bad. Two cruisers and six destroyers had been lost, and with them Rear Admirals Daniel J. Callaghan and Norman Scott, both old friends of Halsey's. But there was good news, too: the Japanese landing was scuttled, the airfield had not been shelled, and the *Hiei* was badly damaged (it would fall victim to American bombers hours later). The price had been high, but he had won a victory.

Minutes after the U.S. triumph was confirmed, Halsey sent a message to every unit in his command. The word went out by radio, by signal blinker, by hand courier, to all the men who served under him:

"YOUR NAMES HAVE BEEN WRITTEN IN GOLDEN LETTERS ON THE PAGES OF HISTORY, AND YOU HAVE WON THE EVERLASTING GRATITUDE OF YOUR COUNTRYMEN. MY PRIDE IN YOU IS BEYOND EXPRESSION."

Bull Halsey was the son of a Naval officer and had lived with discipline all his life, from his days at Pingry School in Elizabeth, N.J., through the Naval Academy at Annapolis, where he was a football star, right on up through the ranks in destroyers and later in the Navy's air arm. He was past 50 years old when he learned to fly. Because he was going to command a carrier, he felt he first ought to learn how to take orders about flying. He never was much of a pilot, although his instructors admitted that, for some reason, the worse the weather, the better Halsey flew. I know why that was: he regarded the weather as just another obstacle to be overcome.

What I learned from Halsey in the war—the lessons of command, the characteristics of leadership—has served me well in all the years that followed, years in which I held a variety of posts throughout the Navy. For example:

Confidence. Bull Halsey possessed to a magnificent degree the intuition that let him know just how to get the best out of his people under any conditions. After the *Saufley* affair, we kept our destroyers going and fought the Japanese as hard as we could. The admiral sensed that, and never bothered us with unnecessary instructions. One night early in 1943, he warned me that a number of Japanese destroyers were coming our way. "Proceed. You know what to do," was all his message said.

We did proceed, at 31 knots, a creditable speed considering the condition of our destroyers' boilers. We found the Japanese force and smashed it. Back at headquarters, Halsey grinned proudly and gave me a nickname: "Thirty-One-Knot Burke." My destroyer squadron had proved what he knew: give men the incentive, the opportunity and the information, and they will excel themselves as we had done that night, fighting for a commander whom we respected and loved.

Self-Control. When Halsey's son, young Lt. Bill Halsey, was reported missing from a carrier in the South Pacific, a member of the admiral's staff brought him the news and waited for special orders for the search. "Get the planes out," said Halsey. "But search for him exactly as you would search for any other father's son in the Pacific."

Not that Halsey didn't worry. He nearly cried when word came that Bill was safe. I remember, too, that when I saw him in Nouméa he was not long recovered from a serious case of shingles, brought on by concern for his wife, Fan, who had fallen ill while he was aboard the *Enterprise*. Halsey had fought on, controlling his illness, until called back to Pearl Harbor on the eve of the Battle of Midway. He would have led his task force at Midway except that the commander in chief of the U.S. Pacific Fleet, Adm. Chester Nimitz, had taken one look at him and put him in the hospital.

Responsibility. Although quick to delegate authority, Halsey always accepted full responsibility. A lot of Naval officers are convinced that he made one of the war's great mistakes at the Battle of Leyte Gulf, when he went off on a wild-goose chase after the Japanese carriers, allowing their surface fleet to attack our landing forces. "It was a hell of a mistake," he said later. "But, given the information I had that night, I would do it again."

I rather lost track of Admiral Halsey after the war. He had quickly retired from the Navy, feeling that his usefulness was over. When he died, in 1959, I offered a few words at the funeral. But, being a tongue-tied Swede, could not say what I really felt: that I loved him and had learned the great lessons of my life from him.

One of those lessons I put into action that very year. When Fidel Castro brought his revolution down out of Cuba's Sierra Maestra, we had word in Washington from a number of American citizens living in Nicaro who feared for their lives. As Chief of Naval Operations, I had the job of getting them out. The only American ship anywhere near the area was a small Navy transport commanded by a very junior reserve officer. I sent him orders to get in and "protect American lives and property." He radioed for further orders. "Your replacement will bring them," I radioed back.

It was all the incentive he needed. He moved his ship in, sent an armed shore party onto the beach and pulled those people out as neatly as if he had been doing it all his life. I chuckled to myself when I got the word. Bull Halsey would have been proud of that youngster.

Kosciuszko: Hero of Two Worlds

by Thomas Fleming

At 4 A.M. early in May 1798, a covered coach carrying the Vice President of the United States, Thomas Jefferson, pulled up to a stop before a Philadelphia rooming house. A slight, gaunt man in a military cloak emerged from the darkened doorway, hobbled on crutches to the carriage and climbed into the seat beside Jefferson. The effort brought rasps of pain to the crippled man's lips. The coach rumbled off into the night.

Poland's Tadeusz Kosciuszko was once more in the service of his "second country"—the United States of America. For six years, without a single furlough, he had fought for America's independence. Now, Jefferson was sending him to Paris as an envoy to help the infant United States avoid a ruinous war with revolutionary France. Jefferson was convinced that only an envoy of considerable stature could keep the peace. Kosciuszko was that man.

Most contemporary Americans recognize Kosciuszko's name. But outside the Polish-American community only a handful of scholars know of the remarkable and romantic role Kosciuszko (Kôs-chōōsh′ko) played in the winning of America's independence. For this gallant, tragic figure was passionately devoted to the cause of freedom, both here and in his native Poland. "He is," Jefferson once remarked, "as pure a son of liberty as I have ever known."

Kosciuszko was 30 when he came to America in the summer of 1776. His own country had been crushed by Russia and had lost one-third of its territory to Russia, Prussia and Austria. Kosciuszko had studied military engineering and artillery in France and, since America's revolutionary army badly needed engineers, Congress gave him a colonel's commission and $60 a month. Maj. Gen. Horatio Gates sent him north to strengthen Fort Ticonderoga, guarding the "invasion highway" from Canada. But the over-confident Americans at the fort ignored Kosciuszko's repeated advice to fortify Mount Defiance, which overlooked Ticonderoga.

Kosciuszko's gentle temperament and the fact that he was a foreigner made it difficult for him to deal with the brash Americans. When they scoffed at his recommendation, he dropped it. "I love peace and to be on good terms with all the world if possible," he told Gates. Rather than get his way by quarreling, he would "return home and plant cabbages." Scarcely more than a month later, the British hauled cannon to the top of Mount Defiance, and Ticonderoga's defenders had no alternative but humiliating retreat.

Instead of blaming them, Kosciuszko worked feverishly to keep the British army at bay. He and his men filled creeks with debris to make them unnavigable, broke down bridges, felled hundreds of trees to slow the British advance. When Horatio Gates became supreme commander of the Northern Army, he ordered Kosciuszko to select a position where they could make a stand. The young Pole soon had 1000 men toiling on fortifications along the Hudson near Saratoga. The British army, commanded by Gen. John Burgoyne, smashed itself to ruins on Kosciuszko's fortifications and surrendered to Gates on October 17, 1777. It was the turning point of the American Revolution.

Kosciuszko's next assignment was West Point, that huge ridge of rock and earth jutting into the Hudson River in the heart of New York's highlands. George Washington called it the most important post in America, and ordered Kosciuszko to make it impregnable. For more than two years, Kosciuszko laid out a series of redoubts and forts—a system depending upon depth, mutual support and use of terrain that was 100 years ahead of its time. The result was "the American Gibraltar," a fortress so strong that the British never even dared to attack it.

Kosciuszko next became chief engineer of the American Army of the South, commanded by the fighting Quaker, Nathanael Greene. He selected encampments and battlefield sites, and supervised the construction of a fleet of boats which enabled Greene's retreating army to escape the hotly pursuing enemy. When the British finally fell back to Charleston, Kosciuszko turned cavalry commander and fought a number of ferocious battles with British patrols outside the city. In one of these clashes, Kosciuszko led a headlong charge against some 300 British infantry backed by cannon. When the fight ended, he found four bullet holes in his coat.

In spite of his remarkable record, Kosciuszko did not receive a promotion from the Continental Congress until after the war. The reason was politics. When the French finally decided to aid the Americans, they sent a group of engineers, who arrived in 1777, led by an abrasive character named Louis le Bègue de Presle Duportail. He demanded and got from a frightened Congress, over the objection of General Washington, the rank of brigadier general and command of the Continental Army's engineers.

Kosciuszko's friends were outraged and began protesting to Congress. Washington himself wrote a letter in which he called Kosciuszko "deserving of notice too." Kosciuszko put a stop to the quarrel with a single letter to Congress. "If you see that my promotion will make a great many jealous," he wrote in his disarming prose, "tell the General that I will not accept of one because I prefer peace more than the greatest Rank in the World."

The good-natured patience with which Kosciuszko bore such Gallic intrigue and his refusal to seek a promotion made him one of the most popular officers in the American Army. Although he himself was the son of a minor Polish noble, he detested aristocratic pretensions. To him, aristocracy was synonymous with the exploitation and corruption which had destroyed Poland. Years later, his will would leave all the money he had received as back pay from Congress—he served throughout the entire war without drawing more than a few months' salary—to the creation of a fund to purchase the freedom of Negro slaves, educate them and give them 100 acres of land and equipment to farm it. Unfortunately, the will was broken by avaricious relatives. But it remains a monument to his conviction that all men are born equal.

After the American Revolution, Kosciuszko returned to Europe with a fierce desire to restore Poland as an independent nation and to create within it the free society he had experienced in America. "We must all unite for one purpose," he wrote to a friend. "To free our country from the domination of foreigners, from the abasement and destruction of the very name of Pole." The Poles began reforming their nation, and he was appointed a major general in a revived Polish army. In 1792, the Russians invaded Poland, determined to crush these stirrings of independence. The division commanded by Kosciuszko distinguished itself repeatedly on the battlefield, but the Poles had no hope of victory over the huge Russian army. When the Polish king surrendered, Kosciuszko fled to Leipzig and organized a resistance movement.

In 1794, Kosciuszko and a small band of followers reentered Poland and proclaimed his "Act of Insurrection," based in part on the American Declaration of Independence. It denounced the tyranny which made Poland's revolt a necessity and declared as its goals "the re-establishment of national liberties and the independence of the Republic." Finally, it outlined a future government for Poland which strongly resembled that of America. Kosciuszko was named military commander in chief to direct the war against the Russians. For his uniform he chose a Polish peasant's white cloak.

Revolutionary France, the one nation that could have helped Poland, refused to come to Kosciuszko's aid. Both Russia and Prussia sent immense armies into Poland. For a while the Poles held their own, but when Austria joined the war with a third army, Poland's doom was sealed. Kosciuszko's forces were crushed in the savage battle of Maciejowice. As charging Cossacks overwhelmed his lines, Kosciuszko rode to meet them, sword in hand. A cavalry saber slashed open his head. A lance was driven deep into his hip. More dead than alive, he was carried off to a Russian prison, as were 10,000 compatriots.

Despite this defeat, Polish historians agree that Poland as a nation was reborn in Kosciuszko's act of insurrection. "Out of nonentity," one wrote, "he extracted an immense force, he demonstrated what the nation, even without foreign help, can accomplish. From a leader of a lost insurrection, he became forever a symbol of national resurrection."

Two years later, a new tsar offered Kosciuszko his freedom if he would swear allegiance. To free his fellow Poles suffering in Siberian prison camps, Kosciuszko agreed. Returning to America, he found dozens of old Army friends begging him to settle in their neighborhoods. The lance thrust in his hip had damaged nerves which forced him to use crutches most of the time. But he responded to Jefferson's plea and returned to Europe in 1798, becoming in the words of one observer, "the first link" in the eventual rapprochement between France and America.

Kosciuszko remained in Europe, hoping that the turmoil created by Napoleon Bonaparte would enable him to strike another blow for Poland. Friends in America, particularly Thomas Jefferson, pleaded with him to return. "My dear friend," Jefferson wrote. "Close a life of liberty in a land of liberty. Come and lay your bones with mine in the cemetery of Monticello." But Kosciuszko refused. Even after Napoleon's defeat, when the great powers brushed aside Kosciuszko's pleas on behalf of Poland, he kept a lonely exile's vigil on behalf of his betrayed country. To the end of his life, he never refused a plea for help from the unfortunate. People said that his horse learned to stop at the sight of a beggar, even before Kosciuszko tugged on the reins.

For two centuries, Kosciuszko's name has remained a living link between the United States and Poland. After World War I, when the Russian communists invaded Poland, a group of American airmen volunteered to help the Poles defend their freedom. They were led by Capt. Merian C. Cooper, a direct descendant of a colonial family at whose house Kosciuszko lived for a time while campaigning in South Carolina. Cooper and his friends called themselves the Kosciuszko Squadron, and they played a dynamic role in the series of little-known but enormously violent battles in which the Poles drove the Russians out of their country, securing for Poland nearly 20 precious years of independence.

"The title of 'an American' will always be sacred to me," Kosciuszko once said. It is abundantly clear that the name Kosciuszko should remain equally sacred to Americans.

Our Legacy from Mr. Jefferson

by Bruce Bliven

ONE NIGHT in 1962, at a dinner for leaders in the arts and sciences, President Kennedy said, "I think this is the most extraordinary collection of talent, of human knowledge, that has ever been gathered together at the White House—with the possible exception of when Thomas Jefferson dined alone."

Thomas Jefferson probably knew more than any single man of his age. In the breadth of his interests he was as amazing as Leonardo da Vinci. When he was in his early 30s a contemporary wrote that he could "plot an eclipse, survey a field, plan an edifice, break a horse, play the violin and dance the minuet."

Out of his prodigious energy came inventions, books, new ideas and new starts in every field of human endeavor. He was an expert in agriculture, archeology, architecture and medicine. He practiced crop rotation, soil conservation and contour plowing a century before these became standard practice, and he invented a plow superior to any other then in existence. He had a profound influence on architecture throughout America, especially when he discarded the Corinthian column in favor of the Ionic, believing it easier for craftsmen to construct. Many of his gadgets are still remembered—a machine for copying documents, an outdoor-indoor weathervane, a rotating desk.

In 1796 Jefferson became president of the American Philosophical Society, which helped to create the American philosophy, with its emphasis on freedom and progress. Members included illustrious men like David Rittenhouse, who built the world's first planetarium, Thomas Paine, author of *Common Sense*, Dr. Benjamin Rush, who anticipated psychiatry, Joseph Priestley, the discoverer of oxygen. They considered Jefferson their master because he knew *all* their fields.

The man whose work and thought were to shape this country so profoundly was born in 1743, son of a prosperous, self-educated man, a public surveyor and a colonel in the militia. His mother was a member of an old Virginia family, the Randolphs. The death of his father left him, at 14, with the responsibilities only the oldest male could, in those days, assume. He was graduated from William and Mary College in Williamsburg, Va., and for a few years practiced law.

His wife, to whom he was deeply devoted, died after ten years of married life; Jefferson in his grief shut himself up in his study for three weeks, pacing the floor night and day. Then he threw himself back into public life with a dedicated zeal that helped heal his wound. He became governor of Virginia, minister to France, Secretary of State, Vice President, then President of the United States.

Jefferson looked more like a philosopher than a President, and he had a philosopher's love of simplicity. When he was inaugurated he arrived alone on horseback, tied his horse to a fence and strolled over to be sworn in. He hated "Your Excellency," insisted on being called "Mr. Jefferson." Once a foreign ambassador called in full-dress uniform; Jefferson received him in slippers.

He was six-foot-two, spare but robust, with a ruddy complexion, angular features, sandy hair and a ramshackle informality of manner that his contemporaries criticized. "His clothes seem too small for him," one wrote. "He sits in a lounging manner, on one hip commonly; his face has a sunny aspect; his whole figure has a loose shackling air. His discourse was loose and rambling; and yet he scattered information wherever he went."

This untidy philosopher was actually quite disciplined. He got up at dawn, usually wrote and read until breakfast, then read for another hour. After a day of work he would burn the midnight oil, reading in Latin, Greek, French, Spanish, Italian and Anglo-Saxon, and laboriously taking notes on everything he read.

His accomplishments as President were prodigious, enabling him to rank with Washington and Lincoln. He sent the Lewis and Clark Expedition to open men's eyes to the riches of the continent. By the Louisiana Purchase he doubled the size of the United States. His administration was run so economically that the Treasury had a large surplus and he was able to abolish all internal taxes. In his Second Inaugural Address he could boast, "What farmer, what mechanic, what laborer ever sees a tax gatherer of the United States?" He helped to end, first in Virginia, then throughout the country, the tax-supported church, and thus made possible true religious freedom.

Of all Jefferson's many talents, one is central, the unifying thread of his career. He was above all a good, and tireless, writer. His complete works, now being published for the first time, will fill more than 50 volumes. He wrote at least 50,000 letters!

His colleagues early learned that he could draft a document better than anyone else, and when the time came to write the Declaration of Independence, at Philadelphia in 1776, the draftsmanship was his. Millions have thrilled to his flaming words: "We hold these truths to be self-evident, that all men are created equal..."

That same year he was called back to Virginia. His state was drafting a constitution, and he was responsible for drawing it up. He was in France when the Constitution of the United States was written, but it was he who later insisted that the Bill of Rights Amendments be drafted, guaranteeing freedom of religion, speech and press, trial by jury, and other safeguards of democracy.

He not only wrote books. He used them and revered them. When the British burned the Capitol and the newly assembled Library of Congress in 1814, Jefferson offered his own magnificent library to Congress, at its own valuation, to replace the lost books. According to historian Arthur E. Bestor, "The Library of Congress is the living monument of this transaction, and of Jefferson's principle of building democracy upon a foundation of vigorous, enlightened, fearless, intellectual effort." After his books went to Congress, Jefferson began gathering another library, which contained 1000 volumes by the time he died 11 years later.

For years Jefferson kept a "literary commonplace book" into which he copied quotations, excerpts and summaries. It was, in fact, by the incessant physical act of writing that Jefferson forged his own thought and his own evolving ideas, which in turn flowed into his never-ending stream of work.

He left his countrymen a rich legacy of ideas and examples—among them his diligent habit of putting thoughts into writing so that they became precise, capable of forming action. He founded libraries and universities because he believed that only a nation of educated people could remain free. The same doctrine applies to the individual: only an informed person, he believed, could help influence events, and so be independent of surrounding pressures. This is the true dignity of man.

America has apparently taken Jefferson's advice to heart, for no other country has devoted so much of its energy to education.

Jefferson believed that a free man obtains knowledge from many sources besides books, and that best of all is personal investigation. When still a young man, he was appointed to a committee to find out whether the South Branch of the James River was navigable by large boats; while the other members sat in the state capitol and studied documents, Jefferson jumped into a canoe and made on-the-spot observations.

At a time when we rely on experts more and more, Thomas Jefferson's belief in seeing for oneself is worth remembering. Experts are needed to get the facts, but it is a basic tenet of democracy that the people are capable of making the decisions once the facts are collected. To exercise this capacity, it is every man's duty to keep informed, to take nothing on trust. See for yourself!

In a day when most aristocrats would not deign to speak to those of humble origin except to give an order, Jefferson went out of his way to talk with gardeners, maidservants, waiters. Putting people at their ease so that they would talk freely was a real art. He told Lafayette, "You must ferret the people out of their hovels as I have done, look into their kettles, eat their bread." If the marquis would only do this, Jefferson told him, he might find out the people's grievances and understand the revolution then brewing in France.

All around are people who know something interesting and useful. Jefferson's habit of learning from everyone is something worth cultivating.

Jefferson repudiated the idea of accepting other people's opinions ready-made. "Neither believe nor reject anything," he wrote to his nephew, Peter Carr, "because any other person or descriptions of persons have rejected or believed it. Your own reason is the only oracle given you by heaven."

Jefferson's statements against censorship have long been our guide: "It is error alone," he observed, "which needs the support of government. Truth can stand by itself." He felt that the people "may safely be trusted to hear everything true and false, and to form a correct judgment. Were it left to me to decide whether we should have a government without newspapers, or newspapers without government, I should not hesitate a moment to prefer the latter."

In a free country there will always be a clash of ideas and this is a source of strength; it is conflict and not conformity that keeps freedom alive. Though Jefferson was for many years the object of intense abuse, he made a lifelong policy of never answering. He summed up his philosophy in letters to his friend, Gen. George Rogers Clark, who was also being viciously slandered: "If you meant to escape malice you should have confined yourself within the sleepy line of regular duty. There are two sides to every question. If you take one with decision and act on it with effect, those who take the other will of course be hostile in proportion as they feel that effect."

Jefferson felt that the present should never be shackled by outworn customs. "No society," he said, "can make a perpetual constitution, or even a perpetual law. The earth belongs to the living generation."

He did not fear new ideas, nor did he fear the future: "How much pain," he remarked, "have cost us the evils which have never happened! My temperament is sanguine. I steer my barque with hope in the head, leaving fear astern."

Jefferson died on July 4, 1826, the 50th anniversary of American independence. He had written his own epitaph: "Here was buried Thomas Jefferson, author of the Declaration of American Independence, of the Statute of Virginia for Religious Freedom, and father of the University of Virginia."

It did not say that he had also been governor of Virginia, minister to France, Secretary of State, President. Why? He told his daughter: "The things that are not on my inscription are things the people did for me. The things that are on it are things I did for the people."

New World

Who Really Discovered America?

by Thomas Fleming

THOUGH MOST AMERICANS believe that their history began with Christopher Columbus, historians have lately discovered hard evidence that Leif Ericson and his fellow Norsemen were exploring Canada and the northern tier of the United States as early as A.D. 1000. But before that date, the history of the New World above the Rio Grande has been a virtual vacuum, inhabited by a few Indian legends.

Now, thanks to the genius of a single man from another hemisphere, all this is beginning to undergo a vast change. In his book, *America B.C.*, New Zealandbred Barry Fell, a marine biologist at Harvard, offers astonishing evidence that there were men and women from Europe not merely exploring but living in North America as early as 800 B.C. They worked as miners, tanners and trappers, and shipped their products back to Europe. In temples in the rugged hills of New Hampshire and Vermont, and in river valleys in Iowa and Oklahoma, they sang hymns and performed sacred rituals to honor their gods. When their kings or chiefs died, they buried them beneath huge mounds of earth in which they left steles—written testimony of their grief carved on stone.

Some of these were discovered in the 19th century: strange inscriptions carved on cliffs from Maine to the Rio Grande, or on stones which lay in obscure museums. But archeologists could not read the writing, and dismissed these mysteries as forgeries or accidents of nature. Fell's expertise in this recondite field (called epigraphy), which requires many of the gifts intelligence men bring to code-cracking, is the tool which has enabled him to add a thousand years to America's past.

Fell first became interested in ancient languages when he was a student at the University of Edinburgh. He learned Gaelic, and began investigating Celtic tombs and ruins in Scotland. Then, in a study of the marine biology of Polynesia, he found hundreds of unreadable inscriptions engraved on rocks and painted on cavern walls.

Intrigued, Fell went to Harvard in 1964 and spent the next eight years ransacking the Widener Library's unique collection of texts on obscure languages and writing systems. He acquired a working knowledge of a half-dozen ancient alphabets, including Egyptian hieroglyphics; Punic (Carthaginian script used by several ancient peoples); and Ogam, an almost-forgotten script used by pre-Christian Celts.

Fell finally proved to his own satisfaction that the Polynesian inscriptions were written in the native language, Maori. But its vocabulary was derived from a mixture of Greek and Egyptian spoken in Libya after Alexander the Great conquered Egypt. The alphabet came from Carthage.

The most remarkable of these Libyan texts was found in a huge cave in New Guinea. There, a navigator named Maui left drawings of ancient but sophisticated astronomical and navigational instruments, as well as a depiction of a solar eclipse which enabled Fell, with the help of Harvard astronomers, to identify the year of the drawings as 232 B.C.

If there were Libyans visiting Polynesia at that time, Fell reasoned, perhaps they sailed on to South America. He accumulated evidence for such landfalls, and began lecturing on it at Harvard. His talks attracted the attention of a group of dogged investigators led by James P. Whittall II, an archeologist who had noted the similarity between numerous crude stone buildings in New England, which farmers often called root cellars, and similar ruins in Spain and Portugal. The European buildings had been identified as creations of Celts who ruled that part of Europe during the Bronze Age, the period of prehistory which dates roughly from 3500 B.C.

Whittall asked Fell to take a look at the Bourne stone, which had been discovered near Bourne, Mass., around 1680. No one had ever been able to make any sense of the writing on it. Now, Barry Fell was able to read it. The letters were a variation of the Punic alphabet found in ancient Spain, for which Fell has coined the word "Iberic." It recorded the annexation of a large chunk of present-day Massachusetts by Hanno, a prince of Carthage. Fell joined in a search for additional inscriptions at one of Whittall's favorite sites, Mystery Hill in North Salem, N.H.—a series of slabstone buildings variously attributed to Norsemen and wandering Irish monks.

Fell began studying the inscribed triangular stones which had previously been found at the site by Bob Stone, owner of Mystery Hill and a researcher there since the early 1950s. He found a dedication to the Phoenician god Baal, written in Iberic. Then suddenly, people began seeing hitherto unnoticed inscriptions. "A shout from Bob Stone told us that he had found another tablet in an adjacent drystone wall," Fell recalls. "As he brushed away the adhering dirt, there came into clear view a line of Ogam script that read 'Dedicated to Bel.'"

Students of ancient mythology had long suspected that the Celtic sun god Bel and the Carthaginian-Phoenician god Baal were identical. Here, for the first time, was evidence not only of this fact, but of a Celtic-Carthaginian partnership in exploration and settlement on a scale hitherto never even imagined.

"Within ten days we were finding dozens of Ogam inscriptions on another more remote site in central Vermont," Fell says. "It became clear that ancient Celts had built these stone chambers as religious shrines, and the Carthaginian mariners were visitors who were permitted to worship at them and make dedications in their own language to their own gods."

Next, Whittall showed Fell a 1940 photograph of an inscription engraved on a cliff above Mount Hope Bay, in Bristol, R.I. Discovered and recorded in 1780, it had been severely vandalized, making it necessary to work from the photograph. Fell soon read a single line, which was written in Tartessian Punic: "Voyagers from Tarshish this stone proclaims."

Tarshish was a Biblical city on the southern coast of Spain, and its men were among the boldest sailors of antiquity, famous for the size of their ships. About 533 B.C., Tarshish was destroyed by the Carthaginians and its trade was taken over by them. Here was evidence of how the partnership between the Iberian Celts and the Carthaginians began.

On Monhegan Island, ten miles off the coast of Maine, another inscription was brought to Fell's attention. Written in Celtic Ogam, it read: "Cargo platforms for ships from Phoenicia." From these and other inscriptions, as well as an intensive study of historical data on the seafaring ability of the men of Tarshish and Carthage, Fell concluded there was a highly developed trade route between America and the Mediterranean for at least 400 years before the birth of Christ. The chief products from North America were probably copper, furs and hides.

"We have evidence of very early mining in the copper fields of Minnesota," Fell says, "as well as of an extensive fur trade. The Carthaginians told everyone that they got their furs from Gaul. But when the Romans invaded Gaul, they found little evidence of a fur trade. I think Gaul was a code word for America."

"American data," as Fell calls it, now began to multiply. Most important was his decipherment of the Davenport stele, which some people compare to the translation of the Rosetta stone—the 19th-century breakthrough which enabled men to read hieroglyphics and grasp the awesome sweep of Egyptian history. On this inscription, which was found in a burial mound near Davenport, Iowa, in 1874, Fell was able to read three kinds of writing. At the top were Egyptian hieroglyphics. Below them was the Iberic form of Punic writing found in Spain. The third line was in Libyan script.

What does this mean? "It means there were Egyptians, Libyans and Celtic Iberians living together in a colony in Iowa in 900 B.C.," Fell says. "It means we have to revise a lot of our ideas about American history in general and American Indian culture in particular."

Fell next turned his attention to native Indian languages. He reasoned that if these pre-Christian visitors colonized parts of America, they must have left behind a deep impression on the language and beliefs of the people they encountered. He soon found evidence to support this conclusion.

From Harvard's Widener Library, one of Fell's colleagues brought him a book by a missionary priest, published in 1866. It contained a document titled "The Lord's Prayer in Micmac Hieroglyphs." Fell saw that at least half of these hieroglyphics were Egyptian. He was able to prove from the written testimony of other priests that the Micmacs were using this writing when the first missionaries arrived. In fact, all the northeastern Algonquians, the family of tribes to which the Micmacs belonged, apparently used it, having acquired this language from Libyan mariners and preserved it for 1000 years.

As Fell began studying the Algonquian language, he found hundreds of Egyptian words in the dialects of the northeastern Algonquians. The verb *na*, to see, is the same in both languages. So is *nauw*, which means to be weak, and *neechnw*, which means child. Celtic is also plentiful. The names of many New England rivers, once thought to be Indian, turn out to be Celtic. Merrimack, for instance, means "deep fishing" in Algonquian. It is too close for coincidence to the Gaelic *Morriomach*, meaning "of great depth."

In the next few years, Fell expects archeologists and interested amateur explorers to report new discoveries and inscriptions from all parts of North America. These findings may help explain exactly what happened to our earliest settlers after the destruction of Carthage in 146 B.C. and the fall of Rome in the fifth century A.D. Meanwhile, Fell and his associates are calling for a national effort to preserve the ancient sites they have already discovered as historic treasures, under the protection of either state or federal government. Such a program, they believe, should begin immediately.

We must also begin trying to assimilate the meaning of Barry Fell's discoveries. No longer can we think of America as developing in cultural isolation. For the first time, we must include in our American heritage fighting Celts from Spain, and daring Semitic seafarers from Carthage, Libya and Egypt. Who knows how many others will be added before the end of Barry Fell's epic voyage into the past?

Homage to the Vanishing Prairie

by Larry Van Goethem

IT WAS NOT, as so many think, just an expanse of worthless weeds blowing in the wind, an open space between East and West. The great American prairie was a distinct, unique ecosystem, as vital in its way as mountain ranges, oceans, lakes or great forests. Some 25 million years aborning, it waxed and waned across the continent, rising like a grass sea to Canada, invading the East. If it were here now, we would try to preserve it; but to our forefathers the prairie was just an obstacle, a way west, or an impediment to farming.

This splendid land! What a gigantic presence it was in the American mind of the last century. You could lose your past in it, find the future, break your heart. The human rivers of immigrants and disaffected Easterners flowed out from the Appalachians like an engulfing tide, but the fair land intimidated them, crushing human spirits with its endless sky and restive wind, and seven-foot rattlesnakes that struck like cannon. It was alien, forbidding, magnificent, alluring. And lonely.

But this was a time like no other, and an entire nation was westering, hoping the next day or year would bring them to a better place. There was an exquisite, uncontrollable sense of anticipation that drove men and teams on, past hope, beyond fear. Unknowingly, their creaking wagons had followed the buffalo west, trekking ancient trails beaten through the forest by the bison in their journeys to graze in the eastern savannas. In time the wagons were called prairie schooners, in tacit recognition that they were venturing west like frail ships on a vast, heaving sea.

Few would have done it except for the land, which the settlers plowed, grazed and domesticated. They mistakenly regarded the native perennial grasses as weeds, and worked hard to eradicate them, ending up with the pesky tumbleweed, crabgrass, brome and cheat that plague us today.

Homage to the Vanishing Prairie

The grassland was big, occupying a third of the continent. It dominated the midsection, in a rough triangle extending from Ohio northwest into Canada and Montana, and southwest deep into Texas. Its western advance ended along the Rockies. It was an ocean of grass, a balanced, self-perpetuating plant and animal world. The whole expanse was a wild garden of nature—but nobody knew it and nobody cared. And now it is gone, less than four percent remaining.

A boy looks at the rolling corn in Iowa and says, "There is the prairie." But that is not prairie. Then what *is* prairie?

The prairie was an ultimate response to a series of conditions, a self-enriching grassland system that evolved over thousands of years by natural selection. Nothing was wasted. Every seed that grew there, every animal, was highly adapted to its time and place. The smallest burrowing owl had its niche. The prairie was born in the sun and wind, nourished in soil, washed in rain.

The prairie's paradox—and one central to its being—was that it was born and reborn again and again in fire, like the phoenix. Set by lightning (and probably also by Indians, to improve hunting), the fires consumed vast expanses of grassland, endlessly returning to the soil not only the virile ashes of grass, herbs and flowers but needed nitrogen and phosphates, earth's ultimate fertilizer. They also consumed all the trees on the land, except the bur oaks that made up the "oak openings" so loved by early settlers in the Midwest.

Two feet of topsoil! exulted pioneers, with some exaggeration. But first there was that dense layer of useless grass that loomed so high it often hid a horse, a herd of buffalo, lurking Indians. It took six yokes of oxen to break the sod, until invention of the steel plow in 1840 by John Deere made it possible for a man and his single team to open the land. Those who saw it said the breaking of the prairie was arduous. Men worked from sun to sunset, the plows rolling back sod in carved black rows, the thick, tough roots popping like wires as the blade bit. That was the beginning of the end of the ancient prairie.

Plowing the earth stopped the fires, which early settlers feared more than tornadoes or blizzards. As the fires ended, scrub brush, oak and weeds took over where fields weren't planted. Count the growth rings in many of those trees and they will likely tell you when the area was first plowed.

The dangers for the settlers were real enough. Prairie grizzlies, now extinct, preyed on bison, and occasional humans. The bison herds themselves were mindless juggernauts when stampeded. The climate was an erratic combination of twisting air currents from the north, south, east and west, and from moist tropics and dry desert, that still produces some of the most extreme mid-continental weather on earth.

These were unknown dangers; the unknown was a haunting specter. Ole Rölvaag tells in his epic novel, *Giants of the Earth*, how a small Norwegian settlement in the Dakotas would suffer spasms of nameless dread. People simply stopped working to look around and stare at the horizon, for they carried into the new land the psychology of the old country. They feared the forces of evil—trolls, the bogyman, harlequin.

The true giants in the earth are captured in layers of time. Paleontologists have unearthed bones of old reptiles, camels, elephants and giant beaver that populated the inland plain from 5 million to 40 million years ago. Before then, as the Rocky Mountains thrust slowly upward, a vast "rain shadow" was created that stopped most Pacific moisture on its easterly way. Deprived of rain, the forests fell back, their remains becoming coal and petroleum as the surface became grassland.

The North American prairie marched north and east again and again with changes in climate. Fire enabled the prairie to take over rain-rich Midwestern land that would have been boreal forest, in Wisconsin, Minnesota, Ohio, Indiana, southern Michigan and Missouri. Millions of buffalo, antelope, elk and deer followed, grazing on the tender shoots of bluestem grass that sprang up after the burning.

The pastures of the Lord. Canada geese, ducks, whooping cranes, sandhill cranes and passenger pigeons were clouds in the sky during migrations. Complex prairie-dog towns covered dozens of miles. One in the Texas plains was reported to have been some 25,000 square miles in size.

The prairie was a cornucopia for the Plains Indians, who lacked for little in the way of food, hides, horses and land. They lived in a kind of symbiosis with the land, eating the prairie potato (a small tuber) and growing corn.

A good many obituaries have been written for the prairie. Still, it has survived timelessly wherever it persists—on the long, narrow lines of railroad right-of-way, for example. Prairie tends to seep back into unplowed fields, but slowly, by several feet a year.

Today, interest in the prairie has revived. It is possible to order seeds of many of the more than 400 species of prairie plants. States have moved belatedly to preserve what natural grassland they still have. Illinois, the Prairie State, had trouble finding prairie to preserve; its sites total only some 3000 acres. An organization called "Save the Tallgrass Prairie," in Shawnee Mission, Kan., is dedicated to its preservation. Nebraska has planted prairie along its interstate highways, Minnesota along its roads and rest areas. Bison, all but wiped out in the 1870s as a hindrance to farming and ranching, are preserved and encouraged here and there like antiques.

The prairie fancier's fondest dream is the creation of a large Prairie National Park, possibly in the Flint Hills of Kansas, where the original prairie has remained because the rocky hills resist plowing. Here is the 13-square-mile Konza Prairie, largest in the nation.

The prairie was difficult to live with, which is why we throttled it. This giant in the earth gave up the land to us, surrendered to our farms and crops and livestock, our cities and towns. But nothing is gained without loss. All that people still seek in the earth's remaining wild places—a restfulness, an inexplicable sense of peace and oneness, grace—was present in the prairie. And now that it's gone we find it impossible to renounce.

"Free Land!" The Saga of the Homesteaders

by Paul Friggens

SPEAKING in the early 1840s, an eloquent member of Congress said of the then unknown and forbidding American West: "What do we want with this vast, worthless area, this region of savages and wild beasts, of deserts of shifting sands, and whirlwinds of dust, of cactus and prairie dogs? To what use could we ever hope to put these great deserts or endless mountain ranges? I will never vote one cent from the public treasury to place the Pacific Coast one inch nearer to Boston than it is now!"

It was a commonly held view. In 1820 Maj. Stephen H. Long explored the Great Plains to the Rockies and dismissed the area on his maps as "The Great American Desert," maybe useful someday as a "barrier against the incursions of an enemy." Appropriately, Congress voted $30,000 to equip the Army with a camel corps for travel over the American Sahara, and before the experiment finally was abandoned one caravan actually made it to California.

But Major Long's desert had a destiny. Within a few years the advancing fur traders, gold seekers and cattlemen had breached the frontier of the Indian and buffalo. Then, in 1862, Congress enacted the Homestead Act, opening the West to farming and final settlement. With a ringing shout, "Free land!" came the expectant sodbusters, driving their plodding oxen into the sunset.

In the spectacular land rush that followed the Homestead Act a million and a half determined homesteaders strung their fences in 17 western states, settled some 270 million acres and gave a vast surge to our industry, population and politics. They made the desert bloom and helped the United States become the greatest food producer on earth.

The idea that the land belongs to the people is as old as our Republic. As early as 1776, Thomas Jefferson advocated

"Free Land!" The Saga of the Homesteaders

the gift of "small quantities" of land to western settlers, and through the years the homestead movement became a national political issue. Events in the 1860s finally forced a showdown. The nation was concerned with turning the vast public lands productive and providing homes for the immigrants flooding our shores. But when a crusading Pennsylvania Congressman, Galusha A. Grow, took up the cause of the Homestead Act, it was bitterly fought in Congress. The bill provided that every U.S. citizen, 21 or over, or person who declared his intention to become a citizen, could file a claim to "one-quarter section" or 160 acres. The homesteader would be required to live and work on his land for five years, after which he could acquire deed.

Southerners opposed the measure for fear of peopling the western territories with anti-slave settlers, while Easterners feared the westward movement would depress land values at home. But the growing power of the Middle West, coupled with the South's secession, finally cleared the way. President Lincoln enthusiastically signed the bill in 1862, and at midnight, on January 1, 1863, the law took effect.

Daniel Freeman of Ohio claimed to be the first homesteader in the United States. Hearing of choice lands out west, Freeman had journeyed to the frontier town of Brownville, Nebraska Territory to look around. Finding the town already thronged with hungry land seekers, he rode 70 miles westward to stake out 160 acres of rich bottom land on Cub Creek. Back in town he went to a New Year's party at the local hotel, where he persuaded one of the land agents to step out from the dance and open the land office a few minutes after midnight. Today, the Freeman farm, four miles northwest of Beatrice, Neb., is a national monument.

The Homestead law was widely advertised in Europe, and before long the promise of opportunity and freedom lured tens of thousands of immigrants.

Take the Lars Hanson family of four, from Norway. They traveled "steerage," were cooped up in foul-smelling bunks below decks, subsisted on moldy bread and tainted meat. From New York they rode the newfangled "cars" to Chicago, then a box car to rail's end. Then they drove oxen overland another 90 miles into the booming Dakota Territory. Lars declared his intention to become a citizen and hurried to stake out his treeless 160 acres. He did his temporary surveying by wagon with a rig tied on the wheel spoke—each revolution counting off 13 feet.

The Hansons dug a well, and from the buffalo grass they plowed squares of fresh clean sod to lay up their one-room habitation. During heavy rains, the earthen home leaked rivulets, and during dry spells the dirt cracked and fell off in chunks. It attracted mice, gophers and snakes. Still this cave-like dwelling provided amazing insulation against 30-below winters and scorching summers, and above all, it was the family's own. Hannah cooked on a sheet-iron stove, for which the children gathered buffalo chips and twisted dry prairie hay. The family ate on a packing box, and the diet was monotonous—cornmeal, salt pork, wild greens and occasional game. Life was primitive and hard. Hannah hungered for the sight of another woman. That winter she nearly died in childbirth—there was no way to reach a doctor, or even a midwife.

The first year the immigrants harvested ten acres of corn, broke more sod, and Lars, standing proudly on his 160 acres, was monarch of all he surveyed. Then drought set in—three searing seasons, with withering fields, dusty stream beds and hope vanishing on the hot prairie winds.

On the heels of drought, in 1874, came grasshoppers—so thick in some sections of the Great Plains that they blotted out the sun. But despite drought, grasshoppers and privation, the Hansons hung on and in five years celebrated two tremendous events—Lars became an American citizen and "proved up" on his 160 acres, worth, with all his other possessions, probably $1000.

Within 15 years, the Dakota "wilderness" boasted a farming population of half a million stouthearted families like the Hansons. Neighboring Minnesota claimed 400 towns with Scandinavian names. Sodbusters spilled from Canada to Mexico, settled most of the choice land, and then, on the sunny morning of April 22, 1889, stampeded into the last native sanctuary of the Indian in Oklahoma. That morning some 20,000 "boomers"—on horseback, bicycles, in buggies, covered wagons and on foot—lined up along the Indian Territory boundary. At a volley from U.S. Cavalry, the boomers thundered across the starting line in a choking cloud of dust. Before night, they had settled on 1,920,000 acres.

Four years later, with the opening of the 200-mile-long Cherokee Strip, another army of landseekers re-enacted the

"Free Land!" The Saga of the Homesteaders

great Oklahoma rush. By 1900, the sodbusters had filed on more than 80 million acres of "The Great American Desert"—double the area of all New England.

The homesteader spurred farm mechanization. Before 1862, the average eastern farm was only 50 acres, worked by one or two men and a plow. But on the 160-acre farms of the Great Plains, the "walking" plow gave way to the gang plow. Then, as homesteaders were consolidated into larger farms, came the revolutionary McCormick reaper, the threshing machine, the twine binder and gasoline tractor. "Within 25 years after the Homestead Act," says the U.S. Bureau of Land Management, "the United States became the greatest grower of farm products in the world."

Although the Homestead Act caused profound beneficial changes, it also had faults, the chief of which was the 160-acre limitation. While a family could wrest a living from a quarter section in subhumid eastern Nebraska or Kansas, it would likely starve on the dry lands west of Dodge City. Eventually, under pressure, Congress increased the homestead grant to 320 acres, and a "stock-raising" homestead to 640 acres. With these changes, homesteading got its second wind in the early 1900s, and a new wave of settlement swept the West. In acreage, it vastly exceeded the first.

As a youth in western South Dakota, I vividly remember the period. My family homesteaded, and our ranch, with its lush feed and water, was a favorite campsite for the Montana-bound "honyockers," as they were then nicknamed (nobody knew why). The honyocker came from all walks of life—there were barbers, carpenters, clerks, schoolmarms. They filed on government land or bought from railroads or speculators, flung up tarpaper shacks, and planted a crop. Before World War I they struck a few good wet years, and towns mushroomed. Then, after a five-year drought I saw the ruined, disillusioned honyockers flocking back East, their scanty belongings jouncing on rickety hayracks, together with their hungry, shabby children.

A handful of the honyockers stuck it out, however, and prospered. Mrs. Bertha W. Ingalls of Colorado Springs, Colo.—until her death at 94, the nation's oldest homesteader—exemplified the quiet courage of these pioneers. "All of my 13 children were born in our sod home and we never had a doctor," Mother Ingalls recalled. "One time when I was alone

I gave birth to twins. Our nearest neighbors were four miles away. We didn't have a tree, and coyotes and wolves prowled around the place." The saga of homesteading is written in women's trials and tears.

By the late 1920s the homesteaders had virtually conquered the "desert," and the supply of desirable land, even for stock raising, was running out. Finally, in 1934 the government closed "the unreserved and unappropriated public domain" and consolidated its remaining holdings for lease under the Taylor Grazing Act. Since that day homesteading has been confined to a few western irrigation projects and Alaska, and we are closing another chapter in the American Dream.

Gone are the plucky pioneers who braved blizzards, drought, floods, twisters, grasshopper plagues, prairie fires, isolation, and, as one recalls, put up "a hard fight with a short stick" to lay claim to 160 acres. The prairie statesman William Jennings Bryan paid them perhaps their finest tribute: "They were men and women who gave the world more than they took from it."

Bold Dreams

The Spivacks Beat the Odds

by John Steinbeck

A WISE and cynical friend of mine handicaps life as seven to five against. I think he is largely right, but when horses or men buck the odds and win, we have champions.

I think I have a good example of this in the creation of a doctor. I have watched it happen year by year, and it makes me a little impatient with the despairing cries of lost or beat generations who lose before they have laid down a bet.

Next door to my little house in New York City is a newsstand and store, so tiny that when two customers are in at the same time they have to move sideways. It is run by Mr. and Mrs. Spivack and their son and daughter. They sell newspapers and magazines, tobacco, candy bars, cards, soda, ice cream, paper clips, glue.

The margin of profit is small, the hours incredibly long—5 a.m. till past midnight and closed only on Sunday afternoons. One member of the family is on duty all the time, two during rush hours.

Starting as customers, we have become friends of the Spivacks and we have been privileged to observe a dogged, gallant, undeviating miracle. For this family—with the odds high against them—have created a doctor.

His mother says that Morty wanted to be a doctor from the beginning. There was never any defection toward cowboy, soldier or pilot. It was medicine from the start. Medicine was simply a fact, an inevitability. So the family, the newstand, constituted itself a creative organism.

Morty got good grades in high school, but that also was a fact of nature. He did his studying behind the counter between customers. Then he went to Cornell. This meant longer hours for the remaining three, except during vacations when Morty took his shift again with his textbooks behind the cash register. His parents gave him the slacker hours when fewer customers interrupted his studying.

Then an accident happened: the building changed hands and the little store ceased to exist. The Spivacks moved their papers to the front of a butcher shop on Third Avenue and held on. It was over a year before they were able to move into another place next door to their old stand, but the process of creation continued. Morty went into pre-medicine, came home, studied behind the counter. He graduated from Cornell with honors and entered Buffalo Medical School.

You can think of this family as an engine aimed at medicine, except that people are not engines. There were debts, worries, illnesses, during which the remaining three had to carry on 19 hours a day, 121 hours a week. But the family functioned—one step at a time. We have known the Spivacks quite a while now, and we have never heard a complaint or a doubt. As for neurosis or self-pity, who has time for it?

Recently Morty received his degree in medicine, head of his class. He will intern at a New York hospital in his chosen field of thoracic medicine. It isn't over, of course. It never is.

The family isn't exactly proud because they never doubted that it would be this way. There's a glow in the newsstand, surely, but it still opens at five in the morning and closes past midnight and if there is any family celebration it will have to be on a Sunday afternoon.

Perhaps, after all, the odds were not against the Spivacks. Given the unassailable determination of every unit of this family, an all-wise handicapper might have considered them ten to one in favor. I doubt whether you could beat an outfit like that, short of bombing it.

"My Name Is Ilya!"

by William Sambrot

EVEN from this distance, across an entire ocean, I could pick her out in the crowd of refugees that waited to climb the ship's gangplank. The fear was on her, now that the tremendous moment was here. Not fear for herself—never had she fear for herself—but for her man, who stood next to her with sagging shoulders and taut blue lips. He was desperately ill, and she feared he yet might not be allowed to go.

Fear had never left her, never in all the black days of the blitzkrieg, when Nazi tanks roared through the midnight quiet of her Polish village, their loudspeakers blaring Wagner's "Ride of the Valkyries."

Ever since that night, when the soulless men of Hitler had taken her name and replaced it with a number, had the terrible fear been with her. They had taken her man, Leo, from her, though she had fought ferociously to stop them. Even when someone knocked her unconscious, she moaned his name aloud.

Through all those bleak years I watched her from afar, a tiny, unquenchable flame, burning steadily, her will to live, to find her Leo, sustaining her while others fell. She did the work of ten women, from prison camp to prison camp throughout the ruined land, suffering indignities without flinching.

Unceasingly, her sharp, black eyes stared at the faces of the labor battalions which marched by, rank on rank—men without homes, without families or memories. Endlessly, her eyes searched for the familiar, dear face. She *knew* he was not dead.

And when at last, my dusty, weary boys had finished their battles and freed her, I watched her start her search again. Her love was a compass, guiding her across the blasted countries where hope was dead, and futility and hunger were a smothering blanket over the land.

When she found her Leo, even from here I felt the leap

44 Bold Dreams

of her heart, the surge of her thanks to God. Even from here, I knew her joy.

How she worked! With her bare hands she scooped aside debris to make their cubbyhole. With loving care she laid her Leo on a pallet. Long hours she searched for food. And her eyes always would turn to the West, and I could see her undying desire for freedom, for a chance to start anew.

And at last, when the Red Cross aide told her that she and her man were to be placed on the list of those allowed to migrate to America, she fell on her knees and kissed the hem of the aide's skirt. From this far, I could see the tears in the aide's eyes as she helped her up.

I heard it, too, when the grave, harassed American doctor, in a major's uniform, told her quietly that there had been a change, that her Leo was too sick to go. Again she dropped to her knees, her anguish too great for tears, and again she pleaded for her man.

She told of the years of struggle, of how she had kept her man alive. She told of her visions of America, of the great sweep of the Montana sky in the pictures she had seen. She fumbled hastily with her calloused, work-scarred hands to show him a letter, a letter from America. She had work on a ranch in Montana, waiting for her.

"But he may not live to reach America," the major told her. "He is very sick. Terribly anemic."

"He *will* live!" she whispered. "The voyage is nothing. Can't you see what we have behind us—the blows we have survived? In Montana, he will become well."

When at last the major nodded, and wrote their two names on the list, even from here I felt his heart wrench as she lifted her hands and blessed him. "I am not God," he murmured.

She stood amid the anxious crowd, with the fear washing over her. Their names would be called next. Her Leo must not stagger, must not fall before they reached the gangplank.

Their names were called, and even from here I could see the sheer strength of her wiry body as she half-pushed, half-carried her man up the gangplank, whispering, praying, begging him to reach the top because she knew the top meant life; it meant America.

They made it, and none called to them to step out of line. She walked to the rail to face the sad land she had left behind forever.

"My Name Is Ilya!" 45

"My name is Ilya!" she cried, and the tears for the first time ran down her lined face. *"My name is Ilya!"*

I watched her, from here, as they came closer and closer on the great ship. How tenderly she cared for him, crouching by his side for hours, sustaining him with little songs, with stories of the magic Montana, where there was no one to demand a card in exchange for the right to live.

And at last, when the New York skyline loomed out of the morning mist, and the moment was at hand, I saw her, tugging and pulling her Leo, crying out at the others, pleading, forcing the well ones aside to obtain a place at the rail so he could see that at last it was over, that the black years were behind and they were born again.

She held him up, watching him as he stared at me. And when she saw the quick light leap into his eyes, she sobbed aloud in her happiness. Oh, the wonder of that moment! But she, Ilya of the great courage, she did not look. She was content to see me reflected in her man's eyes.

Timidly, filled with awe and clinging together tightly, they walked down the gangplank to their new home. Behind them lay the black years, years lighted only by the flame which leaped and blazed within the heart of a woman. She alone had not seen me. And yet the flame within her mingled with my own, and of those who came, the torch I hold so proudly aloft burned most brightly for her.

Moonstruck

by Al Reinert

THEY HAD ALL SEEN the Moon before, of course. Indeed, there was never a druid more obsessed with the Moon than the astronauts in the Apollo program; no fertility cult had ever watched it with such care and close attention, or with greater devotion. For thousands of hours apiece they had rehearsed going there, under the most rigorous conditions that science could devise. Dressed in outlandish costumes, they had lurched around the Arizona desert, pretending it was the Mare Tranquillitatis, carefully selecting and preserving odd chunks of stone as if they were lunar samples, and learning survival techniques. For years they had made believe, with precision and with dedication, yet they always knew it to be unreal. It was the Moon alone that gave meaning to the lives of Apollo astronauts, so when they saw it at night they must have genuinely yearned for it.

Among those men who went to the Moon, even the most insensitive of them, there are certain moments they recall in common, profoundly arresting moments that were stamped alike in their 24 separate lives, during 11 different missions. One of these was that scene, three days out and afar in space, when they first turned and saw their destination.

They had last seen it the morning they launched—still fairly high in the Florida dawn and far away—if they were lucky. "It was just by accident I saw it," remembers Ken Mattingly, the command-module pilot on Apollo 16. "There's a long period before launch where you've done all the things you can do in the cockpit and you just have to wait. So I looked out the window and doggone if the Moon wasn't visible in the daylight. And I thought, 'My God, that's where we're going. Today. For real.'"

Most of the astronauts, though, had their last glimpse of an earthly Moon the night before, just before entering the windowless rooms of the quarantined crew quarters. Without exception they slept easy on that last night: they were that sure of themselves. Awakened after six or seven hours, they began the hurried ritual of physical exams, eating, suiting up, final briefings, last-minute checkouts. They also pre-breathed pure oxygen for several hours, so they felt a shade giddy as they waited atop their Saturn rocket: 36 stories tall and filled with chemicals that can't exist together, primed to explode in an organized way. And most saw no Moon.

They saw next to nothing during the riotous, fiery rush into Earth orbit. At four G's one's field of vision narrows acutely as the corneas compress, producing tunnel vision of the truest sort. All the most important gauges were thus arrayed directly in front of the crewmen, three feet away from them, the only place they could see anything. To see out the windows they had to turn away from their instruments, which they were trained not to do and which could be distracting. Yet the record shows they always did, all of them. The blue-green swirl below was too compelling.

To escape from Earth's gravity they were accelerated to 24,000-plus miles per hour, 11 times faster than a rifle bullet and the fastest humans had ever traveled, yet they had no sense of motion. "We never felt that we were moving after we left Earth orbit," recalls Jim Irwin, who rode Apollo 15. "We felt that we were stationary." There was no up or down, no day or night, no fixed frame of reference except the steadily shrinking ball of Earth.

They traveled away facing backward for two days, rotating slowly to evenly distribute the intense solar heat, unable to see where they were going. Out one side of their ship was the blinding whiteness of the sun across a vacuum—totally colorless, pure-light energy arriving at 240 degrees Fahrenheit. Out the other side, at minus 250 degrees, was a blackness blacker than any ink or dye could reproduce, the utter blackness of an infinite void. "We were outside of ordinary reality," as Jim Irwin puts it very matter-of-factly.

"I thought the strangest aspect of the trip out," says Alan Bean of Apollo 12, "is that you don't really pass anything tangible on the way. You leave the launch pad, then you leave Earth orbit, and about a couple of days later, after apparently passing nothing, all of a sudden you're where you were going. And that lack of way points had the effect of making it seem a little magical and mystical getting there."

48 Bold Dreams

Passing through time more than anything else, they occupied themselves with star-sightings, housekeeping, preparations for arrival. They watched the Earth grow smaller and smaller, farther away, its hold on them weakening. Then, nearly three days from home, they crossed that abrupt but invisible boundary beyond which they entered, in the neatly symbolic term used in orbital mechanics, "the lunar sphere of influence." It now drew them physically as well as emotionally, and their speed began to increase. It was time for final course corrections and navigational adjustments, time to turn around and look at the Moon. They were astonished.

It was a different Moon from any that humans had ever seen. "The Moon I have known all my life," as Mike Collins recalls the moment, "has been replaced by the most awesome sphere I have ever seen. To begin with, it is *huge*, completely filling our window. Second, it is three-dimensional. The belly of it bulges out toward us in such a pronounced fashion that I almost feel I can reach out and touch it. This cool, magnificent sphere hangs there ominously, a formidable presence without sound or motion, issuing us no invitation to invade its domain."

They had arrived at what was for them not only their destination, but their destiny, and not one of those 24 men has ever forgotten the power of that moment. They have forgotten a great deal else about going to the Moon: the technical specifics, the interminable numbers, code names and computer words. They remember instead the surprises, the sights and events that were not in the program.

Jim Irwin registered the presence of God on the Moon, so overwhelmingly and tangibly—"I cannot imagine a holier place"—that he turned to evangelical preaching when he came back to Earth. "We thought with a new clarity, almost a clairvoyance." Ed Mitchell, Alan Shephard's lunar-module (LM) pilot, also had a powerful mystical experience—so much so that, back on Earth, he founded a research center which explores extraordinary human capabilities.

The sense of dislocation was tremendous and profound. Never have men been so estranged from their environment. Any man open to the experience would have difficulty holding it together, no matter how strong-willed he was. Al Bean, the LM pilot on Apollo 12, would cast frequent upward glances at his planet, repeating aloud to himself, "This is the Moon, that is Earth. I'm really here. I'm really here."

Like the other command-module (CM) pilots who followed him on later missions, Mike Collins circled the moon alone while his two Apollo crewmates went down and touched it. Removed from total astronaut self-fulfillment, the CM pilots share a cosmic perspective filled with wonder. As a group they are the most interesting to talk with of all the Apollo astronauts, the ones with the deepest insight. They were the only men during the lunar landings to be truly alone in space. For half of each lunar orbit they disappeared *behind* the Moon, to the side so dark it showed only as an absence of stars, into a universe where the Earth existed only in their minds. They were out of sight and hearing, alone against the stars. They loved it.

Although Michael Collins felt very much a part of what was taking place on the lunar surface, he describes a special feeling of solitude during his sojourns behind the Moon: "I am alone now, truly alone, and absolutely isolated from my known life. I am it, and I feel this powerfully—not as fear or loneliness, but as awareness, anticipation, satisfaction, confidence, almost exultation. I like the feeling...."

"Some of my best memories are from that period," says Ken Mattingly, softly. "People are always expecting you to say it was lonely, but it wasn't. It was incredibly peaceful." Flying three years and five missions after Collins, on Apollo 16, he had both the time and the foresight to anticipate his solitude, and he went prepared to savor it. For Mattingly that meant appropriate music: the Berlioz "Symphonie Fantastique," Holst's "The Planets," Strauss waltzes. Thus equipped did he enter that earthless universe—with his hammock strung in front of the one big window and his tape deck floating beside him, quietly playing—as open and receptive as a poet or a lover.

Most inscrutable of all were the mission commanders—especially Frank Borman, Tom Stafford, Neil Armstrong, Dave Scott, John Young. They were the most intense and least reflective of all the Apollo astronauts, the true zealots of Moon travel. Like Renaissance Jesuits they had rational minds wedded to an absolute faith in their mission, which made them relentless and willful; observant without being sensitive, decisive but never impulsive, they possessed the inner discipline of genuine disciples. It was what made them commanders, because even their peers were impressed with their dedication,

50 Bold Dreams

and humbled a bit by their self-assurance.

So imperturbable were they, in fact, that finally going to the Moon for real never fazed them, hardly changed them, scarcely even seemed to impress them. They took it in stride like the stoics they were, conscious every minute of their responsibilities. Each Apollo mission had been planned and rehearsed to the smallest detail—the procedure for opening the door involved a checklist of 92 steps. Nothing was left to the imagination, and the job of the mission commanders was to bring it off that way. They followed their instructions and performed their assignments with skill and dispatch, always coolly, sometimes cleverly or jokingly, but never with much imagination.

Of the 12 Apollo astronauts who actually touched the Moon, only six appeared really touched by it in turn. These were the lunar-module pilots who rode down to the surface with the mission commanders. Each man handled the actual excitement and danger of the landings in his own way.

"The people in my slot were sort of tourists on these flights," says Jim Irwin, the LM pilot on Apollo 15, with modest exaggeration. "We had time to look out the windows, to register what we saw and felt, and to absorb it."

"I found for me it was most convenient not to look out," recalls Al Bean, another LM pilot, "because when I did I was kind of amazed, and it was also slightly frightening, and I found if I concentrated on the displays that it was more like a simulation, so I could perform more normally. I'd look for about half a second—that was about all I could stand—then I'd look back in and try to work on the job again."

And Jim Irwin: "I kept telling myself, 'Jim, this is really a simulation. You are not really landing on the Moon.' If I had believed I was landing on the Moon, I would have been so excited I don't know if I could have made it. It was really hard not to look."

What they were doing was so audacious, so unearthly, so unimaginable that some had to pretend they were still just pretending. Men of remarkable will and passionate minds—on the verge of making real the most daring dream they were able to conceive—they remained detached and professionally cool. If they succumbed to the wonder of the moment, they might spoil everything.

While the lunar module was carrying Armstrong and

Aldrin toward their historic landing, the practical-minded men in Mission Control felt helpless. On the tapes you can almost hear their collective deep breath, virtually a physical displacement as silence overtook that busiest of rooms. They had imagined it so hard for so long—inventing in their minds what going to the Moon might be like and then acting it out—that it still didn't seem altogether real. Some part of each of them had to believe they were still just pretending.

It was Buzz Aldrin who brought it home to the Houston technicians, when from 200 feet above the Moon he tersely observed, "Got the shadow out there...." It was the first moment those in Mission Control knew for certain that the Moon was truly within the grasp of men. Then the LM was down in the Sea of Tranquility, with eight seconds of fuel to spare, for real.

And the astronauts, those supposedly dull technocrats, were revealed as visionaries, dreamers and, most surprising to some, real heroes after all.

The Source of All Our Strength

by A. Whitney Griswold

SINCE that moment, lost in the mists of time, when man first looked upon himself and saw the image of God, he has struggled against the powers of nature and the supernatural, and against the tyrannies of his fellow men, to fulfill the promise in that image. He has lived to the full the gregarious life to which half of his instincts commit him. And, in response to the other half, he has striven in every element on earth, in the skies above the earth and in the waters under the earth, to express himself as an individual.

Philosophers have long recognized this conflict in the bosom of man and we, like every generation before us, have been witnesses to its political manifestations. Our world is divided by political philosophies which proclaim man's mechanistic fate as a species, and those which proclaim his creative destiny as an individual. Just now the mechanistic idea seems to be in the ascendant. It is propagated at the point of the sword by dictatorships now governing nearly half the peoples of the world and seeking to extend their dominion over the rest. Perhaps never in history has the individual had to defend his birthright against such formidable odds.

This is a dark outlook for a country like ours which by tradition and temperament looks to the individual for the salvation of the race. We may be thankful that it is only an outlook and not a reality. We do not know our strength; and we do not know our strength because we do not know our history. Time and again we have seen the individual apparently ready to exit from the stage, only to return with fresh and more dynamic lines.

We had communism in the Plymouth Colony in 1620, two centuries before Marx wrote his *Manifesto* and three before the Russians ever heard of it; and we gave it up, after a pragmatic test, because, as Governor Bradford wrote in his diary, "the experience that was had in this commone course and con-

The Source of All Our Strength 53

dition, tried sundrie years, and that amongst godly and sober men, may well evince the vanitie of that conceite of Plato and other ancients, applauded by some of later times—that the taking away of propertie, and bringing in communitie into a commone wealth would make them happy and flourishing; as if they were wiser than God. For this communitie (so farr as it was) was found to breed much confusion and discontent, and retard much imployment that would have been to their benefite and comforte."

We had totalitarianism, complete with purges and secret police, in the Massachusetts Bay Colony, three centuries before Hitler, Stalin and Mussolini; we gave it up in revulsion and drafted statutes and constitutions to prevent its recurrence.

In our traffic with foreign nations we have always looked out on a world full of despotisms. As colonies we were their pawns. As a young republic we were surrounded by them. And if the airplane had been invented a century earlier than it was, the chances are we would still be their pawn. Democracy is a very new thing in the world. Our knowledge of man in society goes back to the Neolithic Age, 9000 years ago. Over that span of time man has seen and suffered despotisms of every conceivable variety.

Democracy, the hopeful philosophy, attuned to man's instincts as an individual and addressed to their cultivation for the benefit of society, first appeared in Athens about 500 B.C. It saw fitful revival in the Italian city states of the 11th and 12th centuries, and later in the Swiss cantons, but it did not make its modern appearance until the Puritan revolution in England in the middle years of the 17th century. It did not attain the form in which we know it until the 19th century. Compared with despotism it is but a few minutes old. The remarkable fact is not that it is still opposed by despotism but that it has survived that opposition as vigorously as it has.

It has survived because time and again it has proved, under stress, its ability to harmonize and make productive, in every sphere of thought and action, the individual and the social instincts innate in man. In these respects it has demonstrated its superiority over all other political philosophies. All try to draw the line between the opportunities and responsibilities of the individual and those of society, but none draws it so subtly in accordance with reality as democracy.

And what is that reality? It is that for 9000 years society

has depended upon its members as individuals for those creative achievements of mind and spirit that have guided it along the path of civilization. The spark from heaven falls. Who picks it up? The crowd? Never. The individual? Always. It is he, and he alone, as artist, inventor, explorer, scholar, scientist, spiritual leader or statesman, who stands nearest to the source of life and transmits its essence to his fellow men. Let them tie his hands or stop his mouth or dragoon him in the name of uniformity, and they cut themselves off from that source.

Wisdom and virtue cannot be forced from a crowd as eggs from chickens under electric lights. There is no such thing as general intelligence. There is only individual intelligence communicating itself to other individual intelligences.

And there is no such thing as public morality; there is only a composite of private morality. The Athenian statesman Pericles perceived these truths when he said of democracy in its earliest phase that it trusted "less in system and policy than to the native spirit of our citizens." And so did Thomas Jefferson, when he wrote, "It is the manners and spirit of a people which preserve a republic in vigor." The same could be said of all forms of government, but of none so truly as that in which the voice of the people is the voice of God. This is another way of saying the democracy is fundamentally a moral philosophy, a fact which, more than any other in its nature and history, has enabled it to survive all of its previous incarnations.

We have the means for achieving democracy's promise in the most far-reaching system of education any free people has ever known. We have the material resources to enable this system to fulfill its purpose without diverting a penny from the essential needs of our armed forces or from any other national interest of comparable importance. The problem is to create the will, not the resources.

In the solution of this problem hangs the fate of our nation and our civilization. For the very scientific progress that some think spells the doom of democracy depends for its continuation on two things: first, the continued discoveries of individuals in the realm of pure science, hence the continuation of an educational process that produces those individuals; and second, a social philosophy that converts human energy, newly rescued from drudgery by technological advances, to social uses consistent with this purpose.

This vast store of energy, exceeding in human terms our

greatest accomplishment in the conservation of natural resources, in military and political terms equivalent to the enlistment of a powerful new ally in the defense of democracy, is at hand and ready to use. How shall we use it? Shall we abandon it to the entertainment industry? Shall we forget it in our fear of the ideas of a group of Russian doctrinaires, isolated even from their own people, whose conception of the world is not as sound as Columbus's nor as courageous as Ferdinand and Isabella's?

If we do these things we shall have to answer for them, as have all bodies politic that held their individual members in contempt. For "every tree that bringeth not forth good fruit is hewn down, and cast into the fire."

Xerox—The Invention That Hit the Jackpot

by Don Wharton

IN THE MODERN office, the copying machine has become about as indispensable as the typewriter. No office sight is more familiar today than a secretary inserting a letter into one of these table-top or desklike machines, pushing a button, waiting a few seconds while the machine whirs like a dishwasher—and then out pops a splendid copy. In the United States nearly a million business offices now have copiers, turning out nearly 180 billion copies of documents a year. No fewer than 22 American firms are manufacturing copiers, in more than 88 different models.

Copying has been made so easy and speedy that, says one executive, "it has become a national disease." When you send a check to some stores, it is instantly copied, and the copy is turned over to the bookkeeper, while the check itself is immediately cashed. If you enter a hospital, your case history is likely to be copied; so is your electrocardiogram; maybe even your daily menu. College students use the machines to copy not only term papers but also pages from library books. Some libraries, hotels and motels have installed copiers for the convenience of patrons.

All this has come about mainly because of the remarkable persistence of a spare-time inventor, who in the 1930s worked nights and weekends in a makeshift laboratory in New York City. Chester Carlson became a wealthy man, one of the few to receive millions in royalties from a single invention. In his last years he lived in a beautiful home in upstate New York, in leisure and comfort that were the exact opposite of what he grew up with.

At 12, a thin, gangling boy, Chester was doing odd jobs to help his parents eke out an existence in San Bernardino, Calif. By 14 he was the chief support of the family, rising at

Xerox—The Invention That Hit the Jackpot

5 a.m. to wash store windows before school, sweeping out banking and newspaper offices in the afternoon, working from six to six on Saturdays. He was an only child; his father, an itinerant barber, was unable to work because of arthritis and tuberculosis; his mother had contracted tuberculosis, too.

Carlson was under pressures that would have forced many boys to drop out of school, but he held on, an astonishing example of youthful industry. While a junior in high school, in addition to janitoring he got a job as a printer's devil. In his senior year, still washing windows and sweeping floors, he worked Saturdays and Sundays in a chemical laboratory. His mother died when he was 17. Getting a college education while he had a father to support and help care for seemed almost impossible. But Carlson managed—first at a junior college at Riverside, then at California Institute of Technology. After five years of hard work he emerged with a B.S. degree in physics and $1400 in debts.

It was 1930; jobs were scarce. Letters to 82 firms brought only two replies, no offers. But eventually Carlson got steady work with a New York electronics firm in its patent department. There he became impressed by the inconvenience of getting extra copies made of documents and drawings.

Manuscripts had to be retyped, drawings sent out to photocopying firms—expensive and time-consuming processes. Carlson thought how helpful it would be if offices had a machine into which one could feed an original, then push a button and get a copy. In 1935 he set out to invent such a machine. Then as now it was commonplace for people to say that an individual could no longer amass a fortune, and that important inventions could come only out of large, organized laboratories. Carlson, 29, thin and near-sighted but a hard man to discourage, was to prove the pessimists wrong.

He worked for three years alone, surveying the ways light can affect matter, searching for an unconventional way of transferring images from one page to another. Saturdays, Sundays and evenings were spent in the New York Public Library. He studied on the subway. There was never enough time, for he was carrying a triple load: holding down his regular job, working to get his law degree at night school, and pursuing his dream. His theoretical investigations eventually led him to electrostatics, and in 1937 he filed a patent application for a process he called "electrophotography."

Carlson had the basic concept firmly in hand (as proved when the patent was subsequently issued), but he had yet to reduce it to practice. When his "laboratory"—a closet in his one-room apartment—proved inadequate, he rented a tiny room in Astoria, Long Island, and equipped it with a workbench, metal plates, resins, sulphur, chemicals and a Bunsen burner. Out of his own meager earnings he also hired a physicist, Otto Kornei, to do laboratory work.

In this drab room, on October 22, 1938, the phrase "10-22-38 Astoria" was inked on a glass slide. A sulphur-coated metal plate was rubbed with a cotton handkerchief to give it an electric charge, and exposed to the glass slide for three seconds under a floodlamp. When the plate was then dusted with a powder called lycopodium, the legend "10-22-38 Astoria" appeared on it. And when a piece of waxed paper was pressed down on the plate's sulphur surface, the legend appeared on the paper. This was the world's first electrostatic copying—later named xerography, Greek for "dry writing": copying without moist paper or chemicals.

But for Carlson, years of false starts lay ahead. The versions of a machine that the model makers produced from his drawings never ran to suit him. When he tried to interest backers, they were largely indifferent. From 1939 to 1944 he was turned down by more than 20 companies, including Remington Rand and International Business Machines. The National Inventors Council recognized the need for copying machines but dismissed Carlson's process.

Still, he kept on writing letters, making calls and strengthening his patent position. (He was issued four basic patents which he loaded with tight, all-encompassing claims.) In 1944 he went to Columbus, Ohio, to demonstrate his process to the Battelle Memorial Institute, a nonprofit industrial-research organization. Battelle agreed to undertake development work in return for 60 percent of all proceeds. Manufacturers remained uninterested—some of them called the process "crude" or "toylike."

When Battelle's research expenditures on xerography passed a certain specified limit, according to the agreement, Carlson had to put up $15,000 or see his interest in royalties drop from 40 to 25 percent. He threw in his savings, borrowed, persuaded relatives to let him have funds.

The tide turned when a small firm in Rochester, N.Y.,

Xerox—The Invention That Hit the Jackpot 59

(the Haloid Co., later to take the name Xerox Corp.) began dickering for commercial rights. In April 1947, Carlson received his first royalty check from Battelle—$2500. But no Xerox machine was put on the market until 1950. It was ten more years before the company launched its 914 Copier, a desk-size machine that, with a push of the button, turns out dry copies on ordinary paper.

At that time a number of office copiers were on the market—for example, Eastman Kodak Co.'s Verifax, a "wet" copier which employs chemical developers, and Minnesota Mining & Manufacturing Co.'s Thermo-Fax, a dry method that uses heat from an infrared lamp to form images on special paper. The Xerox machine's advantages were: a dry process that does not use chemicals or require special paper, and that turns out copies of extremely high quality.

This was the machine which touched off "the most sweeping revolution in office copying"—and, with expert exploitation, produced one of the most spectacular business success stories ever. Xerox profits increased tenfold in three years. In 1966 Battelle's block of Xerox stock—about five percent of all outstanding shares—was valued at nearly two million dollars. Carlson earned well over 150 million dollars for his remarkable invention. Before his death in September 1968 he had turned over some 100 million of it to charity.

The office copying machine, as many employers have discovered, reproduces many things besides business forms—from office jokes to love letters to three-dimensional objects. In Detroit the Food and Drug Administration no longer has to make typewritten copies of the labels on bottles and cans. Instead, the bottle (or can) is rolled across the Xerox scanning glass to secure a duplicate of the labels. Some police departments, on booking a prisoner, dump the contents of his pockets on the scanning glass—wallet, coins, knives, keys; the reproduction provides an accurate receipt.

The office copier industry's rentals and sales last year added up to an estimated $7.07 billion. Meanwhile, manufacturers are bringing out more and better machines, pouring extra funds into research—and altering the way we do business. All this is a tremendous change from 40 years ago, when Chester Carlson was knocking on doors with the invention that nobody wanted.

Unforgettable John Wayne

by Ronald Reagan

WE CALLED HIM DUKE, and he was every bit the giant off screen he was on. Everything about him—his stature, his style, his convictions—conveyed enduring strength, and no one who observed his struggle in those final days could doubt that strength was real. Yet there was more. To my wife, Nancy, "Duke Wayne was the most gentle, tender person I ever knew."

In 1960, as president of the Screen Actors' Guild, I was deeply embroiled in a bitter labor dispute between the Guild and the motion-picture industry. When we called a strike, the film industry unleashed a series of stinging personal attacks against me—criticism my wife was finding difficult to take.

At 7:30 one morning the phone rang and Nancy heard Duke's booming voice: "I've been readin' what these damn columnists are saying about Ron. He can take care of himself, but I've been worrying about how all this is affecting you." Virtually every morning until the strike was settled several weeks later, he phoned her. When a mass meeting was called to discuss settlement terms, he left a dinner party so that he could escort Nancy and sit at her side. It was, she said, like being next to a force bigger than life.

Countless others were also touched by his strength. Although it would take the critics 40 years to recognize what he was, the movie-going public knew all along. In this country and around the world, he was the most popular box-office star of all time. For an incredible 25 years he was rated at or around the top in box-office appeal. His films grossed $700 million—a record no performer in Hollywood has come close to matching. Yet John Wayne was more than an actor; he was a force around which films were made. As Elizabeth Taylor Warner stated when testifying in favor of the special gold medal Congress struck for him: "He gave the whole world the image of what an American should be."

He was born Marion Michael Morrison in Winterset,

Iowa. When Marion was six, the family moved to California. There he picked up the nickname Duke—after his Airedale. He rose at 4 a.m. to deliver newspapers, and after school and football practice he made deliveries for local stores. He was an A student, president of the Latin Society, head of his senior class and an all-state guard on a championship football team.

Duke had hoped to attend the U.S. Naval Academy and was named as an alternate selection to Annapolis, but the first choice took the appointment. Instead, he accepted a full scholarship to play football at the University of Southern California. There coach Howard Jones, who often found summer jobs in the movie industry for his players, got Duke work in the summer of 1926 as an assistant prop man on the set of a movie directed by John Ford.

One day, Ford, a notorious taskmaster with a rough-and-ready sense of humor, spotted the tall U.S.C. guard on his set and asked Duke to bend over and demonstrate his football stance. With a deft kick, Ford knocked Duke's arms from beneath his body and the young athlete fell on his face. Picking himself up, Duke said in that voice which even then commanded attention, "Let's try that once again." This time Duke sent Ford flying. Ford erupted in laughter, and the two began a personal and professional friendship which would last a lifetime.

From his job in props, Duke worked his way into roles on the screen. During the Depression he played in grade-B westerns until John Ford finally convinced United Artists to give him the role of the Ringo Kid in his classic film *Stagecoach*. John Wayne was on the road to stardom. He quickly established his versatility in a variety of major roles: a young seaman in Eugene O'Neill's *The Long Voyage Home,* a tragic captain in *Reap the Wild Wind*, a rodeo rider in the comedy *A Lady Takes a Chance*.

When war broke out, Duke tried to enlist but was rejected because of an old football injury to his shoulder—his age (34) and his status as a married father of four. He flew to Washington to plead that he be allowed to join the Navy but was turned down. So he poured himself into the war effort by making inspirational war films—among them *The Fighting Seabees, Back to Bataan* and *They Were Expendable*. To those back home and others around the world he became a symbol of the determined American fighting man.

62 Bold Dreams

Duke could not be kept from the front lines. In 1944 he spent three months touring forward positions in the Pacific theater. Appropriately, it was a wartime film, *Sands of Iwo Jima*, which turned him into a superstar. Years after the war, when Emperior Hirohito of Japan visited the United States, he sought out John Wayne, paying tribute to the one who represented our nation's success in combat.

As one of the true innovators of the film industry, Duke tossed aside the model of the white-suited cowboy/good guy, creating instead a tougher, deeper-dimensioned western hero. He discovered Monument Valley, the film setting in the Arizona-Utah desert where a host of movie classics were filmed. He perfected the choreographic techniques and stunt-man tricks which brought realism to screen fighting. At the same time he decried pornography, and blood and gore in films. "That's not sex and violence," he would say. "It's filth and bad taste."

In the 1940s, Duke was one of the few stars with the courage to expose the determined bid by a band of communists to take control of the film industry. Through a series of violent strikes and systematic blacklisting, these people were at times dangerously close to reaching their goal. With theatrical employes' union leader Roy Brewer, playwright Morrie Ryskind and others, he formed the Motion Picture Alliance for the Preservation of American Ideals to challenge this insidious campaign. Subsequent Congressional investigations in 1947 clearly proved both the communist plot and the importance of what Duke and his friends did.

In that period, during my first term as president of the Actors' Guild, I was confronted with an attempt by many of these same leftists to assume leadership of the union. At a mass meeting I watched rather helplessly as they filibustered, waiting for our majority to leave so they could gain control. Somewhere in the crowd I heard a call for adjournment, and I seized on this as a means to end the attempted takeover. But the other side demanded I identify the one who moved for adjournment.

I looked over the audience, realizing that there were few willing to be publicly identified as opponents of the far left. Then I saw Duke and said, "Why I believe John Wayne made the motion." I heard his strong voice reply, "I sure as hell did!" The meeting—and the radicals' campaign—was over.

Later, when such personalities as actor Larry Parks came forward to admit their Communist Party backgrounds, there were those who wanted to see them punished. Not Duke. "It takes courage to admit you're wrong," he said, and he publicly battled attempts to ostracize those who had come clean.

Duke also had the last word over those who warned that his battle against communism in Hollywood would ruin his career. Many times he would proudly boast, "I was 32nd in the box-office polls when I accepted the presidency of the Alliance. When I left office eight years later, somehow the folks who buy tickets had made me number one."

Duke went to Vietnam in the early days of the war. He scorned VIP treatment, insisting that he visit the troops in the field. Once he even had his helicopter land in the midst of a battle. When he returned, he vowed to make a film about the heroism of Special Forces soldiers.

The public jammed theaters to see the resulting film, *The Green Berets*. The critics, however, delivered some of the harshest reviews ever given a motion picture. The *New Yorker* bitterly condemned the man who made the film. The New York *Times* called it "unspeakable...rotten...stupid." Yet Duke was undaunted. "That little clique back there in the East has taken great personal satisfaction reviewing my politics instead of my pictures," he often said. "But one day those doctrinaire liberals will wake up to find the pendulum has swung the other way."

I never once saw Duke display hatred toward those who scorned him. Oh, he could use some pretty salty language, but he would not tolerate pettiness and hate. He was human, all right: he drank enough whiskey to float a PT boat, though he never drank on the job. His work habits were legendary in Hollywood—he was virtually always the first to arrive on the set and the last to leave.

His torturous schedule plus the great personal pleasure he derived from hunting and deep-sea fishing or drinking and card-playing with his friends may have cost him a couple of marriages; but you had only to see his seven children and 21 grandchildren to realize that Duke found time to be a good father. He often said, "I have tried to live my life so that my family would love me and my friends respect me. The others can do whatever the hell they please."

To him, a handshake was a binding contract. When he was in the hospital for the last time and sold his yacht, *The Wild Goose*, for an amount far below its market value, he learned the engines needed minor repairs. He ordered those engines overhauled at a cost to him of $40,000 because he had told the new owners the boat was in good shape.

Duke's generosity and loyalty stood out in a city rarely known for either. When a friend needed work, that person went on his payroll. When a friend needed help, Duke's wallet was open. He also was loyal to his fans. One writer tells of the night he and Duke were in Dallas for the premiere of *Chisum*. Returning late to his hotel, Duke found a message from a woman who said her little girl lay critically ill in a local hospital. The woman wrote, "It would mean so much to her if you could pay her just a brief visit." At 3 o'clock in the morning he took off for the hospital where he visited the astonished child—and every other patient on the hospital floor who happened to be awake.

I saw his loyalty in action many times. I remember that when Duke and Jimmy Stewart were on their way to my second inauguration as governor of California they encountered a crowd of demonstrators under the banner of the Vietcong flag. Jimmy had just lost a son in Vietnam. Duke excused himself for a moment and walked into the crowd. In a moment there was no Vietcong flag.

Like any good John Wayne film, Duke's career had a gratifying ending. In the 1970s a new era of critics began to recognize the unique quality of his acting. The turning point had been the film *True Grit*. When the Academy gave him an Oscar for best actor in 1969, many said it was based on the accomplishments of his entire career. Others said it was Hollywood's way of admitting that it had been wrong to deny him Academy Awards for a host of previous films. There is truth, I think, to both these views.

Yet who can forget the climax of the film? The grizzled old marshal confronts the four outlaws and calls out: "I mean to kill you or see you hanged at Judge Parker's convenience. Which will it be?"

"Bold talk for a one-eyed fat man," their leader sneers.

Then Duke cries, "Fill your hand, you sonofabitch!" and, reins in his teeth, charges at them firing with both guns. Four villains did not live to menace another day.

"Foolishness?" wrote Chicago *Sun-Times* columnist Mike Royko, describing the thrill this scene gave him. "Maybe. But I hope we never become so programmed that nobody has the damn-the-risk spirit."

Fifteen years ago when Duke lost a lung in his first bout with cancer, studio press agents tried to conceal the nature of his illness. When Duke discovered this, he went before the public and showed us that a man can fight this dread disease. He went on to raise millions of dollars for private cancer research. Typically, he snorted: "We've got too much at stake to give government a monopoly in the fight against cancer."

Earlier this year, when doctors told Duke there was no hope, he urged them to use his body for experimental medical research, to further the search for a cure. He refused painkillers so he could be alert as he spent his last days with his children. When he died on June 11, a Tokyo newspaper ran the headline, "Mr. America passes on."

"There's right and there's wrong," Duke said in *The Alamo*. "You gotta do one or the other. You do the one and you're living. You do the other and you may be walking around but in reality you're dead."

Duke Wayne symbolized just this, the force of the American will to do what is right in the world. He could have left no greater legacy.

Land and People

Country of My Heart

by Donald Culross Peattie

MANY MILLIONS of years ago, in the springtime of the world, this continent creased into a wrinkle like a smile and the Southern Appalachians arose. Other mountains may wear caps of glaciers; many are bleak—treeless and wind-whipped. But the Southern Appalachians are livable and lovable. There are no others quite like them, so deep in forest that you are never out of sound of rustling leaves or whispering needles, so laced with streams that the murmur of running water is almost always with you. And wherever you go there is a pervading odor of lichen and fern, of pine and mushroom, with wood smoke reeking through it from cabins in the laurel.

This is the country of my heart. It is the country where I was young, in my own Appalachian spring, and where I first found my love of nature. I can remember every detail that I ever knew in the Southern Appalachians—the fragrance of each kind of flower, all the many sorts of trillium, the clove-scented pinesaps that grow beneath the leaves, and the shy people and their speech.

For they do not speak as other Southerners do; their r's are not dropped or slurred, but rolled. They say "nary" when they mean "none"; they use certain words as they were once used by Chaucer, Shakespeare and Pepys. A broom they may call a "besom." They say of a town "Hit was thick of houses, thick of people," and you hear in this how lonely are their own cabins. "Far tap yan" is "that distant peak yonder," which may bear a name with a naïve poetry like "Chunky Gal Mountain." A coiled snake is "quirled," and if you don't want to kill it you "surround" it; that is, you walk wide of it. A woman who "don't care to talk" is one who does not mind talking. Azalea is "honeysuckle," mountain laurel is "ivy," but "laurel" usually means rhododendron. A "painter" or "tyger" is a panther or mountain lion.

The older mountain people have led isolated lives in their

coves (small headwater valleys) and do not mind it, since they have all good things and require no gadgets. I once found myself in Happy Valley, Tenn., and I never saw a happier place—children splashing in the creek for turtles and prettystones just as I used to, a happy landscape with a slow horsedrawn plow passing across it, and in a doorway a woman watching, babe on her hip. I met an old codger and asked him if I was on the way to Rainbow Fall. "Reckon you might be," he admitted. "They used to call it waterfall. Now they call it Rainbow Fall." And he went on, shaking his head over this "fotched on" (outlandish) name.

The many waterfalls of the Southern Appalachians are not sensational. But the beauty of a waterfall is not to be measured in its height or volume. It lies in the hypnotic music, in the purity of the water, in the absence of parking areas and litter. I know some white cascades falling amidst hemlock and beech which still have no name and are seldom visited except by the flashing redbird, the talkative chat and the eerily caroling water thrush. And every Appalachian waterfall has a setting of maidenhair which shakes off the spray continuously. Forever the spray sets foamflower and meadow rue to trembling, and the big rhombic leaves of trillium to drumming.

These, of all the mountains of North America, were the first to be seen by white men. On a May day in 1540 Hernando De Soto and his Spanish conquistadors in their glittering armor came looking for gold. He had landed in Florida, and as he pushed northwest the Indians he encountered always said that it was the next tribe farther inland which had the gold. As De Soto extracted this information under torture, he had no choice but to believe it and put his weary columns in march again. That's how he came to see, first of white men, the misty wall of the Blue Ridge rising against the soft sky.

The next white men to come were English traders from the Virginia coast. Settlers came at last, after 1704, mostly Scotch-Irish. Their chief port of entry was Newcastle, Del., where they picked up from the Swedes' colonies the idea of the log cabin. They settled the whole land from the foot of the Appalachians in the east to the valley of the Shenandoah and the Tennessee on the west. These were the future mountaineers, a people still dwelling in the deep coves of the Appalachian ranges.

The settlers brought with them the Bible in one hand,

a rifle in the other. They did not stop to convert the Cherokees; they drove them from their lands, all but a small band that hid out on what is now the borders of the Great Smoky Mountains National Park (the most frequented of all our national parks). They are today a pathetic remnant, who sometimes have to wear Sioux headdresses so that tourists will know they are Indians.

From their old country that we now call Ulster the pioneers brought also the ballads of Scotland, Ireland, and England. "Barbara Allen" is preserved as an antiquity in *The Oxford Book of Scottish Verse*, but in the mountains of the South it is a folksong known to every school child. To these ballads (usually doleful or fatalistic) the Southern highlander had added his own. It's hard to forget the plaint of the wife in one such song:

> No shoes on my feet, no hat on my head,
> And babies sprawling all over the bed.

From the British Isles the women brought the spinning wheel, not the little wheel with which the *Mayflower* was apparently burdened, but the high spinning wheel. The wool for the spun thread was dyed with native dyes, from oak bark, walnut, yellowroot, sumac, and scores of others discovered by long experiment. Then, on the slow hand loom, the women wove the old patterns like the Tudor Rose and the Whig Rose, and new ones that the flora presented to their eyes, such as the famed dogwood pattern.

The pioneer menfolk carried with them two dangerous old customs. One was the clan feud. The cause was usually forgotten, but the feud was kept alive by vengeance. Firing from ambush was considered fair play; women of an enemy clan were not immune. I remember one fierce feud in my own childhood. The Hendersons and the Chatfields were feuding and when, allegedly, old Chatfield killed a Henderson, the sheriff put the Chatfield family off the land where they had been squatters. I remember it because it took away Melissa Chatfield, the only playmate on my mountaintop.

The other perilous import was the fanatical conviction that a man had a right to distill his own whiskey, revenue law or not. I used always to see a plume of smoke rising from "Dark Corners," which possessed the great advantage of being

72 Land and People

situated precisely on the state line that divides the two Carolinas. If a North Carolina sheriff raided you, you just took one step into South Carolina and you were safe from everybody except federal agents; some of those were shot on sight.

In my college days I was collecting botanical specimens on the state line when a man cradling a rifle suddenly cast his suspicious shadow upon me. All mountain people ask you what you are doing because they are curious and interested. I told him that I was gathering plants for Harvard. "Who's he?" asked the sentry of the still that I knew could not be far off. "John Harvard," I explained, "was a benevolent Yankee who died in the year 1638." The sentry smiled. "You're just yarbin' it," he said, "and don't try to fool me no more."

I was, in a manner of speaking, "yarbin' it"; that is, I was collecting herbs, or "yarbs," for their value, though not to sell as the mountain people do. They gathered ginseng—"sang" they call it—whose bifurcated root looks like the rough image of a man. By the ancient doctrine of signatures (a liver-shaped leaf is good for your liver, a heart-shaped leaf for your heart) this underground manikin is good for whatever ails mankind. That is what the Chinese believed, at any rate, and why they bought in quantity, having exhausted their own resources. The mountain people had, indeed, more than 90 percent of all the wild plants which yield real, not fictitious, drugs. These were collected in summer, like the "sang," and sold in bulk to men who went around picking them up at country stores. In winter the Southern Appalachians supply Christmas fern, and above all the beautiful bronze and green galax leaf. So that "yarbin' it" became a leading industry.

Mountain people are not easy to get to know. They wait for you to speak first, but unlike city folk they expect you to speak. They love to ask you questions but don't like it if you question them too much. Like all pioneer people they are hospitable; I have knocked at many a cabin door, as it came on to darken on my walking trips, and asked to be taken in. It is not the best of manners, though, to ask this of wife or daughters; best wait till you can speak to the head of the house. He will not refuse you.

The mountain houses that I knew were very clean, and the people much more moral than the run of folk. Courtship usually had to be carried on in sight of the whole family or at least some adult member. Marriage was supposed to be for life, and divorces were rare. Child brides I never heard of—not among mountain folk. Children were brought up to a politeness that our own youngsters might find taxing. The welcome on the hearth is the warmer for the quickness by which a blaze can be kindled; this is because the kindling is splinters of fat or lighter pine, full of turpentine.

From this region with its high birth rate the young people scatter far and wide. "Hillbillies?" These clans have produced such men as Lincoln and Woodrow Wilson.

Poor the mountain folk may be in the things of this world. It is a "doing without" kind of poor—to use their own idiom. It is no poverty of spirit or inheritance. And they claim as their own one of the fairest provinces in all America, the country of my heart.

Offbeat Wonders of New York

by Gay Talese

NEW YORK is a city of things unnoticed. It is a city with cats sleeping under parked cars, two stone armadillos crawling up St. Patrick's Cathedral, thousands of ants creeping on top of the Empire State building. Nobody knows any more about how the ants got there than they do about the panhandler who rides a taxi to the Bowery; or the dapper man who picks trash out of Sixth Avenue trash cans; or the medium in the West 70s who claims, "I am clairvoyant, clairaudient and clairsensuous."

New York is a city for eccentrics and a center for odd bits of information. Gum chewers on Macy's escalators stop chewing momentarily just before they get off—to concentrate on the last step. A Park Avenue doorman has parts of three bullets in his head—there since World War I. Each month 100 pounds of hair is delivered to Louis Feder at 545 Fifth Avenue, where blond hairpieces are made from German women's hair; brunette hairpieces from Italian women's hair; but no hairpieces from American women's hair which, says Feder, is weak from too-frequent rinses and permanents.

On Broadway each evening a Rolls-Royce pulls up at 46th Street—and out hop two little ladies armed with Bibles, and signs reading, "The Damned Shall Perish." They stand on the corner screaming at the multitudes of Broadway sinners, sometimes until 3 a.m., when their chauffeur picks them up and drives them back to Westchester.

In New York at 6 a.m. Mrs. Mary Woody jumps out of bed, dashes to her office and phones dozens of sleepers to say in a cheerful voice, rarely appreciated: "Good morning. Time to get up." In 20 years as an operator of Western Union's Wakeup Service Mrs. Woody has gotten millions out of bed.

By 7 a.m. a floridly robust little man, looking very Parisian in a blue beret and turtle-neck sweater, moves in a hurried step along Park Avenue visiting his wealthy lady friends—to give them a brisk, before-breakfast rubdown. The uniformed doormen greet him warmly; they know him as a ladies' masseur *extraordinaire*.

Shortly after 7:30 each morning hundreds of people are lined along 42nd Street waiting for the 8 a.m. opening of the ten movie houses that stand almost shoulder-to-shoulder between Times Square and Eighth Avenue. Who are these people? They are the city's insomniacs, night watchmen, cops, hacks, truck drivers, cleaning women and restaurant men who have worked all night. They are also alcoholics who are waiting to pay for a soft seat where they can sleep.

New York is a city of 35,000 cab drivers, 10,000 bus drivers, and one chauffeur who has a chauffeur. The wealthy chauffeur can be seen driving up Fifth Avenue each morning, and his name is Roosevelt Zanders. This man will drive anyone anywhere in his silver Rolls-Royce. Diplomats patronize him, models pose with him, and every day he receives cables from around the world urging that he be waiting at Idlewild, on the docks or outside the Plaza Hotel. Sometimes at night he is too tired to drive. So *his* chauffeur takes over and Zanders relaxes in the back.

Each afternoon in New York a rather seedy saxophone player, his cheeks blown out like a spinnaker, stands on the sidewalk playing "Danny Boy" in such a sad, sensitive way that he soon has people peeking out of windows tossing nickels, dimes and quarters at his feet. In 30 years he has serenaded every block in the city, and some days he has been tossed as much as $100 in coins. He is also hit with buckets of water, eggs and empty beer cans. He is believed to be the last of New York's street musicians.

There are 200,000 stray cats in New York. A large number of them hang around the Fulton Fish Market, or in Greenwich Village, and in the East and West Side neighborhoods where garbage cans abound. But 25 cats live 75 feet below the west end of Grand Central Terminal, are fed by the underground workers and never come up into daylight.

New York is a city in which large, cliff-dwelling hawks cling to skyscrapers and occasionally dive to snatch a pigeon over Central Park or Wall Street or the Hudson River. About 12 of these peregrine falcons patrol the city, some with a wingspan of 35 inches. They have buzzed women on the roof of the St. Regis Hotel and attacked repairmen on smokestacks. Maintenance men at the Riverside Church have seen hawks dining on pigeons in the bell tower. The hawks remain there for only a little while. Then they fly out to the river, leaving pigeons' heads for the Riverside maintenance men to clean up. When the hawks return, they fly in quietly—*unnoticed*, like the cats, the ants, the ladies' masseur, the doorman with three bullets in his head and most of the city's other offbeat wonders.

Along California's Golden Coast

By Earl and Miriam Selby

SOMETIMES, when the world crowds in too much, we pack a lunch—San Francisco sourdough bread, Monterey Jack cheese, red apples—and drive 20 miles from home to our own particular security blanket. It is a piece of the mid-California coast, where a trail takes us to a rocky bluff overlooking the Pacific. At our backs are cypress trees that have hung tough against the worst batterings of winter's storms. A hundred feet below are offshore granite rocks thrusting defiant chins against the surging seas.

When we sit on that cliff, thinking about this endless fight for survival, a certain peace descends upon us, and after a while we go home, refreshed and encouraged.

From Oregon to Mexico, the sea haunts California; its sights and smells and sounds ride over everything. Along its 1341 miles, the shoreline works its magic on visitors: tempting, embracing, seducing. To travel this coast, even if only for a short distance, is to know the excitement of the restless, westering Americans reaching continent's edge. It is walking back in history with the mission-founding "Conquistadores of the Cross." It is savoring solitude amid the driftwood of a lonely beach, climbing the 40-odd hills of San Francisco, dissolving into the throngs at Disneyland. It is sampling in small pieces one of the shoreline's three distinct worlds, each of which has its own mood and heritage.

Pelican Beach to Bodega Bay. Beginning at the beach that flanks Oregon and continuing to the bay above San Francisco, this 391 miles of coast is an arena of wild seas, great trees, windswept cliffs and weathered relics. Here the Pacific once raged up to snuff out the light in a lighthouse perched 196 feet above the water. A tidal wave unleashed by Alaska's 1964 earthquake stormed over sea walls to overwhelm Crescent City's business district. From promontories you can look north, look south, and as far as the eye can see there are spectacular views of the desolate cliffs, the sparse beachline, the rocks cut off from the mainland, all rimmed in mist from the crashing Pacific.

Along this coast are the world's mightiest stands of *Sequoia sempervirens*, the rough, scaly redwoods. Nurtured by winter's rains (up to 110 inches fall on some slopes) and kept moist in summer by fogs, these trees are taller than anything else that grows. One has been measured at 367.8 feet. At ground level they can reach 20 feet in diameter. Some have endured more than 2000 years.

The great forests dominate the region's tradition, going back to the last century when loggers and sailors turned the coast into a lusty, brawling frontier. These men often were Yankees, and the towns around the mills have the feeling of New England: the Victorian architecture, the salt-air weathering. One that still survives is Eureka. Eureka's waterfront has the grimy marks of a mill town, but the rest of the city has touches of Victorian splendor, especially the Carson Mansion. Completed in 1884 for a lumber baron, it is an eye-staggering spectacle of turrets, towers, gables and trim so ornate that even the gingerbread has gingerbread.

Down the coast, there are more ancestral Yankee trappings in the little village of Mendocino. Although the old sawmill has vanished, the thin white spire of the Presbyterian Church still stands, and charming streets thread among art galleries, shops and driftwood-decorated homes.

Whatever the traveler wants, this northern coast delivers. There are 30 state parks, beaches and other recreational facilities where a visitor can share a meadow with some of the last surviving herds of Roosevelt elk, hunt for driftwood, rockhound for jade, cast for salmon, or pry loose from the tidal rocks the abalones, those crustacean delights that take ten years to grow eight inches. From Fort Bragg (north of Mendocino) he can penetrate deep coastal forests aboard an old logging train. The tendon that ties much of this coast together, State Highway 1, ranks among the great scenic roads of America. It chases the sea, bending, dipping, climbing, sometimes wrapped in fog, sometimes walloped by winds, always offering new, challenging, surprising vistas.

Bodega Bay to Point Conception. For decades the only direct link between San Francisco and Marin County to the north was a ferry. It was considered impossible to bridge the Golden Gate because of the swift tides that had scoured a channel more than 300 feet deep, high winds that have peaked at 70 miles an hour, and the sheer distance of the 5346 feet between landfalls. That thinking was proved wrong. Completed in the late 1930s, the Golden Gate Bridge, third-longest single-suspended span structure in the world, some of its foundations built 110 feet under water, now carries over 50 million vehicles a year.

The bay that this bridge spans is what gives the compelling touch to San Francisco, a city so romanticized by writers and artists that it seems to promise everything to everyone. Here all the staples of the picture-postcard trade are alive: the cable cars, Fisherman's Wharf, the ferries. Alcatraz (convicts are out; tourists are in), Chinatown's New Year's dragons, the street-corner mimes and musicians, the downtown flower stalls. Across the perfect natural harbor are Sausalito with its racy waterfront, the bustling port of Oakland (busier than San Francisco's piers), the expensive homes that climb the golden hills.

Beyond Santa Cruz, Highway 1 stabs south through artichoke fields to Monterey, capital of California during both Spanish and Mexican rules. This is where the novelist John Steinbeck's *paisanos* worked and loved and schemed on Cannery Row. The old canneries have shut down, to be succeeded by the restaurants and shops that mobile Americans keep in business. Nearby, the famous 17-mile drive ($3 per car) covers the rim of Monterey's peninsula, for peeks at millionaires' estates, craggy sea knolls, and golf courses made famous by televised tournaments.

On the peninsula's south side is Carmel. Once an artist's colony, Carmel now trades in charm, with the flavor of English cottages, summer traffic jams and the rebuilt mission of San Carlos de Borromeo de Carmelo, springboard into historic California. In California, it was the cross and not the sword that shaped the first settlements. Father Junípero Serra, leader of the missionary padres known as "Conquistadores of the Cross," landed at Monterey in 1770 and then moved his headquarters to Carmel. Frail, in his 50s, Serra walked thousands of miles along this coast, establishing what ultimately grew into a chain of 21 Franciscan missions. They were the center of life: hospitality for travelers, ports of call for ships seeking hides and tallow from mission ranches, compounds to teach religion and a trade to thousands of Indians.

Ten minutes south of the Carmel mission is Point Lobos State Reserve, the microcosm of almost everything that is natural to California's shoreline. It has sea-hollowed arches, covers, islands where cormorants and other fishing birds nest, and reefs and cliffs lashed by the surf's foamy white explosions. Sea lions sunbathe on the rocks, while otters playfully show off in the kelp beds. Within sight is the California gray whales' migration run. Fifty feet long, weighing up to 40 tons, spouting as they make the November-March circuit between feeding grounds in the Bering Sea and the breeding pools of Baja California, these awesome mammals are star performers for the binocular crowd.

For much of the next 80 miles down to San Simeon, Highway 1 hangs on the cliffs of the Santa Lucia Mountains as they bump against the sea. This is the Big Sur area, where the wilderness surrounding the state parks is among the most ruggedly beautiful of our untamed lands. It took California 15 years to carve the roadbed, generally narrow, twisting, two-laned, alternatively at sea level and then abruptly veering upward for 1100 feet before plummeting again.

At San Simeon is the 123-acre estate where publisher William Randolph Hearst began building his home in 1919. Rising on "La Cuesta Encantada" ("the enchanted hill"), 1600 feet above the Pacific, the treasure-stuffed Casa Grande is a palace: 100 rooms, 38 bedrooms, two libraries and one theater, all topped by twin towers. It is now a state park, with daily fee tours.

Point Conception to San Diego. Southern California's weather is typically Mediterranean. Here, real-estate developers grow wealthy touting the sun and sea as the soothing antidote to long, hard winters elsewhere. The affluent retired populate the hills above Santa Barbara, a city of palm trees, adobes, courtyards and patios. The well-to-do take to the sea at Malibu, often from hanky-sized houses costing $100,000. The blond, tanned young people who live in pickup trucks ride their surfboards day after day at Redondo or San Onofre. At the heart of it all is Los Angeles County, with its astonishing proliferation of tract homes spread like wall-to-wall carpeting across every available inch of land.

Los Angeles is the gateway to Southern California's galaxy of amusements. The granddaddy of the fun parks is Disneyland. Knott's Berry Farm offers a "ghost town." The Japanese Village imports the Orient. Wax museums, usually built around nostalgic tableaux from Hollywood's days of glory, draw tourists in both Los Angeles and Orange counties. The city of Long Beach has the old luxury liner *Queen Mary* on permanent display. Marineland, the country's largest oceanarium, perches on the cliffs of Palos Verdes Peninsula. In San Diego is Balboa Park, 1400 acres of zoo, galleries, gardens and the Old Globe Theater, summertime mecca for Shakespeare fans.

For a long time, San Diego was mainly known as a sailor's town, the home port for the Navy's Pacific fleet. Lately, it has emerged as one of California's most appealing cities. Its downtown includes modern highrises, imaginatively designed. A couple of miles north is Old Town, a 16-acre state park, where the automobile is banned and visitors can stroll among landmark houses and see a newspaper museum. Within the scope of San Diego is the Scripps Institute of Oceanography at La Jolla, as well as Mission Bay, a $50 million aquatic park.

San Diego has 70 miles of beach, one part of which is the Silver Strand, pointing down to Mexico. In the summer it is crowded with sun worshippers, but on the January day we walked it we were alone. Sea winds blew in, so gusty that thousands of sea gulls had huddled on the sand to sleep. We stood there, staring at the Pacific's horizon, remembering how pioneers had bridged a continent to come to these shores, thinking of the California dream, and of how that dream still lives.

The Glorious Great Lakes

by Noel Mostert

THE Great Lakes are the immemorial surprise of middle America, its finest color; they are the greatest natural wonder of the whole continent, and yet, I am convinced, the most undervalued and unsung.

My own first introduction to them came some years ago from the spectacular stretch of Canadian Pacific track that runs along the north shore of Superior. The train comes drumming down from the bushland plateau, doubling and turning in the cuttings, and suddenly the emerald water heaves below, spreading from the white empty sands to a horizon as vast and open as the sea. That far horizon has always struck me as being the truest measure of North America's breadth: it is hard to grasp that a land should contain several fresh-water seas so big that a ship can steam out of sight of the shore for a day or more, or even founder in giant waves, as happens from time to time.

Yet there they are, these changing, changeless lakes, flung upon the map, almost dead center, spilling eastward and southward across the Middle West. Ontario, the only Canadian province that fringes them, sprawls along their northern coasts, and eight states—New York, Pennsylvania, Ohio, Michigan, Indiana, Illinois, Wisconsin, Minnesota—crowd their lower shores. More than 40 percent of America's total dollar income from farming, mining and manufacturing is earned around their basins; 80 percent of Canada's industry is settled there—so that in a most literal sense it is the breathing, pulsing, coursing heart of the continent.

This is the largest group of lakes in the world and the biggest body of fresh water, covering 96,000 square miles in surface, draining a 300,000-square-mile area, and flowing to the sea at a rate of 240,000 cubic feet per second—more than the Seine, Thames and Danube combined.

The lakes were the single greatest asset this land endowed to its pioneer man. Their spacious waters were a natural high-

The Glorious Great Lakes 83

way for the exploring French and, two centuries later, for the main westward rush of settlement. And when ore was discovered on Superior's shores, in the mid- to late 19th century, the cheap transportation provided by the lakes became the lever of continental prosperity and boom. It established the American iron and steel industries, and made America the industrial giant of the world.

Let us approach the lakes the best way: along the course of history, up from Montreal along the Saint Lawrence and its Seaway. We book on a big Swedish freighter that has crossed the Atlantic with Scandinavian luxuries for North America and will go into the lakes to pick up grain and general cargo for Australia.

Under way, we slide out of Montreal harbor and nose through the deepening twilight into the first lock of the Seaway, at Saint Lambert. Suddenly a siren wails, bells ring, booms descend, the lock gates start swinging shut, lights flash red, and a drawbridge behind us descends while another in front rises, the heavy road and rail traffic shifting imperturbably and without pause from one to the other. There is a roar of water, the ship rises, and in minutes we have been lifted high enough to sail on.

The Seaway is 110 miles long and has seven locks. Through our first night and the following day, these lift us steadily higher, into Lake Ontario. Ontario is the smallest of the Great Lakes, but it is deep, with a maximum sounding of 778 feet. It is 193 miles long, east to west. While the other lakes have distinct personalities, Ontario's is more elusive. The Niagara escarpment with its sheer thunderous drop has been an effective barrier between this and the other lakes, and the Saint Lawrence sluicing out its eastern end draws Ontario's attention seaward. Its commerce has always been in that direction—or south, to New York. Its mood is sedate. Here no vulgar echoes of the westward push, the immigrant scramble; that essential pioneer familiarity of the upper lakes is missing.

On the bridge, the pilot tells us that the lake sailor speaks a different nautical language. The lakeman came originally from the farm, and he brought with him a homey terminology. He goes steamboating, as he describes his calling; he calls the rail his fence, the bow the front end. When a propeller loses a blade he says the boat has "thrown her bucket." After the Seaway brought in the ocean ships, pilotage was introduced and enforced, and the lakeman has grudgingly come to recognize that the Great Lakes are no longer his private preserve.

In the morning we enter the Welland Canal, whose 27 miles and eight locks will lift us over the Niagara Falls escarpment to Lake Erie. We drift down the canal, past orchards and towns. We sail between backyards. Then past the back porch of a small farmhouse. Some sort of domestic celebration, a table out on the grass, the men in chairs talking. I raise my glass and they nod. A woman comes out with a pie dish and offers it around; she raises it and smiles, and we know that she is sorry she can't offer it to us across the gap of water.

Next morning we break out past the last lock into Lake Erie. The ship suddenly begins to sway. Doors bang and the air pours cold and strong through the porthole. We are at sea.

Though Superior is the worst storm lake, with waves reported as high as 35 feet, Erie is the one that is talked about: a killer of small craft. It has a reputation for treacherous flash storms. The shallowest of the lakes, it can be pale as glass, and as smooth—then a few hours later be insensately churning under a fugitive sky. Its shores are low-lying, its beaches often narrow, and except for the gritty imprints pawed by industry in that dense line of cities between Buffalo and Toledo on the south shore, it is succulently pastoral.

All day we push southwest. By evening the air is much colder, and a rainstorm washes away Cleveland's profile as we pass in through the breakwater and tie up there. A group of officials wait on the sodden dock, all solemnly patient in their wet clothes, motionless as pavement pigeons in a downpour. This is our first American port, and they are here to clear the ship. One man goes down into the holds to look for beetles, a serious matter here in the heart of the continent's farmlands; no vigilance is too small to protect against some unknown blight.

We never really see the city; in the morning it remains hidden in dark mist, and the foghorn on the breakwater sounds steadily. The cargo winches are busy, and the ship lists to starboard as the cranes work the port side, probing and nodding over the hatches like weird skeletal giraffes at feed; crates of beer and canned fish swing upward.

At dusk we pass the Detroit River lighthouse, situated at the junction of river and lake. Detroit lies beside us now, an immense suffusion of light on the mist, with glowing red patches from the torches of the plants at River Rouge. The night rattles and growls with the sleepless discontent of industry on the nearby shore. A strange melody as one lies in one's bunk, listening.

The unity between metropolis and water at Detroit forms an extraordinary junction. The other great cities stand back from the water, seem to bend their gaze inland toward the plains. I feel this in Chicago, even in Milwaukee. But not in Detroit. Nowhere else does human traffic converge so spectacularly with such pace and purpose and pride—the silver streamliners and fast freights, the multicolored cars and trucks and buses, the lake and ocean ships on the water, the jetliners like a constant shower of glinting splinters above as they descend and ascend over Willow Run.

In the next day and night we run the 206-mile north-south length of Lake Huron, the second-largest of the lakes. Its deepest sounding is 750 feet, and its shores are sparsely populated. Except for Bay City, Mich., Owen Sound, Ont., and the twin cities of Port Huron, Mich., and Sarnia, Ont., it is still wild country. You can smell the north here; the wind has the resinous taste of pine, and stings from having blown a long way across cold water.

A dark spirit is in the air; on the bridge one of the Swedes is sorting the charts, and the names marked on them run like an incantation to the presence that suddenly seems manifest about us—Manitowoc, Manitowaning, Manitou North, Manitoulin—and we take our sense of awe below with us, where we slowly and thoughtfully eat the rich meal and listen as the pilot, a Canadian, talks solemnly about ghosts and storm and wreck.

We enter Saint Mary's River at the upper end of Huron at twilight. The river is wide and still. On either side of it the forest comes down to the water, a stony shore; the country behind rises to low, hunched mountains. The overwhelming impression is of absolute silence. Not even Huron itself seemed so wide, so empty, soundless, as these woods pressing thickly to the very edge of the water. A gull, solitary as fear, the only movement in this primeval desolation, rises besides the rail and then wheels and soars high and catches that final light on its wing, floats for a moment, then vanishes.

Our destination now is Fort William, Ont., at the top of Lake Superior. Superior is 360 miles long, the largest fresh-water lake in the world. It is also the deepest of the Great Lakes—with the deepest sounding at 1302 feet, its bottom lies several hundred feet below sea level—and it holds almost half the water of the entire system.

There is an antique stillness on Superior, a feeling of immense brooding age. Round-humped mountains around the shores look like burial mounds of the gods, their surfaces rubbed to a hard polish by glaciers through eons of cold sleep. It is even in the very look of the water, a serene surface overlaid upon inscrutable depths.

Out through these ancestral mists move the long lake barges bearing prairie grain and Minnesota ore. If there is a distinctive sound that man has brought to this region, then surely it is the harsh clanging of shunting freight cars, which re-echoes night and day in the ports—Marquette, Duluth, Superior, Fort William, Port Arthur—where the trains crawl in with their mile-long loads of golden seed or tinted nuggets.

We slowly steam up to Fort William. The town wears the look of any city: sidewalks, paved streets and urban architecture. Yet the gleaming tracks and lines of cars, fringing the wilderness, strike me as being among the most remarkable things we have experienced so far; one feels that one has indeed come to some junction of the continent, between past and present, between frontier and factory.

Forty-eight hours later we pass through the Straits of Mackinac and enter Lake Michigan. Michigan, the only one of the lakes entirely within the United States, is the lake that built Chicago. It is the main route of the ocean-going ships. Its shores are green and tangled in the north, and white with dunes to the east.

Now the whole lake has gone glassy, and the sky black. There are distant rumbles, and suddenly the wind comes. In no time the ship begins to lift and roll. The bulkheads creak; the curtains swing; lightning illuminates the whole ship. From that windless dusk to this black rage. A steward comes in to secure the porthole.

"Tomorrow Chicago," he says, as if to convince himself as well as me. It still doesn't seem true. He should have said Cherbourg or Southhampton. Chicago? I lie and listen to the water.

The Life and Death of Casey Jones

by Tom Mahoney

Come all you rounders, if you want to hear
A story 'bout a brave engineer—
Casey Jones was the rounder's name
On a six eight wheeler, boys, he won his fame.

THUS BEGINS what Carl Sandburg calls "the greatest ballad ever written on the North American continent." Who was Casey Jones? Almost everyone knows that Casey was a railroad engineer who was killed in a wreck. But unless you are a railroad buff or live in Jackson, Tenn., where his old home has been converted into a museum, the chances are that your facts are hazy.

Casey Jones was born Johnathan Luther Jones in southern Missouri in 1863. When he was a boy, his schoolteacher father moved the family to the village of Cayce, Ky. All three of his brothers also grew up to be locomotive engineers, but none of the others was as spectacular, in life or death, as Casey.

A handsome man with blue-gray eyes, six-feet-four-inches tall, Casey was by 1900 one of the best engineers of the Illinois Central Railroad. Since the airplane had not yet been developed and there were few automobiles and no highways, railroads were the quickest means of getting about the country. The engineers who handled the big steam locomotives were among the most glamorous men in the land.

Like jockeys carrying their own saddles from mount to mount, many engineers took their own steam whistles from locomotive to locomotive. A St. Louis admirer gave Casey his whistle, a six-lute calliope affair that played an unusual "whippoorwill" tune. He was so famous for being on time that people up and down the railroad set their watches to the lonesome

88 Land and People

wail of his whistle. He did not drink, but he had a reputation for speed dating from his fast-freight days.

The Illinois Central had four fast passenger trains a day running between Chicago and New Orleans—the Cannonball expresses. Early in 1900, Casey, now 36, drew the assignment of helping to pilot these trains over the 188-mile stretch between Memphis, Tenn., and Canton, Miss., on a 50-mile-an-hour schedule, including stops. He was assigned a worshipful young Negro fireman named Sim T. Webb, and given a new locomotive, No. 382. It was not "a six eight wheeler." There is no such thing. No. 382 was a fast ten-wheel McQueen with six driving wheels six feet high.

On April 29, 1900, Casey brought Cannonball No. 2 north into Memphis exactly on time at 9 p.m. He was scheduled to rest there and take No. 1 south the evening of the next day. But at the roundhouse he learned that Sam Tate, the engineer due to take No. 1 south that same evening, was ill.

"I'll double out," said Casey.

He needed the extra money. He had a wife and three children, and he was planning to move from Jackson and buy a house in Memphis. His only condition for "doubling out" was that he use his own engine, No. 382.

The southbound Cannonball arrived late. About 12:50 a.m., Casey Jones "mounted to the cabin" and the 12-coach Cannonball moved south out of Memphis, at least 95 minutes behind schedule.

> Put in your water and shovel your coal
> Put your head out the window, watch them drivers roll
> I'll run her till she leaves the rail
> 'Cause I'm eight hours late with the Western mail.

"We'll have a tough time getting into Canton on the dot, but I believe we can make it," Casey told his fireman. Sim shoveled on coal. Casey poured on steam. With bursts of speed of more than 100 miles an hour, they made up 60 minutes in the straight, level 102-mile stretch to Grenada, Miss., the first stop. In the 23 miles from Grenada to Winona, Casey made up 15 minutes more. "The old lady's got her high-heel slippers on tonight!" Casey shouted to Sim across the cab.

Casey was almost on time when he made his last scheduled stop at Durant. It was a single-track railroad, and he took the siding at Goodman, a little farther on, to let the northbound Cannonball pass. This delayed him just five minutes, and he sped onward at 75 miles an hour over a supposedly clear track. He was only two minutes behind schedule as he approached Vaughan, just 14 miles from the end of his run. Incredibly, Cannonball No. 1 had made up 91 minutes in 174 miles. "This means," wrote Fred J. Lee, an Illinois Central engineer of the time, "that there were times when she was driving through the night considerably in excess of 100 miles per hour, and hardly below 65 miles per hour at any time!"

Twelve minutes more at the same speed and Casey would have ended his run on schedule. But as he swept around an "S" curve into Vaughan, the red lights of a freight-train caboose loomed up in the foggy night.

"We're gonna hit!" shouted Sim.

Casey Jones reacted swiftly. He shut off the throttle, applied the air brakes, pulled the reverse lever and sounded a blast on the "whippoorwill" whistle.

"Jump, Sim!" he shouted.

As the express slowed from 75 to perhaps 35 miles an hour, Sim jumped. Casey Jones stayed at the controls and just failed to brake his train short of collision.

With a crash heard for miles, his locomotive splintered the caboose. It plowed through a car of hay and on into another loaded with shelled corn, tons of which were scattered over the scene. No. 382 then left the rails and turned on her side. The tender and all of the Cannonball coaches remained on the track.

Casey Jones was found with an iron bolt driven through his neck and bales of hay crushing his body. He was the only person killed. Sim Webb was picked up unconscious, but was only bruised, as were an express messenger, two postal clerks and a woman passenger. The five accepted a total of $31 in full payment of any claim against the railroad. Engine No. 382 was later repaired and returned to service under another number.

How had it happened? Two freight trains had been ordered to a siding at Vaughan, but their combined length was longer than the 3148-foot siding, so that four cars extended onto the main track at the north end. To let a southbound train pass, the freights had to execute a "saw by." They would move south on the siding, permitting the through train to stop alongside on the main track. Then they would pull back until the way ahead was clear.

They were preparing to do a "saw by" to let Casey Jones through when a rubber air hose broke and froze all of one train's wheels, leaving four cars on the track in the path of the onrushing Cannonball. What happened next is still a matter of controversy.

Regulations required that warning torpedoes (cartridges that explode under a locomotive's wheels) be placed on the track "30 telegraph poles away," that a flare be lighted and that a trainman be sent with a lantern to intercept the oncoming train. A flagman named John M. Newberry was dispatched from the stalled freight to do all these things. According to an official Illinois Central investigator's report, Sim Webb and the crews of the trains waiting at Vaughan all agreed that Newberry had done his job and that the torpedoes had exploded.

"Engineer Jones was solely responsible for the collision by reason of having disregarded the signals given by Flagman Newberry," the report concluded.

For many years before his death in 1957, Sim Webb told and recorded a different story, insisting, "We saw no flagman or flare. We heard no torpedoes."

In any event, admirers of Casey rallied to his defense. One of Casey's friends, Wallace Saunders, a Negro engine-wiper at the Canton shops of the Illinois Central, composed a ballad about the wreck and began to sing it: "Casey Jones— Casey Jones, he was all right. Stuck to his duty both day and night...."

William Leighton, an Illinois Central engineer, passed Saunders' ballad along to his brothers, Bert and Frank Leighton, vaudeville performers, who sang variations of the tune and spread it throughout the land. A professional song-writing team, T. Lawrence Seibert and Eddie Newton, copyrighted the best-known version in 1909. It was superior in tune and rhyme but much less accurate than that of Wallace Saunders. They even placed the wreck on a Western line near San Francisco and added a verse suggesting that Mrs. Jones had another husband "on that Salt Lake Line." It was a best-seller just before World War I, and has been a steady seller in records and sheet music ever since.

In the 1930s, a book, a motion picture and a series of

radio dramas based on the Casey Jones story added to the legend. A commemorative stamp was issued in Jackson, Tenn., for the 50th anniversary of Casey's last run. The first-day-sale ceremonies drew the biggest crowd in the town's history, and speakers compared Casey to Paul Bunyan and Johnny Appleseed.

The Casey Jones Museum was opened in 1956, after the city purchased the home where the Joneses lived at the time of the accident. The family gave the museum Casey's watch and other personal relics. A locomotive of the same type as No. 382 was given by the city of Jackson, and many other railroad relics were donated by the Illinois Central. The museum also had a duplicate of Casey's "whippoorwill" whistle.

A memorial marker pinpoints the Vaughan, Miss., wreck site. Placed there by the Mississippi Department of Archives and History, it reads: "Casey Jones: A famous ballad, the folklore of American railroading and a postage stamp commemorate the colorful and courageous engineer who was killed in a wreck here in 1900." Corn grows each year at the scene, self-seeded from the grain scattered by Casey's locomotive.

The Way We Live Now

Name-Changing—It's the Custom!

by Ted Morgan

WHEN I BECAME an American citizen in February 1977, I renounced my title (I was a count in France) and changed my name to Ted Morgan. Sanche de Gramont, my ancestral name, identified me by national origin and social class. I wanted to make my name rather than inherit it. Just as I was choosing my nationality, I wanted to choose my name.

Several years before, a friend of mine who is a whiz at anagrams had drawn up a list of 19 possible names from the nine letters in de Gramont. In addition to Ted Morgan, it included Tom Danger, Rod Magnet, Monte Drag, Mo Dragnet and R.D. Megaton. I felt that Ted Morgan was forthright and practical, a name telephone operators and desk clerks could hear without flinching. Morgan was someone you could lend your car to. He would return it with a full tank of gas. Dogs and small children liked him. Editors knew that if he was not always brilliant, at least he was on time. And so, Ted Morgan.

At the naturalization ceremony, 30 other applicants for citizenship also changed their names. This was not unusual. Indeed, most people don't realize how common name-changing is in this country. It's one of the overlooked freedoms.

In America, changing your name is part of the culture, going back to the Indians, who changed their totemic names according to accomplishment. A chief of the Blackfeet Piegan tribe, for instance, known as Spotted Elk, changed his name to Chief of the Bears after leading a successful war party. A change of name was like a promotion.

Sometimes the change was less formal. Early German settlers names, for example, were often casually anglicized on their arrival. The Rockefellers were originally Rockenfellers from the lower Rhine. Did Ezra Pound, Herbert Hoover and General Pershing know that their people were Pfunds, Hubers and Pfoershings? Does Walter Cronkite know that his ancestral name is Krankheit?

Sometimes the abrasion of everyday speech simply wore down odd names. The De La Noyes, Huguenots from Holland, became Delanos. Boncoeur became Bunker. General Custer was the descendant of a Hessian mercenary named Kuester. Lincoln may have come from a family of Linkhorns.

But just as often, the change was deliberate. Paul Revere's father changed his name from Apollos Rivoire "merely on account that the bumpkins pronounce it easier." The evangelist Billy Sunday translated his name from his German immigrant father's Sonntag.

Shaking off an ethnic encumbrance was one reason for a change of name, but not the only one. Here are a few more:

Accident. When Vice President Walter Mondale's family came here from Norway, their name was Mundal. A clerk at Ellis Island added an "e," and one in Minnesota filled out the name on some homesteading forms as Mondale. To avoid any difficulties proving ownership, the family adopted the changed version.

Flight. In America, people disappear all the time. They are casualties of the success ethic, or have had an overdose of family life, or are suffering from an identity crisis. People say they are going to the corner store for cigarettes, and step out into another life. It's easy enough to change one's name.

Ridicule. A classic example is that of George Philpott, who in 1888 petitioned for a change of surname. He explained that he had a "cumbersome and mirth-provoking name...which suggests to that punning portion of the common public, many and annoying calembours upon utensils more or less intimately connected with the household." His petition was granted.

Movie Names. The right name is part of the discovered-in-the-drugstore success story. Would Marilyn Monroe have made it as Norma Jean Baker? In the labyrinthine minds of Hollywood producers, she needed that extra lift, the booster rocket, and so joined the queens of alliteration.

Impressive Names. One example of a name that works is Learned Hand—for a judge. Not only is the judicial solemnity built in, but it was his real name (Learned was his mother's family name). Sometimes a slight alteration is in order, however. Thomas W. Wilson dropped his first name to become Woodrow Wilson, and Hiram Ulysses Grant (nicknamed "Useless" as a boy) became Ulysses S. Grant.

The doctoral thesis on the correlation between name-

Name-Changing—It's the Custom!

changers and over-achievers has yet to be written. Would Fred Friendly have reached the CBS executive suite as Ferdinand Wachenheimer? Would Mike Nichols have charmed Broadway and Hollywood as Michael Igor Peschkowsky?

Historical Associations. Sometimes history intervenes. During World War II, several Hitlers applied for name changes. But not Master Sergeant Paul Hitler who said, in effect, "Let the other guy change his!"

What if a man wants to change his obscure name for one made famous by the patina of history and the glitter of wealth? This is what Harry H. Kabotchnik decided to do in 1923 when he petitioned the court to change it to Cabot. The illustrious New England Cabots filed suit to prevent him. The objection was overruled by the court on the ground that there was nothing in the law to prevent the adoption of a famous name. Kabotchnik was merely shortening his name. The Cabots should be flattered that their name had been chosen. They could now talk, not only to God and the Lowells, but to Kabotchnik.

In similar fashion, immigrant Abraham Bitle changed his name to Biddle—and I changed mine to Morgan. There was a $25 naturalization fee, with no extra charge for the name change. It was the bargain of the century. I had a new name and a new feeling of self.

There is a gravestone in Virginia's Shenandoah Valley that says: "Here lie the remains of John Lewis, who slew the Irish Lord, settled in Augusta County, located in the town of Staunton, and furnished five sons to fight the battles of the American Revolution." Not being able to claim any comparable achievements, I think I would want my gravestone to read: "Here lie the remains of Ted Morgan, who became an American."

On the Road With Charles Kuralt

by Stuart A. Segal

AMID A SWARM of deer flies and a raucous chorus of crows, an elderly man pushes his wheelbarrow through the dense tamarack swamp in Minnesota. On camera behind him, CBS News correspondent Charles Kuralt spins out the latest installment of his award-winning "On the Road" TV series:

"Gordon Bushnell always thought there ought to be a straight highway from Duluth to Fargo. About 20 years ago, he got tired of waiting for the state to build it. He decided he better just build it himself. Of course, it takes hundreds of people to build a highway. Everyone knows that—except Gordon Bushnell. Here is a retired dairy farmer, with nothing but a wheelbarrow, a No. 2 shovel and an ancient John Deere tractor, building a highway all alone.

"After 20 years of dickering with landowners, obtaining easements, buying the land when he had to—though he's far from a rich man—Gordon Bushnell has finished nine miles. He has 191 miles to go. Gordon Bushnell is 78 years old."

Charles Kuralt is as unique to television news as Gordon Bushnell is to highway building. Producer, director, writer and ultimate decision-maker for "On the Road," Kuralt has become one of television's most popular commentators by providing a rare counterpoint to the grim events that dominate today's news. Kuralt's three- to four-minute segments, spliced into Walter Cronkite's "CBS Evening News," capture the people, places and things that don't make headlines—but that do make America. Conventional newsmen glorify the spectacular; Kuralt looks for what's "old and enduring" and, above all, what's good, in American life.

"Since everybody else at CBS is busy covering the wars and scandals and Senate hearings, they leave the greased-pig contest to us," Kuralt tells his viewers from a Fourth of July celebration in Salina, Kan. In Monroe, La., Kuralt marvels at Arden Chapman, who breaks the world grape-catching record at 252 feet. In South Bend, Ind., he delights in a fireplug painted to look like a toy soldier. A stop in North Fork, Calif., yields three lumberjacks who can split beer cans with logging axes at 50 paces. And in Hoover, Ala., there is Danny Andrade, the "yo-yo man," who dazzles youngsters with his spinning spool.

As a rule, Kuralt once noted, none of these people lives in Washington or New York or Hollywood. "So you might have forgotten that they're there. But they are there—and they're *us*. And who we are is probably worth remembering."

Kuralt has been nudging the nation's memory since October 26, 1967, when his first "On the Road" segment was aired. During the intervening years, he and his cameraman and soundman have traveled 500,000 miles, visited every state and gone through seven mobile vans.

It is people, rather than events, who draw Kuralt's interest. "After all those depressing stories," he says, "I think it's nice for the viewer to be able to relax and see someone like 104-year-old Lula Watson of Siler City, N.C., who goes around entertaining at old-folks homes and doesn't mind paying Social Security taxes on her small wages because she says she's going to need something to retire on. There is something noble and admirable about her—qualities usually missing from other people on the news."

Of all the subjects Kuralt covers, his favorite is the American hero—except that Kuralt's heroes are different. Their faces don't grace trading cards or sell candy bars. These are, he says, just "people questing for something, not necessarily something important, but just something they really want."

Among these heroes is E.W. Kunza, the 83-year-old Ohio butcher who could hold 29 eggs in one hand. Or in New Iberia, La., there is stoic Juan "Hot Tamale" Sanchez, winner of the International Hot Pepper Eating Contest. As Kuralt reports: "Juan Sanchez, who faced the fire with the least outward suffering, accepted a garland of peppers with a wistful smile and gave a kiss that rocked the pretty girl who received it back on her heels. But even kings are human. Our microphone did not catch it, but in Juan Sanchez's outwardly calm and composed moment of victory, I heard him whisper to his son-in-law, 'Quick, man, get me a beer.'"

Hector Barragan, 43, also a Kuralt hero of the human spirit, is a Texas hairdresser who used to dream of fighting bulls. "What makes Hector Barragan different from the rest of us is that he did it," Kuralt notes, "and has become *El Pipo*, one of the best-known *banderilleros* at the Sunday bullfights in the border city of Juarez. Tomorrow, this man, a little too old and a little too fat, will be back cutting hair in El Paso. Today he is young, slender and bold. Today he is *El Pipo*."

Another Kuralt hero, from a 1967 segment, was the late John Franklin Smith of Westerville, Ohio: "He is 87 years old, and he walks across the campus of Otterbein College with the same purposeful stride he must have had when he came here in 1906. He was a professor of speech and dramatics, and when they made him retire at the age of 70 he just kept on working, until last year—as a janitor. Some considered that undignified. But in the philosophy of John Franklin Smith, no honest work is undignified."

Roughly half of the 35 to 40 "On the Road" segments done each year originate from files kept in the mobile van. These files consist of newspaper clippings, memoranda and many of the 200 letters a week that pour into Kuralt's office at CBS headquarters in New York. Serendipity does the rest. "We travel as slowly as we can so as not to miss anything unimportant," Kuralt explains. "We always have a story idea somewhere down the road, but we always hope we don't get there."

To capture his timeless vignettes of America, Kuralt operates on instinct. This was the case the day he and his assistants were driving to an Ohio town, which had a parakeet that supposedly could say, "And that's the way it is" (Cronkite's closing words on the "CBS Evening News"). "On our way there," Kuralt recalls, "we passed a farmhouse with a sign that said, 'Welcome Home, Roger.' We drove on without anyone saying anything. Finally one of us asked, 'I wonder who Roger is?' We were all asking ourselves that, so we stopped, turned around and went back to find out."

The year was 1970 and Roger was 22-year-old Roger Lambert of Carrothers, Ohio, who was coming home from Vietnam. "Time was in America when veterans were heroes," Kuralt told his viewers on Veterans Day that year. "They came home to waving flags and marching bands, and we raised great gaudy monuments to them. But times have changed; wars have changed. Monuments and heroes are out of fashion. Nobody thinks much about veterans anymore except, of course, the people they left behind." Then followed a touching portrait of the people waiting for Roger.

As for the parakeet, it just didn't work out. "When the lights were on and the camera was running," Kuralt says, "the parakeet wouldn't say anything."

Once they go on the air, Kuralt's "postcards," as he calls them, sometimes change the lives of the people he is covering. Deep in the piney woods of Arkansas, for instance, "On the Road" discovered Eddie Lovett, the son of a sharecropper, living in near-poverty, with three children and thousands of books. His tin-roofed shack bore the inscription: *Hic Habitat Felicitas* ("Here Lives Happiness").

"Well, you know a man is happy wherever he loves, and I love to read," Eddie Lovett told Charles Kuralt. "And I think that it's doing me, particularly my children, a lot of good. 'Cause, truth to tell, I'm really living for my children. I want to set good examples for them. I've been told that man's greatest enemy is ignorance. And so, by me pondering in my library, researching, I have declared war upon my ignorance. I aspires to drink very deep."

After this segment was broadcast, fire gutted Eddie Lovett's library—and the "CBS Evening News" duly reported the tragedy. Within days, viewers started sending thousands of books to Lovett.

What kind of national impression is Kuralt left with, after all these years and miles? "It is too rich and varied a country to give it one mood," he muses. "And I don't think I'd be smart enough to put my finger on it anyway, if it did exist. But if there's any feeling I've come away with, it's that people out there believe the country is perfectible, whatever the problems."

Kuralt then recalls when he was a teen-ager and he summoned up enough courage to go see poet Carl Sandburg, who was living out his last years in Flat Rock, N.C. Sandburg told him: "There is always that saving minority—even when the majority gets bamboozled—there are always those few people who still keep the dream...."

Sandburg, of course, had no idea that he was talking to one of them.

Suburbia: Of Thee I Sing

by Phyllis McGinley

TWENTY MILES east of New York City as the New Haven Railroad flies sits a village I shall call Spruce Manor. It is a commuters' town, and the epitome of Suburbia. By day, with the children pent in schools, it is a village of women. They trundle baskets at the A & P, they sit under driers at the hairdressers', they sweep their porches and set out bulbs and stitch up slip covers.

On one side of Main Street are the grocery stores and the drugstores and the Village Spa where teen-agers gather of an afternoon to drink their Cokes and speak their curious confidences. There one finds the shoe repairers and the dry cleaners and the secondhand stores which sell "antiques," and the stationery stores which dispense comic books to ten-year-olds and greeting cards and lending-library masterpieces to their mothers. On the opposite side stand the bank, the firehouse, the public library.

Spruce Manor in the spring and summer and fall is a pretty town full of gardens and old elms. In the winter the houses reveal themselves as comfortable, well kept, architecturally insigifnicant. The population is perhaps four or five thousand. No one is very poor here and not many families are rich enough to be awesome. There is not much to distinguish Spruce Manor from any other of a thousand surburbs outside of New York City or San Francisco or Detroit or Chicago, or even Stockholm for that matter.

But, for some reason, Spruce Manor has become a sort of symbol to writers, a symbol of all that is middle-class in the worst sense, of smug and prosperous mediocrity. I have yet to read a book in which the suburban life was pictured as the good life or the commuter as a sympathetic figure. He is a stock character: the man who "spends his life riding to and from his wife," the eternal Babbitt whose sanctuary is the club locker room, whose ideas spring ready-made from the illiberal newspapers. His wife plays politics at the PTA and keeps up with the Joneses. Or—if the scene is more gilded—the commuter is the high-powered advertising executive with a station wagon and an eye for the ladies, his wife a restless baggage given to too many afternoon cocktails.

These clichés I challenge. I have lived in the country, I have lived in the city. I have lived in a middlewestern small town. But for the best years of my life I have lived in Suburbia and I like it.

We came here from an expensive, inconvenient, moderately fashionable tenement in Manhattan. Our friends were aghast that we could find anything appealing in a middle-class house on a middle-class street in a middle-class village full of middle-class people. To this day they cannot understand us. You see, they read the books. They even write them.

As for being middle-class, what is wrong with acknowledging one's roots? And how free we are! Free of the city's noise, of its ubiquitous doormen, of the soot on the window sill and the radio in the next apartment. We have released ourselves from the seasonal hegira to the mountains or the seashore. We have only one address, one house to keep. I do not insist that we are typical. There is nothing really typical about any of our friends and neighbors here, and therein lies my point.

We could not keep up with the Joneses even if we wanted to, for we know many Joneses and they are all quite different people. The Albert Joneses spend their weekends sailing, the Bertram Joneses cultivate their delphinium, the Clarence Joneses are enthusiastic about amateur chamber music. The David Joneses dote on bridge but the Ernest Joneses prefer staying home of an evening so that Ernest can carve his witty caricatures out of pieces of old fruit wood. We admire each other's gardens but we are too busy to compete. So long as our clapboards are painted and our hedges decently trimmed, we have fulfilled our community obligations.

On our half acre we can raise enough tomatoes and assassinate enough beetles to satisfy the gardening urge. Or we can put the whole place to lawn. We can have privacy and shade and the changing of the seasons and also the Joneses next door from whom to borrow a cup of sugar or a stepladder.

104 The Way We Live Now

Few of us expect to be wealthy or world-famous or divorced. What we do expect is to pay off the mortgage and send healthy children to good colleges.

For when I refer to life here, I think, of course, of living with children. The adjacent waters of Long Island Sound are full of them in summer, gamboling like dolphins. The lanes are alive with them, the yards overflow with them, they possess the tennis courts and the skating pond and the vacant lots. Their roller skates wear down the asphalt and their bicycles make necessary the 25-mile speed limit. They converse interminably on the telephones and make rich the dentist and the pediatrician.

Spruce Manor seems designed for the happiness of children. Better designed than the city; better, I say defiantly, than the country. Country mothers must be constantly arranging and contriving for their children's leisure time. There is no neighbor child next door for playmate, no school within walking distance. An extra acre or two gives a fine sense of possession to an adult; it does not compensate children for the give-and-take of our village where there is always a contemporary to help swing the skipping rope or put on the catcher's mitt.

Of course, our taxes are higher than we like and there is always the 8:11 in the morning to be caught. But the taxes pay for our excellent schools and for our garbage collections and for our water supply. As for the 8:11, it is rather a pleasant train, say the husbands; it gets them to work in 34 minutes and they read the papers restfully on the way.

"But the suburban mind!" cry the die-hards. "The suburban conversation! The monotony!" They imply that they and I must scintillate or we perish. So far as I know, not one of my friends is doing any of the things that suburban ladies are popularly supposed to be doing. Some, undoubtedly, are ferociously busy in the garden. One lady is on her way to Ellis Island, bearing comfort and gifts to a Polish boy—a stowaway who did slave labor in Germany and was liberated by a cousin of hers during the war—who is being held for attempting to attain the land of which her cousin told him. Twice a week she takes this tedious journey, meanwhile besieging courts and immigration authorities on his behalf. This lady has a large house, a part-time maid and five children.

My friend around the corner is finishing her third novel. The village dancing school is run by another neighbor, as it has been for 20 years. Some of the ladies are no doubt painting their kitchens or a nursery; one of them is painting the portrait, on assignment, of a distinguished personage. Some of them are nurse's aides and Red Cross workers and supporters of good causes. But all find time to be friends with their families and to meet the 5:32 five nights a week. They read something besides the newest historical novel and their conversation is for the most part as agreeable as the tables they set. The tireless bridge players, the gossips, the women bored by their husbands live perhaps in our suburb too. Let them. Our orbits need not cross.

And what of the husbands? Do they spend their evenings and their weekends in gaudy bars? Or are their lives a dreary round of taking down screens and mending drains? Well, screens they have always with them, and a man who is good around the house can spend happy hours with the plumbing even on a South Sea island. Some of them cut their own lawns and some of them try to break par and some of them sail little boats all summer with their families for crew. Some of them are village trustees for nothing a year and some listen to symphonies and some think Johnny Carson ought to be President. Some of them are passionate hedge-clippers and some read Plutarch for fun. But I do not know many who either kiss their neighbors' wives behind doors or whose idea of sprightly talk is to tell you the plot of an old movie.

This afternoon my daughters will come home from school with a crowd of their peers at their heels. They will eat up the cookies and drink up the ginger ale. Presently it will be time for us to climb into our very old Chevy—we are not car-proud in Spruce Manor—and meet the 5:32. There is something delightfully ritualistic about the moment when the train pulls in and the men swing off. The less sophisticated children run squealing to meet them. The women move over from the driver's seat and receive an absent-minded kiss. Deluded people that we are, we do not realize how mediocre it all seems. We will eat our undistinguished meal, probably without even a cocktail to enliven it. We will drink our coffee at the table, not carry it into the living room. If a husband changes for dinner here it is into old trousers and more comfortable shoes. The children will then go through the childhood routine—complain about their homework, grumble about going to bed, and finally accomplish both ordeals. Perhaps later the Gerard Joneses will drop in. We will talk a great deal of unimportant chatter and compare notes on food prices; we will discuss the headlines and disagree. We will all have one highball and the Joneses will leave early. Tomorrow and tomorrow and tomorrow the pattern will be repeated. This is Suburbia.

But I think that someday people will look back on our Spruce Manor way of life with nostalgia and respect. In a world of terrible extremes it will stand out as the safe, important medium.

Suburbia, of thee I sing!

Crack! Roar! It's World Series Time

by William Schulz

THE SCENE: New York's Yankee Stadium; Game 5 of the 1956 World Series. Inning after inning, Yankee pitcher Don Larsen retires the Dodger batters in order—Pee Wee Reese, Duke Snider, Jackie Robinson, Gil Hodges. And inning after inning, the tension builds. Ninth inning; the crowd of 64,519 is on its feet, straining with every pitch as Larsen sets down first Carl Furillo, then Roy Campanella. The public address system announces that Dale Mitchell will pinch-hit. A ball. Two strikes. A foul ball. Larsen rears back and throws. Umpire Babe Pinelli jerks his right hand high. Strike 3 called! Don Larsen has done the impossible—pitched the first and only perfect game in World Series history!

- It is the Polo Grounds, September 1954. The hometown New York Giants are meeting the Cleveland Indians, winners of an unprecedented 111 games during the regular season. The Cleveland batter is Vic Wertz, who hits a mammoth shot to the deepest reaches of the park. A young center-fielder named Willie Mays turns and runs. And runs. And runs. Finally, 460 feet from home plate, he looks back, throws up his gloved hand and makes one of the most incredible catches of all time. Their spirits sapped, the Indians lose the Series in four straight.

- October 1975; Fenway Park in Boston. It's the 12th inning of a magnificently played game—the sixth of the Series—as the Red Sox attempt to stave off Cincinnati's Big Red Machine. At the plate is Boston's Carlton Fisk. The pitch is inside. Fisk hits a towering drive down the left-field foul line. He stands at the plate, waving his hands, imploring the ball to stay fair. It hits the foul pole—a home run!—and 35,205 fans jammed into the tiny stadium watch a grown man leap up and down like a little child. The Red Sox have won one of the most dramatic games in baseball history.

108 The Way We Live Now

* * *

These scenes—and many like them—are etched forever in the memories of countless Americans. For over 75 years the World Series has been America's greatest sporting event. Super Bowls, Kentucky Derbies, Indianapolis 500s, spectaculars all, run together in the public mind. Only major heavyweight-title bouts have generated anything like the drama and controversy of the World Series—and with the advent of theater television, the fights are witnessed by only a small number of Americans.

This year, as usual, the World Series will again attract one of the largest audiences in sports history. The stadiums of the American and National League champions will be filled to overflowing, and an estimated 120 million other Americans will be glued to their TV sets.

What is it that makes the World Series so unique? Unlike the Super Bowl, with its 80-odd participants hidden behind heavy armor and metallic masks, the Series is a drama starring visible actors to whom all can relate. Some rise above themselves—an unknown like pinch-hitter Dusty Rhodes coming off the bench to win three games for the New York Giants in 1954, or an entire team like the "Miracle" Mets, who rose from the depths of the National League to win the 1969 Series. And some fail—Fred Snodgrass of the Giants dropping a routine fly more than half a century ago to give the world's championship to the Boston Red Sox. For tens of millions of Americans, these recollections come back every October, images that are crystal-clear despite the passage of years.

It started in 1903, when officials of the 28-year-old National League and the fledgling American League decided to end a bitter feud and meet in a post-season series to determine the world's championship. The Boston Pilgrims (who would soon change their name to Red Sox) captured the first Series, defeating the National League champion Pittsburgh Pirates.

Within just a few years, the Series had become America's favorite sports spectacular. In 1912, tens of thousands jammed Times Square to follow the play-by-play on a modern-day miracle—a huge electric scoreboard. The New York *Times* of October 17, 1912, noted editorially that national attention had been focused on a heated Presidential campaign, "the greatest Naval pageant in the history of this country" and a sensational criminal trial. "Yet, who will doubt that public interest will center on none of these, but on the games of baseball at our Polo Grounds and in Boston?"

In 1919, the Cincinnati Reds staged one of the great upsets, defeating the awesome Chicago White Sox, and it was not until the following year that America knew why. It turned out that seven White Sox stars had conspired with gambler Arnold Rothstein to throw the Series—and jeopardize the very future of baseball.

Two men saved the sport. One was the iron-fisted commissioner, Kenesaw Mountain Landis, who banned the "Black Sox" for life and vowed that scandal would never again tinge the game. But far more important was the spindly-legged, potbellied product of a Baltimore boys' home. His name was George Herman Ruth, and he would revolutionize the game of baseball.

Babe Ruth came to the Red Sox as a pitcher, and he was a great one, setting a record in the 1918 Series for consecutive scoreless innings (29⅔) that stood for more than four decades. But so powerful a batsman was Ruth that he was moved to the outfield. Sold to the New York Yankees before the 1920 season, he became the most prodigious hitter in the history of the game. From 1921 through 1932, he led the Yankees into seven World Series, and his records from those championship games were awesome: 42 hits, 15 home runs (including three in one game in 1926) and a .625 batting average in 1928. But if baseball is a game of statistics, it is also a game of Gargantuan personal feats, and Ruth saved the best for last.

That was 1932, and in the third game, before a jeering, hostile crowd at Chicago's Wrigley Field, Ruth came to bat with the score tied 4-4. In a gesture of defiance, he pointed to the center-field bleachers, then smacked a mighty homer deep into those seats. Cynics say that Ruth was not really promising a home run, that the famous "called shot" has been magnified out of proportion by hero-building reporters. But it matters little. For nearly half a century, Americans have recalled the picture of Ruth, right hand pointed to the stands, just before smashing out his most famous homer.

Although this was Ruth's last World Series, the Yankees were far from dead. A magnificent young rookie named Joe DiMaggio came up from the minors in 1936, leading the Yankees to four straight World Championships. In 1949, with DiMaggio in the twilight of his career, a baseball genius by the name of Charles Dillon (Casey) Stengel took over as manager. A new generation of Yankee greats—Yogi Berra, Mickey Mantle, Whitey Ford—arrived on the scene, and the Yankees kept on winning. In the 16 years ending in 1964, the Yankees won 14 pennants and 9 more World Championships.

Fans in other cities have not been so fortunate. Until the 1980 Series, the Philadelphia Phillies had won a grand total of one Series *game* in their entire history. The Chicago Cubs have not captured a Series since 1908, seven times making the fall classic only to lose to the American League champion. There are fans in some cities who have spent the better part of their lives waiting for a championship.

The Pittsburgh Pirates won the National League title in 1927, were demolished in four straight games by the Yankees' Murderers' Row, then entered into what can only be described as a prolonged slump. Not for 33 years did the Pirates win the pennant, and the 1960 Series went into the bottom of the ninth inning of the seventh game all tied up. Then second baseman Bill Mazeroski hit the most dramatic homer in Pittsburgh annals, a mighty drive over the left-field wall at Forbes Field, and Steel City embarked upon its longest, most boisterous celebration ever.

Mazeroski is only one of many players over the years who have risen to new heights during the Series—but none more dramatically than Johnny Bench in the 1976 clash. Plagued by injuries, the Cincinnati catcher—a certain Hall of Fame member after he retires—had suffered through his most disappointing season, hitting a pathetic .234. But as the Reds swept the Yanks, Bench played as well as any catcher ever has. His rifle arm nailed down Yankee runners. At the plate, he batted a stupendous .533 and slugged a pair of massive homers in the fourth and final game. "I feel redeemed," Bench said later in the jubilant Cincinnati dressing room. "I thank God for this opportunity to finally do something for my team."

Preparations for each year's World Series begin many months in advance, long before anyone could know who would win the National and American League pennants. In mid-August of 1977, for example, baseball commissioner Bowie Kuhn summoned to his New York office representatives of the 13 clubs he felt had a shot at the series, and directed them to begin making plans. Then his office made hundreds of hotel reservations in different cities, selecting one hotel in each to be the Series headquarters. No detail was left uncovered, from selection of the singers of the national anthem to accommodations for more than 750 writers and reporters.

All season long, that year, ABC looked toward the World Series, its first after 30 years of coverage by NBC. By opening day of the Series, more than six miles of television cable had been laid in the two home parks. An ABC team of more than 75 technicians and crewmen manned nearly $5-million worth of equipment. Outside the stadium, in a giant trailer, producer Chuck Howard sat in a swivel chair wearing a headset that enabled him to coördinate with his 12 camera crews—including one aboard the Goodyear blimp. It was Howard's job to select the shots and orchestrate the coverage watched not only by a majority of Americans but by Little Leaguers in Venezuela, fishermen in Japan, GIs in the Philippines.

The World Series long ago became big business. Sponsors pay $150,000 a minute for TV advertising during the games. The players' pension funds are enriched by approximately $8 million. Members of the winning team walk off with $25,000 or more, losers with an estimated $19,000. And stars from each year's Series can be expected to make tens of thousands of additional dollars from off-season appearances and endorsements.

But dollars don't tell the whole story, and nothing better explains just what the World Series is all about than the Cincinnati Reds' clubhouse after that fabulous sixth game of the 1975 World Series. It has been called the greatest game in the history of the autumn classic, marked by magnificent defense, gritty pitching, timely hitting and, finally, Carlton Fisk's game-winning homer in the bottom of the 12th inning. Now the Reds faced possible defeat in the seventh and final game.

"Why are you looking so down?" the Reds' Pete Rose asked a teammate. "This game had *everything*—hitting, fielding, an incredible home run. Hell, it was a pleasure just to watch!"

Comeback of the Small Town

by Roul Tunley

In 1976, a man almost unknown to the rest of the country came out of a small town in rural Georgia and captured the Democratic nomination and then the Presidency of the United States. It was a stunning feat, people said, for a man who grew up in a community of barely 600 inhabitants.

Yet anyone who knew the hometowns of the candidates Jimmy Carter had defeated for his party's nomination would not have been surprised. Almost all the other contenders—Humphrey, Udall, Wallace, Bayh, Muskie, Harris and Church—came from small towns, too. Moreover, except for John Kennedy, every President we've elected since Taft, in 1908, has had a similar background. The plain fact is that small towns have always produced leaders out of proportion to their size. And they are still doing so today.

In spite of this phenomenon, big cities have, for over a hundred years, acted as magnets for Americans seeking sophistication, culture and, of course, jobs. But that's changing. Both rural communities and small towns are suddenly growing faster than cities and their suburbs. For example, Census Bureau data show that between 1970 and 1975 metropolitan areas gained 4.1 percent in population, while non-metropolitan areas gained 6.6 percent.

Why are small towns suddenly attractive to more and more Americans? Experts cite these factors:

- People are fed up with the violence, crime and pollution of the cities.
- They feel they can control their lives more effectively in a smaller community, especially their work, schools and government.
- With new interstate- and state-highway systems providing easy access to metropolitan areas, the isolation of small towns is no longer as much of a problem.
- Between 1960 and 1970, half of all new manufacturing jobs

Comeback of the Small Town 113

opened up *outside* metropolitan areas. Employers like small towns because wages, taxes and living costs are lower. They have also found greater employee loyalty, fewer work stoppages and higher productivity.

• Community colleges have put higher education within commuting distance of just about everybody.

Perhaps more important than any of these reasons is the feeling most Americans have that we are small-town people at heart. A recent Gallup sampling showed that nearly 90 percent of Americans would prefer to live in a small city, town or village, or in a rural area.

Even those of us who live in metropolitan areas tend to congregate in neighborhood clusters, and to act and think as people do in smaller communities. "We exaggerate the citification of this country," says New York University urbanologist Irving Kristol. "We have an urban culture, but we are not really a city people."

Recently, I visited a number of small towns around the country to discover for myself the qualities that have made, and are making, small-town life so appealing.

My first stop was Edgefield, S.C. (pop. 2750), a magnolia- and mimosa-scented place that has produced an extraordinary number of successful politicians. From this tiny town on the western edge of South Carolina have come ten governors, five lieutenant governors and numerous senators, representatives, justices and other high officials.

I asked Edgefield's Rep. Butler Derrick why political success is easier in small towns. (At 41, Derrick had already twice been elected to Congress.) "I think it's because the small-town person doesn't know he can't do something," he replied. "He just goes ahead and does it."

Harvard University's urbanologist, James K. Wilson, agrees. He feels it's simpler to carve out a political career in a small town than in "cutthroat cities" where people get discouraged before they begin. "In a small town, you get confidence," he added. "You learn the intricacies of government more quickly and have a better understanding of how the whole thing works. It seems easier to make a contribution."

My next stop was Cadiz, Ohio, a town of 3060 persons in the eastern end of the state. Cadiz is virtually unknown outside Ohio, and yet no one who visits it can help but be astonished by what it has contributed to American life.

One wonders, for one thing, what President Lincoln would have done without Cadiz (pronounced kā'diz). It gave him his Secretary of War, Edwin Stanton. It provided a general (George Custer) who helped turn the tide at Gettysburg, as well as a Methodist bishop (Matthew Simpson) who was the guiding spirit behind the Emancipation Proclamation.

After the Civil War, the town went right on turning out talent. Charles Hanna became one of America's most influential financiers. In baseball, two young Cadizites, Cy Young and George Sisler, won immortality. The town gave Hollywood its "king," Clark Gable, and provided an education for George V. Patterson, onetime head of American Electric Power, one of the nation's largest electric utilities.

Like many small towns, Cadiz today has little unemployment. "Employment in non-metropolitan areas has increased faster than in metropolitan areas in every major industry except government," says a recent Department of Agriculture report. What with coal mining, diversified manufacturing, and its position as a trading center, Cadiz is sitting pretty. Years ago, citizens placed a bronze plaque in front of the courthouse stating that "Cadiz is the proudest small town in America." They still feel that way.

Next, I visited Amherst, Mass., a town known for its contribution to world literature. Someone once said it would be hard to swing a bat in the main square "without hitting a poet, possibly a major one." Certainly there is no denying that this community of 26,794 has produced writers. Its most famous was Emily Dickinson, the eccentric recluse who lived most of her life behind a high hedge on Main Street, secretly writing poems which, published after her death, caused her to be recognized as one of the greatest American woman poets. Noah Webster came to Amherst in 1812 and wrote his dictionary here. A host of other writers, including Robert Frost, also found inspiration in the town.

In its peaceful river-valley setting, Amherst today is a powerhouse of education. Three great colleges are set here: Amherst, Hampshire and the University of Massachusetts. Two others, Smith and Mount Holyoke, are nearby. Louis Hayward, the town manager, chose to bring up his family in Amherst because "the values are more clearly defined here than in a big city." Asked why Amherst has always been a hotbed of literary production, he said he thought it was the same quality that had attracted him: "Stimulation without pressure."

My last stopping place, Columbus, Ind. (pop. 27,468), embodies the kind of industrial innovation that has made America great. It was here that Clessie Cummins, a chauffeur and auto mechanic, adapted the hitherto stationary diesel engine for use on the highway—an invention that gave birth to the modern trucking industry. Today the Cummins Engine Company is the largest independent producer of diesel engines in the world, and employs one third of the town's citizens.

Even so, Columbus is far from a one-company town. Arvin Industries, Cosco, Saps Bakery (the biggest raised-doughnut factory on earth) and other smaller companies make this one of the busiest and most prosperous small towns in America.

But what make Columbus most exciting is that this town, set down amid the cornstalks of southern Indiana and "so flat you can spot a grasshopper on its knees," is also a place of startling architectural innovation. Two decades ago, when it became necessary to build several schools, Irwin Miller, the head of Cummins Engine, made a unique offer: he would pay the architectural fees for any building, provided the architects were chosen from a panel of the best-known names in the country. The school board agreed and, since then, 46 buildings—schools, churches, libraries, sports centers, malls and industrial plants—have been constructed. They are among the most daring and handsome in America, imaginatively landscaped and dotted with sculpture by Henry Moore and others. Columbus has been dubbed "America's architectural showcase." It is a mecca for tour buses the year round.

Yet Columbus remains small town in spirit. Its newspaper, *The Republic*, reports such things as who gets traffic tickets and who goes in and out of the hospital. It's a place where people still live close to family, church and the flag. Part of the Bible Belt, it has 131 churches. Its charity drives raise twice as much per person as the national average. It also has a first-rate school system, a four-year university, and a symphony orchestra.

No small town is exactly like any other; each has its own flavor, intimacy and set of values. Nor can one point to any single factor that makes people return to small towns in ever greater numbers. But from those I talked to, one feeling emerged more frequently than any other: a sense that small towns had been better able to preserve a way of life that Americans had come to cherish.

Whatever the reason, the small town is making a big comeback.

Native Wits

Old Ben Franklin and His Miserable Maxims

by Mark Twain

BENJAMIN FRANKLIN was one of those persons whom they call philosophers.

He early prostituted his talents to the invention of maxims and aphorisms calculated to inflict suffering upon the rising generation of all subsequent ages.

His simplest acts were contrived with a view of their being held up for the emulation of boys forever. It was in this spirit that he became the son of a soap-boiler, and probably for no other reason than that the efforts of all future boys who try to be anything might be looked upon with suspicion unless they were the sons of soap-boilers.

With a malevolence without parallel in history he would work all day, and then sit up nights, and let on to be studying algebra by the light of a smoldering fire so that all boys might have to do that also. Not satisfied with these proceedings, he had a fashion of living wholly on bread and water, and studying astronomy at mealtime—a thing which has brought affliction to millions of boys since.

His maxims were full of animosity toward boys. Nowadays a boy cannot follow out a single natural instinct without tumbling over one of those everlasting aphorisms. If he buys two cents' worth of peanuts, his father says, "Remember what Franklin has said, my son: 'A groat a day is a penny a year,'" and the comfort is all gone out of those peanuts. If he wants to spin his top before his work is done, his father quotes, "Procrastination is the thief of time." If he does a virtuous action, he never gets anything for it because "virtue is its own reward."

A boy is robbed of his natural rest because Franklin said once:

> Early to bed and early to rise
> Makes a man healthy, wealthy and wise.

As if it were any object to a boy to be healthy, wealthy and wise on such terms. The legitimate result of this maxim is my present state of general debility, indigence and mental aberration. My parents used to have me up before nine o'clock in the morning, sometimes, when I was a boy. If they had let me take my natural rest, where would I be now? Keeping store, no doubt, and respected by all.

And what an adroit old adventurer he was. In order to get a chance to fly his kite on Sunday, he used to hang a key on the string, and let on to be fishing by lightning, and a guileless public would chirp of the "wisdom" and the "genius" of the hoary Sabbath-breaker. He invented a stove that would smoke your head off. He was always proud of how he entered Philadelphia with nothing in the world but two shillings in his pocket and four rolls of bread under his arm. Really, anybody could have done this.

Franklin did many notable things for his country, and made her young name honored in many lands as the mother of such a son. It is not the idea of this memoir to ignore that. No. The idea is to snub those pretentious maxims of his, which he worked up with a great show of originality out of truisms that had become wearisome platitudes as early as the dispersions from Babel.

I merely desire to do away with the prevalent calamitous idea among heads of families that Franklin acquired his great genius by working for nothing, studying by moonlight, and getting up in the night instead of waiting until morning, and that this programming, rigidly inflicted, will make a Franklin of every father's fool. It is time these gentlemen found out that these execrable eccentricities are only the evidence of genius, not the creators of it.

I wish I had been the father of my parents long enough to make them comprehend this truth, and thus prepare them to let their son have an easier time of it. When I was a child I had to boil soap, notwithstanding my father was wealthy, and I had to get up early and study geometry at breakfast, and peddle my own poetry, and do everything as Franklin did, in the solemn hope that I would be a Franklin someday. And here I am.

The Night John Alden Spoke for Himself

by Russell Baker

WHEN CUSTIS CURTIS, public-relations man for the Plymouth Colony, heard that Myles Standish and his colleagues were planning a day of Thanksgiving, he hopped the first horse to Plymouth Rock.

"Myles," he said, "it's a sweet idea and I love it. There's just one thing: it's all wrong for this particular colony. In the first place, you've got to come up with a better name."

"What's wrong with calling it Thanksgiving?" asked Standish.

"It has no dynamism, Myles, no thunder. This is a big country for big men capable of big dreams. When people think of Plymouth Colony, you want them to think of he-men roaring through Marlboro country with tigers in their cougar tanks. But what does 'Thanksgiving' suggest? Pussycats."

If the name created a too passive image, Standish said, the colony was open to suggestions. "We'll call it Thunderherd Day," said Curtis. "With a name like that, you'll get people from all over the country pouring in to see the fireworks."

But no fireworks were contemplated, Standish explained.

"I know, Myles," said Curtis. "I wanted to talk to you about that. You say you want to have a little worship, then have the Indians in for turkey and pumpkin pie. It's a great idea. But, believe me, Myles, it's strictly a nothing bit."

Standish asked what was wrong with it.

"Turkey, Myles. Turkey! You know who eats turkey? Frenchmen. But they call it pheasant, or guinea hen. You're living in *red meat* country, Myles. How are you going to put this colony on the map by sitting around eating turkey? We'll ship in a load of buffalo steak from out West. Then you'll be able to throw a Thunderherd Day with point to it."

Standish asked whether it would hurt the image to invite the Indians.

"Indians!" snorted Curtis. "You're still in the 16th century, Myles. Wait a minute." He entered a convenient dressing room and reappeared a few minutes later wearing a red jacket, red knickers, red nightcap, white beard and black boots.

"*Santa Claus*, Myles! On Thunderherd Day, Santa Claus is going to arrive—right here in Plymouth Colony, with eight tiny reindeer."

Myles said he could not understand how Santa Claus related to the festivities of Thunderherd Day.

"This colony," said Curtis, "is going to be packed with tourists who have come in to be part of Thunderherd Day, part of red-meat country. Their pockets are going to be loaded with wampum. What do we do? Deliver old Santa Claus, to sell them beads and souvenir Pilgrim blunderbusses and those funny black hats you fellows wear. They're going to need Christmas presents anyhow, and the more you can get them to buy right here, the sooner Plymouth Colony is going to move up to dynamic living."

Standish pointed out that Thunderherd Day would occur a full month before Christmas, and it was unlikely that anyone would spend good wampum so long before the holiday.

"You're exactly right, Myles," said Curtis. "And that is why Thunderherd Day is not going to be just one single isolated day on the calendar. *It is going to be the kickoff day for Thunderherd Month.*"

That night Myles, John Alden and the others thought it over. "There be no doubt," said a church elder, "that this Curtis knoweth whereof he speaketh, but the question be whether we on this rocky shore truly wish to be held responsible for creating Thunderherd Month."

"Speaking for myself," said John Alden, "I think the image would be very bad."

And so, three centuries elapsed before Thunderherd Month was finally created.

Wit and Wisdom From Vermont

by Allen R. Foley

Many years ago, I moved from New Hampshire, where I was teaching, across the Connecticut River to Norwich, Vermont. Soon I began to roam the back-country and visit with local people of all ages and walks of life, collecting quips and yarns from them and about them. This is a sampling of the characteristic Vermont stories I've heard.

An old Thetford farm family was gathered around the kitchen table to fill out the insurance forms for the farmer who had fallen off the barn roof, broken his neck and died. They recorded all the facts as best they could—date, hour and nature of the accident, and so on—and finally, under the heading *Remarks*, solemnly wrote: "He didn't make none."

Sometimes I rib fellow members of the state legislature by reporting the exchange between two old boys at a political rally where a candidate for office was going on at great length. One of them, a bit hard of hearing, asked his friend, "What's he talking about?"

He received the response: "He don't say."

A tourist inquired of an old-timer the way to Wheelock and was told. "Well, Mister, if I was going to Wheelock, I'd be damned if I'd start from here."

And Walter Piston, the great musician and composer at Harvard, tells of taking a rather back-roads route from a concert at Tanglewood in the Berkshires to Hanover, N.H., for an engagement. He came to a fork that had signs pointing in both directions saying White River Junction. "Does it make any difference," he inquired of an old-timer standing nearby, "which road I take to White River?" If not enlightened, Piston was duly impressed by the answer: "Not to me it don't."

A minister went way back in the hills to substitute at a service at which one man proved to be the entire congregation. The preacher asked him if he thought they should go on with the service.

The man thought a while, then replied, "Well, Reverend, if I put some hay in the wagon and go down to the pasture to feed the cows and only one cow shows up, I feed her."

So the good brother went through most of the service, including a full-length sermon. Afterward he asked the lone member of the congregation what he thought of it.

"Well, Reverend, I'll tell you. If I put some hay in the wagon and go down to the pasture to feed the cows and only one cow shows up, I don't give her the whole damn load."

Our local road commissioner told me of stopping in Beaver Meadow to visit with an old bachelor who lived alone in squalor but who, at the urging of his friends, had had a telephone installed. The phone was ringing insistently—one long and three short—and Charlie asked him, "Ain't that your ring?"

The old-timer guessed it was, whereupon Charlie said, "Then why don't you answer the damn thing?"

"Charlie," came the deliberate reply, "I had that phone put in for *my* convenience."

Among older natives of the Green Mountains, thrift is about as deep-seated as the spirit of independence. A favorite story concerns the farmer who went into the little bank in Chelsea to borrow some money. When asked how much he wanted, he indicated he'd like "'bout a dollar." The banker expressed surprise at the size of the request, but agreed to the deal, explaining that the bank would have to have some security. The farmer said he had a $1000 government bond; the banker agreed that this would be adequate coverage for such a loan. As for interest, six percent would be the charge. The farmer allowed as how he would like to pay in advance, so he put down the bond and the six cents, took the dollar and went his way.

A year later, he asked to renew the loan, and paid another six cents in advance. The year after that, when he again requested renewal, the banker said, "It's very peculiar that you, with this thousand-dollar bond, keep renewing this one-dollar loan."

"Well, it's damn peculiar," said the farmer, "that you, being a banker, ain't figured this out. I was paying five dollars a year for a lockbox to keep my bond. Now I've found a way to keep it safe for six cents."

Some 100 years ago, Mark Twain (Samuel Langhorne Clemens) came to Brattleboro to give one of his famous humorous lectures. According to the account, the response was not what Clemens thought it should be. He stopped talking a little ahead of schedule, went out the stage entrance and around front, and is reported to have found out what the trouble was in short order.

Out came a nice old couple who had driven down from their hill farm with the horse and buggy, and he heard the old gentleman say to his wife, "Wan't he funny? Wan't he *funny!* I had all I could do to keep from laughing."

And there's the story about a man from Quechee who, late in the afternoon in the North Station in Boston, was taking a train to come back to White River Junction. The train was crowded, and a well-dressed city man sat down beside him. After getting acquainted, the Bostonian said: "You say you are just a Vermont farmer, bu I am impressed with your general intelligence and common sense. To pass the time I suggest we play a little game."

"Well, what's your game?"

"I suggest we each ask the other a question, and if we can't answer the other fellow's question, we give him a dollar."

"Well, now, that might be a good game. But I don't think the terms quite fair. You're a city man, probably well educated and traveled. I'm just a poor Vermont farmer—only went through grammar school, and spent all the rest of my life on the farm. So I suggest that if you can't answer *my* question, you give *me* a dollar, but if I can't answer *your* question, I give *you* 50 cents."

"That seems fair enough. Let's play. You ask the first question."

"Well, I'd like to know what it is that has three legs and flies."

After some thought, the city man said, "Damned if I know. Here's your dollar."

"All right," said the Vermonter, "what's *your* question?"

"I'd like to know *what it is* that has three legs and flies."

"Damned if I know. Here's your 50 cents."

Our Town's Only Republican

by Turner Catledge

THE LONE Republican in my home town in Mississippi was Mr. Eustace Eubank. Mr. Eubank was an odd individual in many ways. For one thing, he always attended strictly to his own business, which quickly set him apart in our community. But the oddest thing about this old man was his being a Republican. He never admitted being a Republican, but every four years one Republican vote would turn up in the local ballot box and we never doubted who had cast it.

Mr. Eubank lived over west of the railroad tracks in a little unpainted house with his second wife and three daughters. One of his daughters was in school with me. She was very smart and I'm certain she won most of the literary contests we had at school. But she never got the prize, because the teachers didn't think it would be right to give prizes to a Republican's daughter. Eubank's only work was his gardening, and he grew the biggest tomatoes in town. They would slice out as big as saucers. My Uncle Homer used to sell those tomatoes in his grocery store, but he never told customers who'd grown them, as he figured no one would want to eat a Republican tomato. Eubank walked with a limp which, the town legend said, was because he had a wooden leg. The story went that Eubank had been a Union soldier at the battle of Shiloh and had his leg shot off. His fellow Yankees—as we told the story—had run off and left him, but he had been so fortunate as to survive and make his way to our compassionate little community. And yet he'd repaid us by casting that lone Republican vote every four years!

Such was the situation one hot summer in the early 1900s, when Eustace Eubank's saga came to a close. That summer my uncles Homer and Joe had bought a Ford car and converted it into a truck, and I was having a wonderful time delivering groceries in it. One hot July day, about noon, I was out in front of the grocery, polishing the Ford, when my Uncle

Joe said that he wanted to see me. I went inside the store and found a gathering of the local power structure: the town marshal, the county sheriff, the owner of the furniture store, a livery-stable keeper, our leading physician, and my Uncle Joe.

Uncle Joe put his hand on my shoulder and said, "Turner, Mr. Eubank was found dead in his bed this morning, and I want you to take the truck, go over to his house, get the remains and take them out to the cemetery."

Suddenly the reason for this assembly became clear. The town elders wanted to ensure that our lone Republican was properly laid to rest. I felt proud to be part of this ceremony, which combined civic, political and religious significance. A younger boy, Clifford Sanford, was to assist me, but I was in charge. Clifford and I jumped into the Ford, went by Mr. Spivey's furniture store for a coffin, and then I drove us out to the Eubank house. His family led me into a little front room, where a body was lying on a bed under a heavy quilt. I lifted the quilt and there he was, our lone Republican, stiff and cold. I had been born and bred a Democrat, and I couldn't suppress a moment of triumph at the sight.

After we got Mr. Eubank and the coffin out to the Ford truck, I faced a problem. The Eubank family would be coming to the cemetery in a wagon drawn by mules. Should I drive the Ford slowly, so the mules could keep up in a funeral procession, or should I hurry on to the cemetery and let the family follow as best it could? It was our town's first motorized funeral, so I had no precedent to follow.

I decided to respect tradition and have a funeral procession. So I drove very slowly, wondering what sort of religious ceremony would be held. Mr. Eubank had never been seen in church, and we assumed that, being a Republican, he was bound to be an atheist too. I wondered if Mr. Eubank would be laid to rest in the respectable part of the graveyard or across a little gravel road in the Potter's Field. When our procession arrived, I was pleased to find mourners waiting around a newly dug grave in the respectable part of the cemetery, although only three feet from the gravel road.

Standing at the head of the grave was Brother Arnett, the Presbyterian preacher. He led us in a hymn, and read from the Psalms, and then read Tennyson's "Crossing the Bar." Then we lowered the coffin into the grave and everyone present helped shovel dirt onto the coffin. It was a sort of community project.

When I drove the Ford back to the grocery store, a lot of people came around to congratulate me on a job well done. A great sense of relief came over the entire community. The Lord had taken away our Republican, and we were pure again.

Thus things stood until November of that year, when the balloting was held in the Presidential election.

I was standing in front of my uncle's grocery when I noticed a commotion in the courthouse yard where the balloting was being held. In those days, when you heard shouting at the courthouse on election day, you waited for the shooting to begin. Then, suddenly, I saw the chancery clerk break out of the crowd, race across the courthouse yard, jump over the fence, and come running into my uncles' store, waving his arms and shouting.

"My God, my God," he cried, "that Republican vote has showed up again!"

We had buried the wrong man.

Genesis Passes Congress

by Russell Baker

IN THE BEGINNING, God sent a Creation bill to the Congress. It proposed a crash program under which everything from light to man would be created in six days. It ran into trouble almost immediately.

The powerful light lobby was unhappy with the bill's language, which said, "Let there be light." This suggested light was going to be free. So the lobby demanded that the bill clearly spell out the light industry's right to sell light, without divine interference, at whatever price the free market would bear. This provoked powerful opposition from consumer lobbies, which insisted that the price be regulated by God with infinite mercy—and from business groups, which wanted the light tax-deductible if used for business purposes.

Another fierce struggle developed in the House Firmament Committee about the creation of the dry land. The bill said, "Let the earth bring forth grass, the herb yielding seed, and the fruit tree yielding fruit upon the earth." All very nice, House members noted, but the bill was suspiciously silent on such matters as oil. It was quickly amended to read, "Let there also be oil."

The issue of where the oil was to be placed was not so readily settled. Congressmen from Louisiana and Texas wanted the oil created in their states, while those from New England wanted it created under Route 128 outside Boston. Eventually, under the Proxmire compromise, Texas and Louisiana got the oil and New England got the great whales.

All this by no means solved God's problems, however, for the Joint Committee on Man was faced with lobbies fighting over the design characteristics of man. Women objected: they wanted the committee's name changed to the Joint Committee on Person. They won, chiefly with the assistance of the medical lobbies, led by the A.M.A., which wanted the specifications to include an appendix and a gall bladder.

Consumer lobbyists argued that the only conceivable purpose for putting in an appendix and gall bladder was to provide work for surgeons. However, when the feminist lobby agreed to support the appendix-and-gall-bladder amendment—in return for the A.M.A.'s agreement to support renaming the committee—the fight was settled.

There were many more. One of the bitterest was over the proposal that man be created "in the image of God." Foundations and fund-raising groups contested it. Since God was perfect and eternal, they pointed out, a man designed in His image would also be perfect and eternal. And a Creation peopled exclusively by perfect and eternal persons would be unbearably dull.

Consumer groups argued that the foundations and fund-raisers were less interested in having an exciting Creation than in having a variety of human ailments, whose alleviation would provide jobs for the foundation-and-fund-raising industry. But the funeral industry sided with the fund-raisers, arguing that in making man temporary instead of eternal, Congress would enrich his existence by encouraging him to dwell on philosophy.

The matter was finally settled when a deal was made about jaw design. The dental lobby had proposed an absurd scheme in which three or four dozen small pieces of bone would be awkwardly planted in the jawbone where they would be subject to quick decay and easy loss. The drawings for this design looked so ridiculous that the Subcommittee on Mastication discarded them after a glance, and instead chose a sensible two-piece cutting-and-grinding device of durable titanium.

The dental lobby carried the day, however, when it formed a coalition with the funeral and fund-raising industries. Which is why to this day we are imperfect, temporary, and found at the dentist's twice a year.

Congressmen are, too. Which suggests that justice isn't entirely dead.

Last of the Big Spenders

by Art Buchwald

PERCIVAL FLAGSTONE, scion of the Flagstone chewing-gum fortune and noted playboy, checked into Peppermint Hospital yesterday for a gallbladder operation. In keeping with his reputation for free-spending, Percival demanded a private room. When asked what his operation would cost, Percival just chuckled and said, "If you have to ask what an operation will cost, you can't afford one."

The young millionaire has been noted for spending money like water. Last month he took a movie actress to dinner and they both had T-bone steaks. When the papers got wind of it, Percival was indignant and said, "It's my money and I can do anything I want with it. Just because most people can't afford T-bone steaks is no reason why I can't eat one if I feel like it."

Percival was left a fortune of $20 million, which his bankers estimate is now down to five. One of the trustees told this reporter, "The man has no idea that if he keeps spending at the present rate he won't have anything left in two years. He had strawberries for dessert three nights in a row, and he bought two pairs of shoes this year."

But Percival has no intention of slowing down. He told this reporter, "My theory about money is, if you've got it, flaunt it."

Percival just bought a two-bedroom, split-level brick house on a quarter-acre of land in Washington, D.C., that is estimated to have cost him $5 million. The estate, which once was owned by a conductor on the Penn Central railroad, has two bathrooms, one on the top floor and one in the basement. It also has a dining room.

"Is it true you're buying a four-door Toyota?" I asked him.

"I might. Ever since I was a kid I've wanted a car, and I may sell the bonds my grandmother left me if I can break

Last of the Big Spenders

the trust. No one said anything when the Rockefellers bought a VW last summer for $2 million, yet when they hear I put in a bid for a Toyota it's a front-page story."

Percival is also known for the lavish gifts he gives the women he is seen with around town. Just the other day he bought a necklace from J.C. Penney for $800,000, and last month he gave a well-known model a rhinestone-covered compact from Montgomery Ward worth $600,000.

My final question to Percival before he was wheeled into his private room was, "Percival, you seem to have done it all. You've eaten a T-bone steak, you own a two-bedroom house and you may even buy a car. Is there anything left?"

He thought a moment and said, "Well, I've always wanted to own a crate of California lettuce, but even for someone like me that's out of the question."

Heritage of Freedom

Dark Yesterdays, Bright Tomorrows

by Martin Luther King, Jr.

AFTER a particularly strenuous day, my wife had already fallen asleep at a late hour and I was about to doze off when the telephone rang. An angry voice said, "Listen, nigger, we've taken all we want from you. Before next week you'll be sorry you ever came to Montgomery." I hung up, but I could not sleep. It seemed that all of my fears had come down on me at once.

I began to walk the floor. Finally, I heated a pot of coffee. I was ready to give up. I tried to think of a way to move out of the picture without appearing to be a coward. In this state of exhaustion, I determined to take my problem to God. My head in my hands, I bowed over the kitchen table and prayed aloud. The words I spoke to God that midnight are still vivid in my memory:

"I am here for what I believe is right. But now I am afraid. The people are looking to me for leadership, and if I stand before them without strength and courage, they too will falter. I am at the end of my powers. I have nothing left. I've come to the point where I can't face it alone."

At that moment I experienced the presence of the Divine as I had never before experienced Him. I seemed to hear the quiet assurance of an inner voice, saying, "Stand up for righteousness, stand up for truth. God will be at your side forever." Almost at once my fears began to pass from me. My uncertainty disappeared. I was ready to face anything. The outer situation remained the same, but God had given me inner calm.

Three nights later, our home was bombed. Strangely enough, I accepted the word of the bombing calmly. I knew now that God is able to give us the interior resources to face the storms and problems of life.

Let this affirmation be our ringing cry. When our days become dreary with low-hovering clouds and our nights become darker than a thousand midnights, let us remember that there is a great benign Power in the universe who is able to make a way out of no way, and transform dark yesterdays into bright tomorrows.

Realizing that fear drains a man's energy and depletes his resources, Emerson wrote, "He has not learned the lesson of life who does not every day surmount a fear."

But I do not mean to suggest that we should seek to eliminate fear altogether from human life. Were this humanly possible, it would be practically undesirable. Normal fear protects; abnormal fear paralyzes. Normal fear motivates us to improve our individual and collective welfare; abnormal fear constantly poisons and distorts our inner lives. Our problem is not to be rid of fear but rather to harness and master it. How may it be mastered?

First, by looking squarely and honestly at our fears, we learn that many of them are residues of some childhood need or apprehension. A person haunted by a fear of death or the thought of punishment in the afterlife discovers that he has unconsciously projected into the whole of reality the childhood experience of being punished by parents, locked in a room, and seemingly deserted. Or a man plagued by the fear of inferiority and social rejection discovers that rejection in childhood by a self-centered mother and a preoccupied father left him with a self-defeating sense of inadequacy and a repressed bitterness toward life. By bringing our fears to the forefront of consciousness, we may find them to be more imaginary than real.

Second, we can master fear through one of the supreme virtues known to man: courage. The determination not to be overwhelmed by any object, however frightful, enables us to stand up to any fear. Courage faces fear and thereby masters it; cowardice represses fear and is thereby mastered by it. Courageous men never lose the zest for living even though their life situation is zestless; cowardly men, overwhelmed by the uncertainties of life, lose the will to live. We must constantly build dikes of courage to hold back the flood of fear.

Third, fear is mastered through love. The New Testament affirms, "There is no fear in love; but perfect love casteth out fear." Racial segregation is buttressed by such irrational fears as loss of preferred economic privilege, altered social status, intermarriage, and adjustment to new situations. White people attempt to combat these corroding fears by diverse methods. Some seek to ignore the question of race relations. Others counsel massive resistance. Still others hope to drown their fear by engaging in acts of violence and meanness toward their Negro brethren. But instead of eliminating fear, these remedies instill deeper and more pathological fears. Neither repression, massive resistance, nor aggressive violence will cast out the fear of integration; only love and goodwill can do that.

Only through Negro adherence to love and non-violence will the fear in the white community be mitigated. A guilt-ridden white minority fears that if the Negro attains power, he will without restraint or pity act to revenge the accumulated injustices and brutality of the years.

The Negro must show white men that they have nothing to fear, for the Negro forgives and is willing to forget the past. *The Negro must convince the white man that he seeks justice for both himself and the white man.* A mass movement exercising love and non-violence and demonstrating power under discipline should convince the white community that were such a movement to attain strength its power would be used creatively and not vengefully.

Fourth, fear is mastered through faith. All too many people attempt to face the tensions of life with inadequate spiritual resources. When vacationing in Mexico, Mrs. King and I wished to go deep-sea fishing. For reasons of economy, we rented an old and poorly equipped boat. We gave this little thought until, ten miles from shore, the clouds lowered and howling winds blew. Then we became paralyzed with fear, for we knew our boat was deficient. Multitudes of people are in a similar situation. Heavy winds and weak boats explain their fear.

One of the most dedicated participants in the Montgomery bus protest was an elderly Negro whom we affectionately called Mother Pollard. Although poverty-stricken and uneducated, she possessed a deep understanding of the meaning of the movement. After having walked for several weeks, she was asked if she were tired. With ungrammatical profundity, she answered, "My feets is tired, but my soul is rested."

On one particular evening, following a tension-packed week, I spoke at a mass meeting. I attempted to convey an overt impression of strength and courage, although I was inwardly depressed and fear-stricken. Mother Pollard came to the front of the church afterward and said, "Come here, son." I went to her and hugged her affectionately.

"Something is wrong with you," she said. "You didn't talk strong tonight. I know something is wrong. Is it that we ain't doing things to please you? Or is it that the white folks is bothering you?"

Before I could respond, she looked directly into my eyes and said, "I done told you we is with you all the way." Then her face became radiant, and she said in words of quiet certainty, "But even if we ain't with you, God's gonna take care of you." As she spoke these consoling words, everything in me quivered and quickened with the pulsing tremor of raw energy.

Since that dreary night in 1956, Mother Pollard has passed on to glory, and I have known very few quiet days. But as the years have unfolded, the eloquently simple words of Mother Pollard have come back again and again to give light and peace and guidance to my troubled soul. "God's gonna take care of you."

This faith transforms the whirlwind of despair into a warm and reviving breeze of hope. The words of a motto which a generation ago were commonly found on the wall in the homes of devout persons need to be etched on our hearts:

> Fear knocked at the door.
> Faith answered.
> There was no one there.

The Right to Speak Out

by Albert Q. Maisel

GEORGE L. Rockwell is a professional hate-peddler. Now and then he emerges from the shabby headquarters of his vestpocket American Nazi Party to spew forth threats of gas-chamber extermination for those who oppose his stormtrooper ideas.

Yet, when New York's mayor refused him a permit to stage a "rally" in Union Square, scores of outstanding Americans rose in protest. The New York *Times* urged the mayor not to deny free speech even to this "miserable and contemptible hate-monger." The New York Civil Liberties Union, while rejecting everything that Rockwell stands for, fought his case all the way to the Supreme Court of the United States to win a clear-cut reaffirmation of the right of anyone to place his views before the public.

Behind such prompt and vigorous defense of free speech as the inalienable right of all Americans lie a faith and a tradition as old as our nation itself.

Historians trace the *idea* of freedom of speech back to the Greek city-states and especially to Athens, the world's first democracy. They quote the words of Socrates in 399 B.C.: "The sun could as easily be spared from the universe as free speech from society. Life that is not tested by discussion is not worth living." Yet it was the Athenians who condemned Socrates to death for speaking his mind or, as their hypocritical verdict put it, "corrupting the young" with ideas.

Later, free speech flourished for a time in Rome, for the few who were freemen. Then the long night of the Dark Ages descended, and in the feudal world the serfs were voiceless and even the knights were bound to unquestioning support of their brigand lords by solemn oaths of vassalage.

Centuries later, the very idea of free speech had to be born anew. It developed by tiny increments as kings and barons struggled for power in medieval Europe. In England the barons assembled in 1215 on the meadow at Runnymede and forced

King John to sign the Magna Carta. It was no democratic constitution, merely a relisting of the barons' customary privileges. But, to preserve their reasserted powers, the rebellious barons set up a standing committee of 25. Thus, unwittingly they helped bring to birth the institution of Parliament.

Parliament, the "speaking place," remained a puny tool against royal tyranny for more than 500 years—as long as the kings could punish its members for what they said within the Parliament Hall. Yet time and again brave members defied the kings and spoke their minds despite threats and punishments.

Typical was the courage of Peter Wentworth, who, in 1575, rose to assert his right—and that of every member of Parliament—to criticize the government, the queen's ministers, even the queen herself. He was seized, tried in a packed court and cast into the Tower of London. But so loud were the protests throughout the country that the cautious Queen Elizabeth quietly released him after a few weeks of imprisonment.

The right to criticize *inside* Parliament grew. When, in 1688 William and Mary ascended the throne, Parliament permitted them to do so only after they agreed to sign a "Bill of Rights." Within that great bill no clause was more important than the one that read: "The freedom of speech and debates in Parliament ought not to be impeached or questioned in any court or place out of Parliament." There the fateful words "freedom of speech" were finally frankly emblazoned.

It was another parallel struggle—the struggle for religious freedom—that led men to demand freedom of speech *outside* the Parliament Hall. When King Henry VIII broke with Rome, he punished any who hesitated to follow him into this schism. His Catholic daughter, Queen Mary, persecuted Protestants with even greater vigor. But the Pandora's box he had opened when he asserted his own freedom of religion could not be closed.

By the tens of thousands, Englishmen became convinced that their religious beliefs were to be dictated only by their own consciences. Thus, when Queen Elizabeth succeeded Mary and once more separated the English Church from Rome, she could not restore conformity though hard she tried. Puritans and other dissidents grew in numbers. All over England the unending debate on religion established freedom of speech in religious matters—in practice if not in written law.

The New World quickened the cause of free speech. To

encourage settlement in America, the English kings granted a long series of royal charters, specifying the people's rights. Maryland's Charter of 1632 incorporated certain provisions for religious liberty nearly 60 years before Englishmen in the home country obtained equivalent guarantees. Freedom of speech in England's Parliament was still not firmly established when the Massachusetts Body of Liberties of 1641 guaranteed the right of every "Inhabitant or fforeiner, free or not free" to speak out in town meetings.

Not all of the first-comers were ready to grant a right of dissent to any who differed with them. In Massachusetts, for example, the Puritan elders quickly became embroiled in disputes with Roger Williams and his Baptist followers. But Williams had only to journey 50 miles southwestward to gain freedom of thought and speech in his own Providence Plantations. And, like Williams' little band, tens of thousands of others over the next century found in the slowly advancing frontier the perfect guarantor of their right to speak out, however pigheaded, wrong-minded or misled they might be.

On the very eve of the American Revolution, and even during the years of bitter war, the colonists were careful to protect their opponents' right of free speech. In 1765 the Virginia House of Burgesses met to vote on a set of ringing resolutions condemning the Stamp Act as an unbearable oppression. But when Patrick Henry proposed that anyone asserting Parliament's right to tax the colonists should be deemed an enemy of the people, the Burgesses decisively voted his resolution down. The colonists wanted to assert their own rights but not to seal the mouths of even the Tories among them. As late as 1777, for example, the Rev. Edward Winslow of Braintree, Mass., was able to pray publicly for George III without interruption.

Once independence was declared, the former colonies hastened to write state constitutions incorporating bills of rights. The Pennsylvania constitution, adopted in August 1776, was the first in history to provide explicitly that "the people have a right to freedom of speech." Behind all these guarantees lay the deep conviction of America's revolutionary leaders that democracy could function only if freedom of speech was secure. Jefferson, Madison, Franklin and others had been deeply influenced by philosophers like Rousseau, who thought of governments as the result of social contracts in which the people yielded only some of their natural rights to the state, carefully reserving others as inviolable rights of each individual. Paramount among these they placed freedom of speech, because by its exercise alone could all the other personal liberties be preserved from abridgment by tyrannically inclined officials.

Thomas Jefferson best phrased the common view when he drafted Virginia's Statute of Religious Liberty in 1786. "Truth," he wrote, "is great and will prevail if left to herself. She is the proper and sufficient antagonist to error and has nothing to fear from the conflict of free argument and debate."

The convention that drafted our national Constitution omitted any further guarantees of individual liberties. Most delegates felt that personal rights would find adequate protection under the state constitutions. When Congress submitted the Constitution to the states, however, a storm of opposition arose. Ratification was secured only by the promise that Congress would make the passage of Bill of Rights amendments its earliest order of business.

To young James Madison fell the task of drawing up these amendments. Urged on by a barrage of letters from Thomas Jefferson, at that time our ambassador in Paris, Madison framed the First Amendment as far more than a mere endorsement of the ideal of free speech. "Congress shall make no law," he wrote, "abridging the freedom of speech."

The words and actions of our founding fathers touched off profound repercussions throughout the world. As early as 1789, while Congress was still considering our Bill of Rights amendments, the States-General of France adopted the Declaration of the Rights of Man, modeled upon the bills of rights already woven into most of our state constitutions.

Since then virtually every independent country on earth has adopted similar guarantees. Even the Soviet constitution, adopted in 1936, blandly states that "the citizens of the U.S.S.R. are guaranteed freedom of speech." Yet the bitter experience of the people behind the Iron Curtain, and of others in many of the newer states, amply testifies that such guarantees may not be worth the paper they are written on unless men are willing to struggle to preserve them.

Our own freedom-of-speech guarantee met its first great test only seven years after adoption. In 1798 war with France seemed imminent, and a spy hysteria swept the country. Pressed to do so by President John Adams, Congress passed the Alien and Sedition Acts. The Sedition Act made it a crime—for the next three years—to criticize the government or to bring the Congress or the President into "contempt or disrepute."

The result was a short but fierce reign of terror. Congressman Matthew Lyon of Vermont was imprisoned for saying that President Adams had "a thirst for ridiculous pomp." A number of other men were dealt with similarly for even more trivial outspokenness. Public revulsion soon led to the defeat of Adams' party and the election of Jefferson in 1800. The new President promptly pardoned all those who had been convicted, and the new Congress quietly allowed the Sedition Act to expire.

During the trials of Lyon and the other offenders, their counsel got nowhere with objections to the validity of the Sedition Act because the federal courts had not yet established their power to decide whether acts of Congress were unconstitutional. In 1803, however, the Supreme Court assumed that right and, ever since, has served as the main guardian of the rights of the people against Congressional or Presidential usurpation.

Thus, over the decades, scores of Supreme Court decisions have clarified the precise meaning of freedom of speech, establishing its limitations where it comes into conflict with other community values and, more often, extending its scope to fit new conditions that the founding fathers could not have foreseen.

Today the limitations are few. If you utter gross obscenities in public, you may be charged with disorderly conduct. If you utter "fighting words"—the kind which virtually force your opponent to take off his coat and belt you—you may be restrained until you cool off. If you slander someone, he may sue you. If your words invoke a "clear and present danger" of inciting a breach of the peace or overthrow of the government by force—if, for example, you urge immediate mob violence—the police have the right to step in and halt you.

On the other hand, the courts have struck down a whole series of local ordinances that tended to restrict free speech. They have ruled, for example, that a public hall cannot be open to one party and closed to its rival; that no one need take out a permit to hold a meeting or speak in any private place; that states and cities must permit the use of parks and streets for speechmaking, setting only such rules as are absolutely necessary to avoid traffic jams or to preserve peace and quiet.

When motion pictures were new, many communities set up censorship boards to review pictures in advance of their public showing and eliminate what they thought to be obscene or sacrilegious scenes. In 1952 the Supreme Court held that the right of free speech made such advance censorship unconstitutional. Today, in most states, an exhibitor needs no prior permission to show a picture, but once he has shown it he may be tried for obscenity.

Every year, as many as a dozen cases involving free speech may come before the Supreme Court. Some years ago, for example, a test case concerning Connecticut's law prohibiting the giving out of birth-control information reached the highest court. The court had to decide whether Connecticut's law, in its restrictions upon the giving of information, was an unconstitutional abridgment of free speech.

Another problem, which has also been investigated at Congressional hearings, concerns the censorship of the speeches of military officers on active duty. Is such a censorship a denial of an officer's civil right to speak his mind? Or is it a legitimate control of military policy by civilian authority?

Visitors from abroad, noting all the attention we give to such issues, sometimes conclude that free speech in this country is in imminent danger of destruction. They could not be more wrong. Local lawmakers and even our Congress may, at times, enact statutes that tend to abridge free speech. Misguided police officers or public officials do, at times, violate a citizen's right to speak freely. But our courts strike down invalid laws and reverse illegal denials of free speech.

It is this constant concern—of our courts, our press, our people—to preserve and extend free speech that most fundamentally distinguishes our open society from all totalitarian regimes, where only those who unquestioningly support the party in power can speak out. As Soviet Russia's Andrei Vishinsky, Stalin's purge prosecutor, put it: "In our state, naturally, there is and can be no place for freedom of speech for the foes of socialism."

In the United States we accept no such weird standard. Our faith, today as when the Constitution was written, rests upon *full* freedom of speech for critics of our government and the governing party as well as for its supporters.

What America Means to Me

by Theodore H. White

I AM HOME in New England after many weeks on the campaign trail. From Boston's Faneuil Hall, through the hives of Florida's sun-washed condominiums, to the fashionable parlors of Manhattan, I have been listening again to the men who want to be President. This year more than ever they perplex me—for there must be some thread, some common concern that binds Americans together beneath the crackling overgrowth of party politics and clashing visions.

The only clue to an answer comes through a window as I sit looking down over a valley in my Connecticut town of Bridgewater. Beyond, a low gray ridge hides the cleft through which runs the Housatonic River. And beyond rises the hazy blue lines of the Berkshires, and beyond that flows the Hudson. Still farther away lift the unseen Appalachians; and yet farther come the Great Plains, the Rockies, the tawny slopes that run down to the far edge of California.

I have crisscrossed this America for many years, looking for meaning. But it started here in New England. When I clear brush, I come across the overgrown stone walls of abandoned farms. How other men's backs must have ached as they cleared fields, pulled the stumps, piled the stones! Then up over the ridge and down into the next valley rolled their wagons, over the next river, over the next range. On and on for 200 years—questing. Seeking opportunity for themselves and a promise for their children. They were followed by millions and millions more from Europe, and are followed today by what is the largest wave of immigrants in our history, legal and illegal alike, seeking the same opportunities, demanding the same promise for their children.

Only it is harder now. Not harder physically, to be sure. The men and women who pushed their plows with horses or oxen through unturned bottomland died young. But if they persisted, and they did, they could raise their own church, choose their own schoolmaster, and pass on their farms to their children—with no interference from a distant government. And if opportunity ran out, it was off and over the next ridge, all the way to the Willamette Valley in Oregon.

But, to get that far, government had to help—with the Cumberland trail over the Alleghenies, with subsidies to the railroads, with irrigation works to water the parched West. Government knew its role was to help.

It is harder now to think clearly about government in this third century of our republic. It strikes me now that we are crossing some vast invisible ridge of the mind, that an era is ending. We are locked into a crush of big organizations that squeeze us all—Big Government, Big Business, Big Unions. From the candidates of the Right to the candidates of the Left, all are trying to pry open or keep open the opportunity which once lay only over the next ridge.

But it is far more complicated today. There will be no opportunity for black children in the ghettoes unless the government reorganizes our big cities; yet the cities will become all-black ghettoes if the government forces policies that drive white families away. If the government mangles American industry with controls, it can halt the engines of prosperity; yet if it does not restrain Big Business, there will be no little businessmen seeding the future with new enterprise.

This valley I see from my window needs government to keep its water clean and its air clear. This vast country needs government to save its cities and defend its shores and skies. But if government crushes opportunity—what then?

All these months I have been listening to men, one of whom will certainly be our next President, making their promises and seeking to keep opportunity open. None have real answers, as yet. All their discourse reduces to questions.

Perhaps that is the meaning of America: the unending question of how to enlarge opportunity while yet maintaining an orderly, balanced government of free men. That was the question with which America began. And the enduring vitality of the question is as important to the spirit of America as the answer any new President can give.

Your Bill of Rights

by Donald Culross Peattie

THE MOST significant piece of paper in the life of every American is on display in its shrine in the Archives Building in Washington. Millions of citizens over the years have gazed in reverence on the original document that promises us, in ink that has faded but in words that never dim, most of what we mean by our "Constitutional rights."

Few of those rights are found in the Constitution itself. They are in the first ten amendments, adopted in 1791. The single sheet that bears on its yellowing face these precious liberties is called the Bill of Rights. And it means more to the American citizen than the Constitution itself, which is the blueprint for our governmental machinery. You might, for instance, change the way by which, under the original Constitution, Senators are elected (indeed, it has been done) without causing the national blood pressure to jump. But lay one finger on, say, Article I of the Bill of Rights, to kill freedom of utterance, and every good American should be up in arms.

It is the same with the other nine amendments; take away one and you weaken all; take freedom from your neighbor and you enslave yourself. "Liberty," said William Allen White, "is the only thing you cannot have unless you are willing to give it to others."

To Americans, the first ten amendments have the force of moral law, on a higher plane than ordinary legislation. They are our fundamental articles of faith. They cannot be abridged or abolished even by Congress. They are the supreme law of the land, and we set the Supreme Court to prowl around the liberties they promise and to nullify any laws that would lessen their force. Yet, marvelous to relate, they are not written in lawyer language. Anybody can understand the Bill of Rights, just as anybody can understand the Ten Commandments: "Thou shalt not kill. Thou shalt not steal."

150 Heritage of Freedom

Take Article I, which sets forth in one sentence enough freedoms to make dictatorship impossible here:

"Congress shall make no law respecting an establishment of religion, or prohibiting the free exercise thereof; or abridging the freedom of speech, or of the press; or the right of the people peaceably to assemble, and to petition the Government for a redress of grievances."

There in one breath a government took the unprecedented step of protecting the citizens against itself. It freed religion from all interference by the state; and by promising free speech and press it exposed itself, as no dictatorship dares do, to the bracing winds of open criticism.

So you may with impunity criticize and roundly denounce Congress, the President, even the Supreme Court, provided that you do not slander or libel individual persons. One hardly knows what to admire more in this—the wisdom of providing a safety valve for the pressures that inevitably build up in a complex society, or the way such freedom operates to keep government on its toes.

True, some other countries permit most or all of the rights in these immortal amendments. But in other countries they are usually found in tradition, precedent or common law. Our government was the first to collect them all in one place and write them into its Constitution.

No confiscation of your property by the Government, says the Bill of Rights, unless you are indemnified for it; no searching of your house without a warrant; no accusation by witnesses unless they can be produced in open court; no putting you on trial twice for the same accusation. The Bill of Rights promises you freedom from excessive bail, freedom from torture to obtain confessions, freedom from cruel and unusual punishment. It gives you the right to a speedy trial by jury, to a definite written accusation if you are tried, and to have counsel and subpoena witnesses in a criminal trial. So, as long as we remain vigilant, we are the freest people on earth.

But we didn't get our Bill of Rights because some high-minded gentlemen penned self-evident truths shortly after our country was founded. Our democratic liberty was conceived ages ago in the dark of dungeons where brave mind whispered to unbroken soul. It was wrenched into birth when limbs were pulled apart on the torturer's rack, and knew the screams of women who saw their men butchered. It drew its breath of life as the ill-trained farm boys choked their last, pinned to the earth by the bayonets of Hessian mercenaries.

The fight to gain recognition of these "unalienable rights" is as old as man's faith in them. Tyranny is a sleepless foe. Always somewhere in the world men are being told they have no rights but what the State allows. Such a State gives you but one liberty—to obey. What a world of difference from our belief that "governments derive their just powers from the consent of the governed"!

The limitations on the power of government which we have defined in the Bill of Rights are foreshadowed in earliest laws and morals. Some are suggested by Magna Carta. Some are written into the Roman code which maintained the essential dignity of the free citizen however poor. Some are implicit in the teachings of Christ which set human values above property values. Over and over the Old Testament tells us that all men are created equal—not alike, naturally, but equal in the sight of a just God before whom kings stand naked as their slaves.

Actually the American people had been hammering away at the problems of democratic self-government for 150 years before our Revolution. Rocking on the wild Atlantic, the *Mayflower* Pilgrims in 1620 drew up, in their famous Compact, the first instrument of our republic—imperfect, but an honest beginning. The primary mistakes of the Puritans were corrected by Roger Williams' statement of religious freedom in 1644. Then there followed William Penn's famous Charter of Liberties granted to his Pennsylvania colonists. The words "inviolable rights" turn up in a petition signed by the inhabitants of Anson County, North Carolina, in 1769. The Virginia Bill of Rights (1776) and the Massachusetts Declaration of Rights (1780) were but the elder sisters of the first ten amendments to the Constitution.

No wonder that, when the Founding Fathers signed the Constitution that enumerated only a few rights of the common citizen, the people were indignant. They had fought a bloody war, ill-armed, starving, barefoot, for more than this—they had fought to secure their individual liberties, their *rights*. And they knew what they meant by them.

So did some of the delegates to the Constitutional Convention, who refused to sign the original document because it contained no Bill of Rights. So did Thomas Jefferson, who wrote from Paris (where he was ambassador) indignant protest at this crying lack. Some of the states ratified the Constitution only on the understanding that a Bill of Rights would be added.

In his first inaugural address George Washington reminded Congress of this duty. That is how, on June 8, 1789, James Madison came to present nine amendments to the Senate. They drew largely on the earlier Virginia Bill of Rights authored by George Mason, one of Washington's neighbors on the Potomac, and on Madison's own work for religious freedom in Virginia. In the House, 17 amendments were offered. Eventually House and Senate agreed on 12, but the states failed to ratify the first two recorded on the original amendment. So the remaining ten amendments became the law of the land.

Sometimes you hear that your Bill of Rights "guarantees" you your liberties. I asked the then Attorney General of the United States, Tom C. Clark, about the word, as we stood one afternoon examining the grand old document in the Archives Building. That night I asked Justice William O. Douglas of the Supreme Court the same question. Both gave the same answer: The Bill of Rights *promises* much, but it is up to the American people to make that promise good.

Somewhere in the country the Bill of Rights is violated almost every day. Its most dangerous foes are not foreign dictators but those of us who while claiming every privilege of democratic liberty would deny it to others. To rise to a neighbor's aid in defense of his rights is a first duty of citizenship. A second is outspoken criticism of every form of local and federal government when it fails in its duty to the first ten amendments. When the people think, and say what they think, this government obeys. The great liberties of the Bill of Rights were paid for in agony and blood, and can be kept safe only by restless conscience and the courage to speak out.

"... Our Lives, Our Fortunes and Our Sacred Honor"

by Henry Lee

ON THE Fourth of July, more than two hundred years ago, the men of the Continental Congress risked everything they held dear to proclaim the independence of the Thirteen Colonies. It was not an easy decision: defeat could mean a hangman's rope; victory would mean years of hardship in a struggling nation.

Faced with such a grim future, some delegates understandably had hesitated. How well the resolute leaders of the Congress rallied the fainthearted was shown in the crucial vote of July 2 in the State House (now Independence Hall), Philadelphia. The delegates of ten colonies voted unanimously for independence, a majority of the Delaware and Pennsylvania delegations supported the resolution, and the New York representatives abstained. Then, on the Fourth of July, the Congress approved Thomas Jefferson's draft of the Declaration of Independence.

That act alone stamped the members of the Congress as traitors to Britain's King George III. But 56 delegates, including some who arrived in Philadelphia too late to take part in the voting, went even further: they flaunted their rebellion by affixing their signatures to the historic document which concluded: "And for the support of this Declaration...we mutually pledge to each other our Lives, our Fortunes and our sacred Honor."

In effect, these 56 men might have been signing their own death warrants. Yet every delegate who was in Philadelphia on the day set for the signing—August 2—walked to the table on which the parchment rested and boldly penned his name.

The men who had the most to lose set the example. John Hancock, president of the Congress and one of the wealthiest

154 Heritage of Freedom

men in the colonies, wrote in the boldest hand of all. When even wealthier Charles Carroll, a Maryland delegate, stepped up, a mischievous colleague said, "There are two Charles Carrolls in Maryland. How will King George know which one to hang?" Carroll had an eloquent answer; he simply added, "of Carrollton"—the family estate—to his name. "Now the king can make no mistake," he said.

Early or late, most of the 56 men who placed their names on the Declaration of Independence paid a high price for their audacity. But these men were so passionately dedicated to the cause of freedom that nothing could distract them from whatever sacrifices might be demanded. Take John Hancock. When the American command debated bombarding Boston to dislodge the British, Hancock said, "Burn Boston and make John Hancock a beggar if the public good requires it." His offer was not just bombast; he put it in writing to George Washington.

A dedicated Virginia signer, Thomas Nelson, Jr., actually directed an artillery bombardment against his own mansion during the colonial Army's siege of Yorktown. He was commanding his state's militia and the British had seized his home as their headquarters.

Nelson did even more. When the colonial government desperately needed two million dollars to provision the French fleet, which was helping Washington on the seas, Nelson raised almost the entire subscription on his own security. After the war he redeemed the loans, at the cost of his estates and fortune. He was never reimbursed by his country, and he was placed in an unmarked grave at his death.

Carter Braxton, planter, trader and, like Nelson, a Virginian, also went from riches to rags for his belief. First, the British chased all his ships from the seas. Then, when wartime inflation undermined the value of his plantations' produce, his properties right down to his slaves and furniture were plastered with attachments and mortgages. He lost everything.

Another signer who suffered for his beliefs was Richard Stockton of New Jersey, a noted swordsman, horseman and jurist. The British descended on Morven, the Stockton great house (which still stands, a stone's throw from Princeton Inn), burned Stockton's library, devastated his rolling lands, stole his stableful of blooded horses, even decapitated his portrait with a saber swing. Stockton went into hiding. But late one winter's night, on a neighbor's tip, the British seized him and

"... Our Lives, Our Fortunes..." **155**

threw him into jail at Perth Amboy, where he suffered greatly from lack of food and heat. Eventually he was released in an exchange of prisoners; but he was a pain-racked, impoverished shell of the dashing signer of '76—and died in 1781.

Four other signers were captured by the British—first, in 1778, George Walton of Georgia, who was exchanged for a British Navy captain. Thomas Heyward, Jr., Edward Rutledge and Arthur Middleton, all of South Carolina, were trapped in the fall of Charleston in May 1780. After some preliminary retaliation on their property, the British packed them off to a prison camp in St. Augustine, Fla., where they languished for more than a year.

The only other South Carolina signer was shy, studious Thomas Lynch, Jr., 27, who served in the colonial army and permanently ruined his health through swamp fever. After he signed the Declaration his health continued to worsen, and in 1779 he embarked for France with his wife; their vessel was never heard of again.

Unlike most of his suave colleagues at Philadelphia, 68-year-old John Hart was a simple farmer. For years he had peaceably tended his 400 acres in Hopewell Township, N.J. Within a few months after the signing of the Declaration the Hessians reached Hopewell. Hart was driven from his dying wife's bedside, and his 13 children were scattered in all directions. His fields were laid waste, his precious grist, saw and fulling mills were razed. He was hunted through New Jersey's wild Sourland Mountains.

For more than a year the tough old man lived in forests and caves, refusing to leave the state because of his wife. Not until the Americans won at Trenton and Princeton in December 1777 was Hart able to return home. By then his wife was dead, and all that remained of his property was blackened acreage.

Everywhere it was the same story of sack and family flight before the enemy. At Bordentown, N.J., the family of gentle Francis Hopkinson barely escaped when the Hessians seized his home. William Ellery's house at Newport, R.I., George Clymer's place in Chester County, 25 miles out of Philadelphia, Lewis Morris's 3000-acre New York estate (Morrisania, located in what is now the Bronx), the Georgia plantations of Lyman Hall and Button Gwinnett—all suffered from Redcoat vandalism.

When Sam Adams of Massachusetts lost his only son

to the cause, there was bitter irony in his loss, for he had said: "I should advise persisting in our struggle for liberty though it was revealed from Heaven that 999 were to perish and only one of a thousand to survive and retain his liberty! One such freeman must enjoy more happiness than a thousand slaves; let him propagate his like and transmit to them what he has so nobly preserved."

Always, it seemed, the signers of the Declaration felt a moral responsibility to carry through what they had started. Those who did not fight worked like men possessed to supply the troops, to administer the government, to combat sickening inflation. Two or three of them were popularly believed to have died of overwork, and it is easy to credit. John Adams, who was to be the second President of the United States, served, for example, on 90 Congressional committees in 1776 and 1777, and was chairman of 25!

Rarely did the statemen and diplomats let an opportunity pass to show their defiance of the enemy. In the fall of 1776, before sailing for France on diplomatic business, 70-year-old Benjamin Franklin entrusted his entire fortune to Congress—as a gesture of his confidence in the new country.

Most of the signers, of course, went on after the war to shape the country they had brought to birth. At last there were only three left, and on the Fourth of July, 1826—50th anniversary of the Declaration of Independence—two of them lay dying: a man of 83 in Virginia and one a few months short of 91 in Massachusetts. At 12:50 p.m. that day Thomas Jefferson succumbed. At four o'clock John Adams followed, and among his last coherent words was the toast he proposed: "Independence forever!"

On a November day six years later the signers' story finally ended. At the age of 95, Charles Carroll of Carrollton died, the last of them all.

Actually their story will never die so long as Americans take courage and example from it. Even if we go back to the first signer to succumb, a man almost forgotten by history because he had so little time to give his country, we find the ultimate quality that possessed every man who placed his signature on the Declaration: faith in the land for which he pledged his all.

In April of 1777, when Revolutionary hopes were bogged in the spring mud, John Morton of Pennsylvania lay dying.

"...Our Lives, Our Fortunes..." 157

His last thoughts were of the Tory friends who had turned against him after he voted for independence. "Tell them," he said, "that they will live to see the hour when they shall acknowledge it to have been the most glorious service that I ever rendered my country." Then he died, in faith.

Only Yesterday

The Night the Martians Landed

by Edwin H. James

OCTOBER 30 began no differently from any other Sunday of 1938. Picnickers and Sunday drivers swarmed out onto the highways; millions attended worship; others stayed home and read their newspapers.

The news was concerned with such items as David O. Selznick's confession that he still sought an actress to play Scarlett O'Hara. Thomas E. Dewey, the young racket-buster, was running for Governor of New York. A month before, Great Britain's Prime Minister Chamberlain had returned from his Munich talk with Adolf Hitler guaranteeing "peace in our time." But in the news columns there was no mention of 23-year-old Orson Welles, whose radio adaptation of H.G. Wells' *The War of the Worlds* that peaceful Sunday evening was to spread wild disorder and terror from coast to coast.

The radio play was hardly more fantastic than the pandemonium it created. Welles used the technique of "news bulletins" and "eyewitness reports," with which listeners had become familiar during the recent Munich crisis. The production started innocently enough with a speech by Welles: "We know now that in the early years of the 20th century our earth was being watched closely by intelligences greater than man's and yet as mortal as his own.... With infinite complacence human beings went about their little affairs, serene in the assurance of their dominion over this small spinning fragment of solar driftwood.... Yet across an immense ethereal gulf, intellects vast, cool and unsympathetic regarded our globe with envious eyes and drew their plans against us. In the 39th year of the 20th century came the great disillusionment."

An announcer then read a weather report. The scene shifted, picking up a dance orchestra, which was interrupted by a "news" bulletin stating that an astronomer in Chicago had observed "several explosions of incandescent gas, occurring on the planet Mars." This was followed by an interview with a Princeton University astronomer (played by Welles), who was unable to account for the gas eruptions.

A "special news bulletin" followed: "It is reported that a huge, flaming object fell on a farm near Grovers Mill, N.J., 22 miles from Trenton. The flash was visible for several hundred miles, and impact was heard as far north as Elizabeth."

An incredibly short time later, the eyewitness broadcast began. A crowd had already converged, the reporter said, around a huge cylinder. The reporter speculated on the nature of the cylinder, interviewed several persons, and consumed perhaps three minutes of air time until the limits of theatrical tension had been reached.

"This is the most terrifying thing I have ever witnessed!" the announcer shouted. "Something's crawling out of the cylinder from Mars. I can see two luminous disks peering out of a black hole.... Are they eyes? It might be a face. It might be—something's wriggling out. There's another one, and another. There, I can see the thing's body. It's large as a bear and it glistens like wet leather. But that face. It... it's indescribable! I can hardly force myself to look at it! The mouth is V-shaped, with saliva dripping from rimless lips that seem to quiver and pulsate!"

After the wet-leather Martians had crawled out of the space machine, police sought to approach it but were cremated by a heat-ray. The announcer himself died at his post when the entire countryside was ignited.

A few minutes later in the broadcast, the New Jersey State Militia was called out. In what must have been a record for rapid mobilization, eight battalions of infantry arrived and attacked the Martians. The space machine itself developed legs and walked through the army, trampling soldiers or charring them with its heat-ray. Of the 7000 troops who opposed the monster, 120 survived.

Having crushed the militia, the monster plodded off toward New York, tearing up bridges, razing cities, killing thousands with its heat-ray and clouds of poison gas.

An announcer "speaking from the roof of Broadcasting Building, New York City," described the destruction of the metropolis. "Enemy now in sight above the Palisades. Five great machines, wading the Hudson like men wading a brook.... A bulletin's handed me.... Martian cylinders are

The Night the Martians Landed

falling all over the country—Buffalo, Chicago, St. Louis. ... Now the machines, tall as a skyscraper, are on the West Side.... This is the end now. Smoke comes out.... black smoke, drifting over the city. People in the streets see it. They're running toward the East River... thousands of them, dropping in like rats... falling like flies.... The smoke's crossing Sixth Avenue... Fifth Avenue... a hundred yards... it's 50 feet..." The announcer choked to death.

Soon a large part of the eastern seaboard was "reported" to be in ruins, its people wiped out.

Statisticians later estimated that six million listeners heard the broadcast and nearly two million believed it was true. As this program began on the Columbia Broadcasting System, the National Broadcasting Company presented Edgar Bergen and Charlie McCarthy. They were the biggest hit on radio, with perhaps ten times as many listeners as Orson Welles. It is shuddering to think what might have happened that night if Welles had been as popular as the ventriloquist on NBC. However, about the time Welles' "reporter" began describing the Martians' terrifying emergence from the space machine, Edgar Bergen introduced a singer, and a million or so listeners twirled their dials to see what was happening on CBS. Having missed all the preliminaries, they, too, believed the invasion was real. These millions of believing listeners were spread so widely that panic struck almost every community in the United States.

Police headquarters, newspapers and radio stations were swamped with anguished calls. Sobbing mothers clutched their children in a last embrace, convinced that horrible death at the slimy hands of Martian monsters was about to overtake them. Whole neighborhoods were evacuated as inhabitants rushed into the streets with wet handkerchiefs pressed to their noses to defend themselves against poison gas. Motorists careened through the night to escape incineration from Martian flamethrowers. Families huddled in desperate prayer.

There was a clamor for casualty lists from people who had relatives or friends living in New Jersey. In San Francisco a man called the police: "My God—where can I volunteer my services? We've got to stop this awful thing!" A young man in a New Jersey town borrowed a car to speed to his priest—"so I could make peace with God before dying." He hit a curve at 80 miles an hour; the car rolled over twice, but he was unhurt. "I thought it didn't matter that the car was wrecked," he said. "The owner would have no more use for it."

The mayor of a large midwest city, by sheer luck having managed to call into the clogged CBS switchboard in New York, demanded to talk to Orson Welles. Mobs were stampeding in his city's streets. If this was a hoax, the mayor would come to New York and punch Welles in the nose.

Not all listeners were frightened. Two Princeton professors of geology preserved such academic detachment that they set off for Grovers Mill with the intention of buying the Martian cylinder for an exhibit at the university's laboratories.

The second 30 minutes of the broadcast told of the rebuilding of the world after the destruction of the Martian invaders, who were killed, "after all man's defenses had failed," by the "humblest thing that God in his wisdom had put upon this earth"—bacteriological action. Despite this less gloomy theme of the second half hour, frantic telephone calls to radio stations, newspapers and police throughout the country only increased in volume.

At 8:48 p.m. the Associated Press wired its editors that queries from radio listeners were the result of a studio dramatization. Assurance that "The War of the Worlds" had been a play and not a news report was broadcast repeatedly the rest of the night by a harassed and worried CBS.

Recalling the program's aftermath in a *Harper's Magazine* article, John Houseman, co-founder of Orson Welles' Mercury Theater, described it as a nightmare. "The building is suddenly full of people and dark-blue uniforms. We are hurried out of the studio, downstairs into a back office. Here we sit incommunicado while network employes are busily destroying or locking up all scripts and records of the broadcast. Then the press is let loose upon us, ravening for horror. How many deaths have *we* heard of? (Implying they knew of thousands.) What do we know of the fatal stampede in a Jersey hall? (Implying it is one of many.) What traffic deaths? (The ditches must be choked with corpses.) The suicides? (Haven't you heard about the one on Riverside Drive?) It is all quite vague in my memory and quite terrible."

Although none stood up in court, damage suits to the tune of $750,000 were filed by citizens who claimed to have suffered injuries as a result of "The War of the Worlds." Millions of words were written in an effort to explain the furor. And days passed before people again concerned themselves with such realities as the quest for a Scarlett O'Hara, jitterbugging and the WPA.

Campaign Buttons U.S.A.

by William Schulz

WHEN George Washington was elected President for the first time, his supporters fastened tiny brass buttons initialed G.W. to their waistcoats. When John Adams ran successfully in 1796, his backers distributed cologne dispensers carrying his likeness and soliciting support.

From these simple beginnings, campaign gadgetry has mushroomed into a multimillion-dollar business with an enormous impact on the selection of our leaders. By election day, each four years, Presidential candidates will have handed out 100 million buttons, 50 million bumper stickers and countless other items from balloons to beer mugs, from emery boards to silver spoons.

One can learn much about America's political history by poring through her campaign memorabilia. Nothing better summarizes Herbert Hoover's successful 1928 campaign than his poster, "A chicken in every pot, two cars in every garage." Equally telling, next time out, was the Democrats' button: "In Hoover We Trusted, Now We Are Busted." Politicians learned early to use gadgets and gimmicks to mold vote-getting images. Brass medals bearing the slogan, "Hero of New Orleans," celebrated the gallantry of Andrew Jackson, who made his name in the War of 1812. By the time William Henry Harrison ran for President in 1840, the image-makers were in firm control.

When a newspaper suggested that Harrison, "given a barrel of hard cider and a pension of $2000 a year, would be content to sit the remainder of his days in his log cabin," his supporters turned the attack into a campaign theme. College-educated, scion of one of Virginia's first families, Harrison was presented to the electorate as a rough-hewn man of the frontier, a dirt farmer clad in the humblest of garb. The log cabin became his campaign symbol—despite the fact that he lived on a 3000-acre plantation. Log-cabin buttons and whiskey bottles were widely distributed, and campaign workers wearing coonskin hats dragged miniature cabins through the streets of major cities. Poor Martin Van Buren, ridiculed as a "lily-fingered aristocrat," never had a chance.

Twenty years later, in 1860, a perennially unsuccessful politician named Abraham Lincoln used buttons and banners, song and slogans, to shape his image. Capitalizing on Democratic corruption, Lincoln was cast as "Honest Old Abe," with flags portraying him as the sinewy, hard-working "rail-splitter of the West."

Bitterness and name-calling have been endemic down through American political history—and our campaign memorabilia vividly record it. There is the Grover Cleveland banner of 1884 denouncing James G. Blaine as the "Continental Liar from the State of Maine." There is the Democrats' less-than-subtle taunt at 330-pound President William Howard Taft—a pin depicting a pig with a wide-open mouth.

But for sheer vituperation, few campaigns have matched the 1940 Wendell Wilkie-Franklin Delano Roosevelt contest, when F.D.R. sought to become the first President to serve three terms. "No Third Termites," proclaimed GOP buttons—and "We Don't Want Eleanor, Either." F.D.R. buttons responded, "Better a Third Termer Than a Third Rater."

Today collectors and historians are digging through the nation's attics for artifacts of our political past—now worth far more than at the time of distribution. A George Washington commemorative button that cost a penny to make goes for $300 and more today. An 8-by-12-inch placard urging the election of William McKinley commands $130. A Chicago collector has turned down $1000 for a button from F.D.R.'s unsuccessful campaign for Vice President in 1920.

Thousands of buttons and banners, gimmicks and gadgets have been collected by the Smithsonian Institution's Museum of History and Technology and National Portrait Gallery. To the historian and the political scientist they are, of course, invaluable. Even more important, perhaps, they provide all Americans with a mini-history of a republic that has for two centuries chosen its leaders in a process unique among nations.

Baseball Stories for a Rainy Afternoon

by Roger Angell

THE TARPAULIN IS DOWN, and a midafternoon rain is falling steadily. Play has been halted. The lights are on, and the wet, pale-green tarp throws off wiggly, reptilian gleams. The players are back in their locker rooms, and both dugouts are empty. A few fans have stayed in their seats, huddling under big brightly colored golf umbrellas, but almost everybody else has moved back under the shelter of the upper decks, standing there quietly, watching the rain. The huge park, the countless rows of shiny-blue wet seats, the long emerald outfield lawns—all stand silent and waiting. By the look of it, this shower may hold things up for a good half-hour or more. Time for a few baseball stories.

For a continuous baseball melodrama, there probably never was a better theater than the Philadelphia Phillies' shabby little park, Baker Bowl, which was finally abandoned in 1938. The field was better suited for a smaller, narrower game—croquet, perhaps—and its very short right-field wall, a bare 280 feet from home, was detested by every pitcher and outfielder in the league. One afternoon in 1934, the starting hurler for the visiting Brooklyn Dodgers was Walter (Boom-Boom) Beck, and the dangerous starboard garden was being defended by Hack Wilson.

Always a robust slugger, Wilson unfortunately got to spend far less time at the plate than afield, where he was, to put the matter kindly, less than adequate. Hack was also known to spend an occasional evening at his local tavern, pondering this injustice. On this day, he had experienced a particularly trying afternoon in pursuit of assorted line drives and scorching grounders rifled in his direction off Boom-Boom's deliveries—often getting extra practice as he spun around and tried to field the caroms and ricochets, off that extremely adjacent wall, of the same hits he had missed outward-bound.

Dodger manager Casey Stengel watched several innings of this before he called time and made his familiar journey to the mound, where he suggested to Beck that he take the rest of the afternoon off. Beck's performance had been perfectly within his genre, but for some reason he was enraged at this derricking, and instead of handing the ball over to Stengel he suddenly turned and heaved it away in a passion. Fate, of course, sent the ball arching out into right field, where Hack Wilson, with his head down and his hands on his knees, was quietly reflecting on last night's excesses and this day's indignities. Boom-Boom's throw struck the turf a few feet away from Wilson, who, although badly startled, whirled and chased manfully after the ball, fielded the carom off the wall, and got off a terrific, knee-high peg to second base—his best fielding play, Casey always said, of the entire summer.

A more recent epochal disorder came in a game played in an instructional league. This time, things began with an outfielder's peg to a rookie catcher, who grabbed the ball and made a swipe at an inrushing, sliding base runner at the plate. As sometimes happens, the catcher missed the tag and the base runner missed the plate. The runner jumped up, dusted himself off, and trotted to his dugout, convinced that he had scored. The umpire made no call either way, which is the prescribed response, and after a moment or two the pitcher and the infielders, analyzing the situation, hurried in and implored the catcher to make the tag.

"Tag who?" asked the catcher.

"The runner, the runner!" they cried. "You missed him. He didn't score. Go tag him!"

"Ah," said the young receiver, the light bulb over his head at last clicking on. Still holding the ball, he ran eagerly toward the enemy dugout, with the umpire close behind. When the catcher got there, however, he gazed up and down the line of seated fresh-faced rookies without recognizing anyone who looked like a recent passerby. He went to one end of the bench and tagged the first three men sitting in line. He looked around at the umpire, who was watching with folded arms. The umpire made no sign. The catcher tagged four more players. The ump shook his head almost imperceptibly. Now the erstwhile base runner, seeing the catcher inexorably working up the line toward him, leaped up and made a dash for the plate. The pitcher, who had been standing bemused near home, screamed for the ball, and he and the catcher executed a rundown, in the style of stadium attendants collecting a loose dog on the field, and tagged the man out in the on-deck circle.

The New York Mets, of course, have been the progenitors of many legendary baseball disasters. Some of the legends were true. During the early stages of their terrible first summer, in 1962, their center fielder Richie Ashburn suffered a series of frightful surprises while going after short fly balls, because he was repeatedly run over by the shortstop, the enthusiastic but modestly talented Elio Chacon. Ashburn eventually concluded that Chacon, who spoke very little English, simply didn't understand what it meant when he saw his center fielder waving his arms and yelling "Mine! Mine! I got it!" Richie thought this over and then went to Joe Christopher, a bilingual teammate, and asked for help.

"All you have to do is say it in Spanish," Christopher said. "Yell out *'Yo la tengo!'* and Elio will pull up. I'll explain it to him, too. You won't have any more trouble."

Before the next game, Ashburn saw Chacon in the clubhouse. *"Yo la tengo?"* Richie said tentatively.

"Sí, sí! Yo la tengo! Yo la tengo!" Chacon said, smiling and nodding.

In the second or third inning that night, an enemy batter lifted a short fly to center. Ashburn sprinted in for the ball. Chacon thundered out after it. *"Yo la tengo! Yo la tengo!"* Richie shouted.

Chacon jammed on the brakes and stopped, happily gesturing for Ashburn to help himself. Richie reached up to make the easy catch—and was knocked flat by Frank Thomas, the Mets' left fielder.

Then there's Tom LaSorda's story. LaSorda, manager of the Los Angeles Dodgers, grew up in Norristown, Pa., and became a serious baseball fan at an early age. When he was 12 or 13, he volunteered for duty as a crossing guard at his parochial school because he knew that the reward for this service was a free trip to a big-league ball game—an event he had yet to witness.

The great day came at last, the sun shone, and the party

of nuns and junior fuzz repaired to Shibe Park, where the Phillies were playing the Giants. Young Tom LaSorda had a wonderful afternoon, and just before the game ended he and some of his colleagues forehandedly stationed themselves beside a runway under the stands. The game ended, the Giants came clattering by, and Tom extended his scorecard to the first hulking, bespiked hero to come in out of the sunshine.

"C'n I have your autograph, please, mister?" he asked.

"Outta my way, kid," the Giant said, brushing past the boy.

When Tom LaSorda tells the story now, the shock of this moment is still visible on his face. "I couldn't *believe* it," he says. "Here was the first big-league player I'd ever seen up close—the first one I ever dared speak to—and what he did was shove me up against the wall. I think tears came to my eyes. I watched the guy as he went away toward the clubhouse and I noticed the number on his back—you know, like taking the license of a hit-and-run car. Later on, I looked at my program and got his name. I never forgot it."

Seven or eight years went swiftly by, during which time Tom LaSorda grew up to become a promising young pitcher in the Dodger organization. In the spring of 1949, he was a star with the Dodger farm team in Greenville, S.C., and took the mound for the opening game of the season at Augusta Ga., facing the Augusta Yankees. Tom retired the first two batters, and then studied the third, a beefy right-handed veteran, as he stepped up to the box.

LaSorda was transfixed. "I looked," he says, "and *it was the same man!*"

The first pitch to the unsuspecting batter nearly removed the button from the top of his cap. The second, behind his knees, inspired a beautiful sudden *entrechat*. The third, under his Adam's apple, confirmed the message, and he threw away his bat and charged the mound like a fighting bull entering the plaza in Seville. The squads spilled out onto the field and separated the two men, and only after a lengthy and disorderly interval was baseball resumed.

After the game, LaSorda was dressing in the visitors' locker room when he was told that he had a caller at the door. It was the former Giant, who now wore a peaceable but puzzled expression. "Listen, kid," he said to LaSorda, "did I ever meet you before?"

"Not exactly," Tom said.

"Well, why were you tryin' to take my head off out there?"

LaSorda spread his hands wide. "You didn't give me your autograph," he said.

Tom LaSorda tells this story each spring to the new young players who make the Dodger club. *"Always* give an autograph when somebody asks you," he says gravely. "You never can tell. In baseball, anything can happen."

Thanks, Hazel

by Emil Petaja

IT WAS 20 BELOW, with a Montana blizzard snarling out of Blackfoot Canyon. Twilit little Milltown was already snugged down for the night after its frugal wartime dinner. The only human movement abroad was an angular girlish form moving between snowbanks, clutching her coat around her chin.

Hazel. Our Milltown librarian. Seven o'clock Tuesday night and, blizzard or no blizzard, there would be those who would want books, *need* books—to hold back the grinding fear for their loved ones overseas. It was 1918, and for Milltown mothers and wives there was no radio to bring news. No television. Just the cutting cold and banked-up snow, oil lamps and hearth fires.

And Hazel's books. Twice every week her village customers came to the attic room over the bakery—every Tuesday evening at seven, every Saturday afternoon at two. They counted on her. How could she let them down?

Hazel kept her coat on and blew on her fingers while she lifted the nickel-plated ornamented lid off the corner wood stove and started a fire. She used kindling she'd chopped herself with a big blunt kitchen knife. Then she opened the somber bookcases against the walls, to display all that wealth of thought and silent action. All the treasures of the world. Courtesy of Hazel.

It had started only a year before, in 1917. Hazel Beadle was just 18 and still in high school when she startled Missoula County library officials by gravely demanding that her sawmill hamlet, seven miles from the county seat, be given a library. Not a big one. Just a start—a few books.

No money, they frowned. Didn't she know there was

a war on? Couldn't the Milltown folk come in to Missoula for their books—that is, if that handful of immigrant sawmill workers *really* wanted books? Hazel's dark brown eyes flashed behind her thick horn-rims. Her Finns and Norwegians and Swedes and the French Canadians might be uneducated, but yes, they *did* want books! It was a hard rough seven miles to Missoula, and winters they were often snowed in. Books would give them something to dream on, so they could forget their sawmill drudgery and the Kaiser.

Hazel got her books. But everything else—housing, service—was left up to her. That was the deal, take it or leave it.

The Milltown Branch Library (first of its kind in the whole state) began in 1917 with a small collection in the home of a local teacher. When the teacher moved away the next year, Hazel's bookcases were carted up to the bakery attic.

But then the baker decided he needed his attic room. Sorry, Hazel. There were no more than 10 or 12 functioning business establishments at the little crossroads on the highway. Hazel knocked on every door. It looked hopeless. Finally, as a last resort, she marched into the town restaurant.

The customers looked up as the awkward, lath-thin girl with the bunned black hair said to the proprietor, Yalmar, a big, blue-eyed, white-bearded Finn, "You've got two empty rooms upstairs. I need them!"

"You, Hazel? What in *perkele* for?"

Hazel's thin lips tightened. "For our library. I need those rooms, Yalmar."

She got the rooms. She scrubbed them down with strong soap. Her Scottish ancestors might have recognized the stubbornness. This was Hazel's dream; it must not die.

It was in 1920 that, backed up by a handful of rugged Scandinavian housewives and their squirming spouses, Hazel marched into the august offices of the Northern Pacific Railway Co., then the Western Lumber Co., then the Anaconda Copper Mining Co. itself. It was time to give the Milltown Branch Library a permanent home of its own. These three companies were the reason for the town's existence. It was their duty, Hazel said, to keep their employes' brains active as well as their hands and feet.

She got her way. It wasn't easy to say no to Hazel when

those solemn brown eyes had you pinned to the wall. The new library was a solid frame building with a wide inviting porch, set back a ways from the bustling postwar highway. It was a monument to Hazel's dream—and a relief, too, from the sometimes raucous noise of Yalmar's restaurant downstairs.

I was five when I went to the "liberry" for the first time, and peeked up over that wide desk with the neat card-file boxes and date stampers on it and saw Hazel. She was tall, bony and very severe. Those heavy black-rimmed glasses perched on her nose looked down at me awesomely, and if she hadn't smiled just when she did I would have scampered out and never come back.

Lazy Saturday afternoons in August, when the other kids were fishing up Deer Creek or swimming by the covered bridge, I would steal in among the musty book smells. Outside, the bees were buzzing in the hollyhocks Hazel had planted at the windows. Idling along the book shelves, I let my fingers just touch them with pleasure. Sometimes Hazel would come and gently remove *Pride and Prejudice* from my ten-year-old hands and replace it with *Treasure Island*.

I wanted to be a writer. I didn't dare tell Hazel about it, but I think she guessed and pointed the way. She saved out books that were special, just for me.

Of course Hazel had to work, and of course she became a schoolteacher. She was my third-grade teacher and my favorite. I remember sloshing home with Emily Halvari, whose books I carried, through the spring snow-melt, and having Emily burst into tears because she had graduated to the fourth grade. She wanted to stay with Miss Beadle. So did I.

Hazel married the town butcher. Young Eino Karkanen was a handsome, muscular man who liked fishing and hunting. He was quite a catch, and there were those who sighed and wondered why he had married the plain, grave-eyed librarian who used no rouge. I knew why. Hazel had beauty and character she didn't advertise. It was just there.

Years went by. Winter and summers, Depression. War. Still, Hazel never missed a Tuesday evening or a Saturday afternoon. It was a rock to cling to in a world of frightening changes.

Eino Karkanen died one bleak March night. For a few weeks Hazel never left that big frame house by the butcher shop with the CLOSED sign on it. Then, one Tuesday night, the library was open again. Hazel's hair was streaked with gray, and she walked a little more slowly. But she was back with us.

I had gone away to college by now, and resettled in California. I kept in touch through my sister, but I was too busy working and eagerly seeking out all the magic things Hazel's books had told me about to give much more than a fleeting thought to Milltown.

Then, on a visit back home, I found myself in front of that square little library. It was summer. The bees were buzzing around the hollyhocks. The wide porch and the open door invited me.

The aura of the library came rushing over me like a mingled whisper of a thousand voices. David Copperfield and Micawber. Long John Silver's parrot. Ilmarinen hammering away at his magic forge. Captain Nemo's sombrous underseas organ. All of them. Lifted down from those very shelves, from among Hazel's books.

Her clucking laugh came from behind her desk.

"Look, Emil!" Hazel said. "Here's your card. After all these years! In the active file."

A few years ago, the Missoula County Library gave a banquet for Hazel Beadle Karkanen. They presented her with a beautiful orchid corsage; there were sincere speeches of gratitude. But how can anyone say the thousand and one things that must be said but for which there are no words? We can only remember how that thin high-school girl *knew* Milltown's people must have books, and was determined that they would get them. How, back in 1923, old Widow Tekkinen's cow got sick and she couldn't afford a vet, so Hazel found the right remedy in one of her books. How once a demented youth who had killed his brother holed up in the locked library and Hazel persuaded him to come out.

It was no great surprise to learn that Hazel has never received one single penny for all of her 50-plus years of work with the Milltown Branch Library. After all, that was the deal she made with those county library officials in 1917. They would provide the books. Everything else was up to Hazel.

We thought, in this world where books don't seem to be the rare treasures they were then, and people are by and

Thanks, Hazel

large too busy to do anything for somebody else, you might like to know about Hazel and her dream. Even more, we wanted her to know, before it is too late.

Thanks, Hazel. Thanks, from all of us.

Melting Pot

My Search for Roots

by Alex Haley

MY EARLIEST memory is of Grandma, Cousin Georgia, Aunt Plus, Aunt Liz and Aunt Till talking on our front porch in Henning, Tenn. At dusk, these wrinkled, graying old ladies would sit in rocking chairs and talk, about slaves and massas and plantations—pieces and patches of family history, passed down across the generations by word of mouth.

The furthest-back person Grandma and the others ever mentioned was "the African." They would tell how he was brought here on a ship to a place called "Naplis" and sold as a slave in Virginia. There he mated with another slave, and had a little girl named Kizzy.

When Kizzy became four or five, the old ladies said, her father would point out to her various objects and name them in his native tongue. For example, he would point to a guitar and make a single-syllable sound, *ko*. Pointing to a river that ran near the plantation, he'd say "Kamby Bolongo." And when other slaves addressed him as Toby—the name given him by his massa—the African would strenuously reject it, insisting that his name was "Kin-tay."

Kin-tay often told Kizzy stories about himself. He said that he had been near his village in Africa, chopping wood to make a drum, when he had been set upon by four men, overwhelmed, and kidnapped into slavery. When Kizzy grew up and became a mother, she told her son these stories, and he in turn would tell *his* children. His granddaughter became my grandmother, and she pumped that saga into me as if it were plasma, until I knew by rote the story of the African, and the subsequent generational wending of our family through cotton and tobacco plantations into the Civil War and then freedom.

At 17, during World War II, I enlisted in the Coast Guard, and found myself a messboy on a ship in the Southwest Pacific. To fight boredom, I began to teach myself to become a writer. I stayed on in the service after the war, writing every single night, seven nights a week, for eight years before I sold a story to a magazine. My first story in The Digest was published in June 1954: "The Harlem Nobody Knows." At age 37, I retired from military service, determined to be a full-time writer. Working with the famous Black Muslim, I did the actual writing for the book *The Autobiography of Malcolm X*.

I remembered still the highlights of my family's story. Could this account possibly be documented for a book? During 1962, between other assignments, I began following the story's trail. In plantation records, wills, census records, I documented bits here, shreds there. I visited our encyclopedic matriarch, "Cousin Georgia" Anderson in Kansas City, Kan. I went to the National Archives in Washington, the Library of Congress, and the Daughters of the American Revolution Library.

By 1967, I felt I had the seven generations of the U.S. side documented. But the unknown quotient in the riddle of the past continued to be those strange, sharp, angular sounds spoken by the African himself. Since I lived in New York City, I began going to the United Nations lobby, stopping Africans and asking if they recognized the sounds. Every one of them listened to me, then quickly took off. I can well understand: me with a Tennessee accent, trying to imitate African sounds!

Finally, I sought out an expert in African languages. The sound "Kin-tay," he said, was a Mandinka tribe surname. And "Kamby Bolongo" was probably the Gambia River in Mandinka dialect. Three days later, I was in Africa.

In Banjul, the capital of Gambia, I met with a group of Gambians. They told me how for centuries the history of Africa has been preserved. In the older villages of the back country there are old men, called *griots*, who are in effect living archives. Such men know and, on special occasions, tell the cumulative histories of clans, or families, or villages, as those histories have long been told. Since my forefather had said his name was Kin-tay (properly spelled Kinte), and since the Kinte clan was known in Gambia, they would see what they could do to help me.

I was back in New York when a registered letter came from Gambia. Word had been passed in the back country, and a *griot* of the Kinte clan had, indeed, been found. His name, the letter said, was Kebba Kanga Fofana. I returned to Gambia and organized a safari to locate him.

My Search for Roots

There is an expression, "the peak experience," a moment which, emotionally, can never again be equaled in your life. I had mine, that first day in the village of Juffure, in black West Africa.

When our 14-man safari arrived within sight of the village, the people came flocking out of their circular mud huts. From a distance I could see a small, old man with a pillbox hat, an off-white robe and an aura of "somebodiness" about him. The people quickly gathered around me in a kind of horseshoe pattern. The old man looked piercingly into my eyes, and he spoke in Mandinka. Translation came from the interpreters I had brought with me.

"Yes, we have been told by the forefathers that there are many of us from this place who are in exile in that place called America."

Then the old man, who was 73 rains of age—the Gambian way of saying 73 years old, based upon the one rainy season per year—began to tell me the lengthy ancestral history of the Kinte clan. The villagers had grown mouse-quiet, and stood rigidly.

Out of the *griot's* head came spilling lineage details incredible to hear. He recited who married whom, two or even three centuries back. I was struck not only by the profusion of details, but also by the Biblical pattern of the way he was speaking. It was something like, "—and so-and-so took as a wife so-and-so, and begat so-and-so...."

The *griot* had talked for some hours, and had got to about 1750 in our calendar. Now he said, through an interpreter, "About the time the king's soldiers came, the eldest of Omoro's four sons, Kunta, went away from this village to chop wood—and he was never seen again...."

Goose pimples came out on me the size of marbles. He just had no way in the world of knowing that what he told me meshed with what I'd heard from the old ladies on the front porch in Henning, Tenn. I got out my notebook, which had in it what Grandma had said about the African. One of the interpreters showed it to the others, and they went to the *griot*, and they all got agitated. Then the *griot*, went to the people, and *they* all got agitated.

I don't remember anyone giving an order, but those 70-odd people formed a ring around me, moving counterclockwise, chanting, their bodies close together. I can't begin to describe how I felt. A woman broke from the circle, a scowl on her jet-black face, and came charging toward me. She took her baby and almost roughly thrust it out at me. The gesture meant "Take it!" and I did, clasping the baby to me. Whereupon the woman all but snatched the baby away. Another woman did the same with her baby, then another, and another.

A year later, a famous professor at Harvard would tell me: "You were participating in one of the oldest ceremonies of humankind, called 'the laying on of hands.' In their way, these tribespeople were saying to you, 'Through this flesh, which is us, we are you and you are us.'"

Later, as we drove out over the back-country road, I heard the staccato sound of drums. When we approached the next village, people were packed alongside the dusty road, waving, and the din from them welled louder as we came closer. As I stood up in the Land Rover, I finally realized what it was they were all shouting: "Meester Kinte! Meester Kinte!" In their eyes I was the symbol of all black people in the United States whose forefathers had been torn out of Africa.

Hands before my face, I began crying—crying as I have never cried in my life. Right at that time, crying was all I could do.

I went then to London. I searched and searched, and finally in the British Parliamentary records I found that the "king's soldiers" mentioned by the *griot* referred to a group called "Colonel O'Hare's forces," which had been sent up the Gambia River in 1767 to guard the then British-operated James Fort, a slave fort.

I next went to the Public Record Office in London, where doors were opened for me to research among old maritime records. I pored through the records of slave ships that had sailed from Africa. Volumes upon volumes of these records exist. One day, during the seventh week of searching, I was going through my 1023rd set of records. As I picked up a sheet that reported the movements of 30 slaves ships, my eyes stopped at No. 18, and my glance swept across the columns. This vessel had sailed directly from the Gambia River to America in 1767; her name was the *Lord Ligonier;* and she had arrived at Annapolis (Naplis) the morning of September 29, 1767.

Exactly 200 years later, on September 29, 1967, there was nowhere in the world for me to be except standing on a

My Search for Roots

pier at Annapolis, staring seaward across those waters over which my great-great-great-great-grandfather had been brought. And there in Annapolis I inspected the microfilmed records of the *Maryland Gazette*. In the issue of October 1, 1767, on page 3, I found an advertisement informing readers that the *Lord Ligonier* had just arrived from the River Gambia, with "a cargo of choice, healthy SLAVES" to be sold at auction the following Wednesday.

In the years since, I have done extensive research in 50 or so libraries, archives and repositories on three continents. I spent a year combing through countless documents to learn about the culture of Gambia's villages in the 18th and 19th centuries. Desiring to sail over the same waters navigated by the *Lord Ligonier*, I flew to Africa and boarded the freighter *African Star*. I forced myself to spend the ten nights of the crossing in the cold, dark cargo hold, stripped to my underwear, lying on a rough, bare plank. But this was sheer luxury compared with the inhuman ordeal suffered by those millions who, chained and shackled, lay in terror and in their own filth in the stinking darkness through voyages averaging 60 to 70 days.

This book has taken me ten years and more. Why have I called it *Roots?* Because it not only tells the story of a family, my own, but also symbolizes the history of millions of American blacks of African descent. I intend my book to be a buoy for black self-esteem—and a reminder of the universal truth that we are all children of the same Creator.

The Happiest Man

by Danny Kaye

JACOB KOMINISKI never achieved fame, never accumulated wealth. He was a simple tailor, and pleased to be one. He walked the streets of our Brooklyn neighborhood with great dignity, but always with a glint of laughter in his eye. He was my father, and the most successful human being I ever knew.

As a child I didn't fully understand his worth. When I saw how hard he worked for so little material reward I felt sorry for him and a little ashamed at his lack of ambition. I was wrong on both counts.

He worked for a Seventh Avenue dress manufacturer, and one summer evening he brought home an enormous sketch pad, a handful of soft pencils, and some wool and silk and cotton swatches. He announced that the boss was giving him a chance to become a dress designer, something he had long hoped for.

Night after night he worked until midnight or later. A slight man with thin blond hair and shoulders rounded by his trade, he stood by the kitchen table, bending over the sketch pad to make quick, swirling lines while Mother sat nearby, mending. She was a beautiful woman with long, auburn hair piled high above a serene face.

Supposedly asleep in the next room, my two brothers and I listened to the nightly routine: the sibilance of pencil on paper for a long time, then Pop calling Mother, "Chaya, come look."

Her dress rustled as she moved to stand beside him. Sometimes she made a suggestion for a change: usually she said, "I think it's just fine." And sometimes Pop would draw an outlandish ornament so they could both laugh. Laughter was a part of everything he did.

When at last the sketches were finished, he took them off to work. Nothing more was said about them. Finally I asked him, "Pop, what happened to the drawings?"

The Happiest Man

"Oh," he said, "they weren't any good."

Seeing my dismay, he said, "Danny, a man can't do everything in this world, but he can do one job well. I found out I'm not a good designer, but I *am* a good tailor."

And there I found the key to the man, the key that let me understand him better as I grew older. Jacob Kominiski never pretended to be something he wasn't. Free from vanity or unrealizable ambition, he was able to enjoy each day as it came.

The core of Pop's happiness was his family. Almost any event served as an excuse for a reunion with all our uncles and aunts and cousins. Such laughter and jokes and sheer loving exuberance—and all sparked by my mother and father. They were always the first couple on the floor to dance, and the first to start singing the old folk songs while the rest of us clapped hands to the rhythm. Part of Pop's pleasure was showing off his wife, with a shy sort of reverence. He thought no one in the world could match her. He once said of her, "Where she walks there is light."

Every night at dinner he reported the amusing things that happened to him during the day (we never heard of any defeats or frustrations). The most ordinary events were hilarious when Pop told about them.

There were serious days, of course—as when Pop received his naturalization papers. He burst into the house. "Chaya! Come here. Bring the children."

We all came running to find him holding a large and very official looking certificate. "What does it say, Pop?" I cried.

"It says that Jacob Kominiski is a citizen of the United States of America! What do you think of that?"

We all thought it was wonderful. He framed the certificate and hung it in the living room for all to see. Thereafter he voted in every election, putting on his best suit for the occasion. One election day he was ill, and Mother insisted he stay in bed. "It's raining and very cold. Surely you can miss voting this once."

He saw me standing in the doorway and spoke for my benefit as well as hers. "In Russia I was not allowed to vote, but here I can help select men who will govern this great America. Do you know how many votes the President of the United States can cast? One! The same number as Jacob Kominiski! Isn't that a remarkable situation?"

Then he dressed and went to the polls.

Pop enjoyed all men, but he reserved his friendship for a few—especially five cronies who had emigrated with him at the time of World War I. Once a month they gathered in our kitchen for an evening of talk. All these men had achieved business success. Yet in many matters it was to Jacob Kominiski they turned for advice, knowing that he saw life clearly and his opinions could not be warped by envy.

They came to our rather shabby neighborhood in big automobiles, wearing expensive suits, and smoking 25-cent cigars. I once asked my mother, "Why do they come here instead of meeting in their own big houses?"

She thought a moment, then said, "I think maybe they left the best part of themselves here. They need to come back to it every now and then."

When I was 13 my mother died. Through my own grief I was aware of the great loss this was to Pop. But he made only one reference to his almost insupportable sadness. He said, "To be happy every day is to be not happy at all." He was saying to his sons that happiness is not a state you achieve and keep, but something that must be won over and over, no matter what the defeats and losses.

In my early teens I ran away from home, for the simple reason that I was bursting with curiosity about the world outside of Brooklyn. I talked a pal of mine into going along. Our thumbs got us rides, we sang for food, and at night we appeared at the local police station to announce we were hitchhiking to relatives and asked to be put in a cell until morning. It worked fine until we hit a small town in Delaware.

The chief of police said, "You kids look like a couple of runaways. You say you're from Brooklyn? I'll just telephone and see if there's a 'wanted' on you."

He found that there was indeed a missing-persons alarm for me. He soon had my father on the phone. After hearing I was all right, Pop seemed to relax. "You want me to send him home?" the chief asked. "Oh, no," Father said. "He wants to find out something. He'll come home when he's ready."

I was on the road two weeks, and when I finally walked down the familiar street toward our house I began to get apprehensive. I was afraid I had hurt Pop by running away. How could I find the right words to explain to him why I went?

As it turned out, it was Pop who found the right words. When I stepped in the front door he looked up from his newspaper, and a wonderfully warm and relieved smile went over his face. Then he gave me a wink and said, "There's food in the icebox, Danny"—the words he had always greeted me with when I came home from school or play. So nothing had changed between us. He understood me, and my searchings and longings, so unlike his or my brothers'.

His patience with me during my late teens was infinite. Both my brothers had jobs and were hard-working, responsible citizens, but I was moody and restless and couldn't settle down. I wanted to express myself, but I didn't know how. Pop supported me uncomplainingly; once a week I found a $5 bill tucked beneath my pillow, to save me the embarrassment of openly receiving spending money.

My shortcomings did not escape the notice of Pop's cronies. Every time they gathered in our kitchen they would ask, "Danny got a job yet?" Pop would shake his head and change the subject.

One evening I heard a voice say, "Jacob, I speak to you as a friend must speak. Danny is becoming a bum. You should not allow this to happen."

Pop said, "My son is searching for something he can devote his life to. I can't tell him what it is. He'll never be happy unless he finds it for himself. It may take him longer than others, but he'll find it. I do not worry about him."

Later that year I got a job as an entertainer on the borscht circuit, and suddenly I knew this was the career I had been searching for. The world of the theater was far removed from the world of Jacob Kominiski, the tailor, yet I found myself returning to him time and again, for the same reason his cronies did.

When I was 20 I got what every actor dreams of—a permanent job! The A. B. Marcus show, *La Vie Paree*, was an extravaganza that had been touring the world for a quarter of a century, and I joined the cast. We played the Orient for a couple of years and then returned to the States for a series of one-night stands. When we finally hit Newark I went home to see Pop.

I had a problem, and I placed it before him. This was at the depth of the Depression, actors were out of work by the hundreds, yet I wanted to quit the show because I needed new experiences and challenges. But also I was scared.

Pop heard me out, then said, "It's very comfortable to have a steady job. You shouldn't be ashamed of liking it. But there are some people who always have to test themselves, to stretch their wings and try new winds. If you think you can find more happiness and usefulness this way, then you should do it."

This advice came from a man who never left a secure job in his life, who had the European tradition of family conformity and responsibility, but who knew I was different. He understood what I needed to do and he helped me do it.

For the next few years I worked in nightclubs, and then I got my big theatrical break, appearing in *Lady in the Dark* with Gertrude Lawrence. After that I went to Hollywood, but even the glamour of the movie capital did not awe Pop.

For some of the time between his retirement and his death at the age of 80, Pop lived with me and my family there. We had a big party one evening, and soon there was a crowd around him listening to his stories about Brooklyn and his Ukrainian legends.

That night I thought Pop might enjoy hearing some of the old folk songs we used to sing at home. When I began to sing, the music and the memories were too much for him to resist, and he came over to join me. I faded away, and he was in the middle of the room singing alone—in a clear true voice. He sang for 15 minutes before some of the world's highest-paid entertainers. When he finished there was thunderous applause.

This simple, kindly old man singing of our European roots had touched something deep in these sophisticated people. I remembered what my mother had said about Pop's rich cronies: "I think maybe they left the best part of themselves here. They need to come back to it every now and then."

I knew the applause that night was not just for a performance; it was for a man.

Our Newest Americans

by Albert Q. Maisel

As ALEXANDER WASHCHENKO pored over a history of the United States, preparing for his citizenship examination, the story of the Pilgrims' exile and their first Thanksgiving here set his thoughts adrift. He recalled how the Russians' "liberation" of his Polish-Ukrainian village in 1939 had been quickly followed by the confiscation of his family's farm. He remembered a second "liberation," by Hitler's *Wehrmacht* in 1941. The Nazis deported him, his wife and daughter in a baggage car to a Bavarian slave-labor camp.

Then he thought of that unforgettable night in 1949 when, after four years of anxious waiting in a Displaced Persons Center, he and his family finally saw New York's lighted skyscrapers, gleaming with the promise of the first real liberation the Washchenkos had ever known. Five happy years had rushed by since then. Washchenko, who had arrived owning only the clothes on his back, had become a Class A spot welder in a Chicago factory. He had bought a car and a tree-shaded home. Now, while he studied on a November evening, his children slept untroubled by the fears that had haunted so much of his own life.

Impulsively, Alex took up a pencil and began to write. On the day before Thanksgiving a paid notice, signed A. Washchenko, appeared in the Chicago *Sun-Times*. The message voicing his gratitude to his new homeland concluded: *"I thank God for such sympathetic human beings in this wonderful God-blessed America."*

Alexander Washchenko spoke not for himself alone. Hundreds of thousands of refugees from Fascism or Communism have found a haven among us since 1933. Their presence here is living proof that America has never abandoned its role as a refuge for those who have suffered in other lands. When Hitler unleashed his persecutions, America saved nearly 300,000 from almost certain extinction by quietly giving them priority under our quota laws. Soon after World War II, by Presidential directive, 90 percent of all quota visas for central and eastern Europe were issued to the uprooted who dared not return to their homes behind the Iron Curtain.

Through the Displaced Persons Act of 1948 and again under the Refugee Relief Act of 1953, Congress set aside quota restrictions to allow for the entrance of additional immigrants. Countless individual Americans (usually strangers to the people they aided) have voluntarily signed up as "sponsors," guaranteeing a job and a place to live for DPs—aptly called "Delayed Pilgrims" by Rhode Island's Governor Dennis J. Roberts.

Upon these, the uprooted and homeless, no greater gift could have been bestowed than the chance to build their lives anew in a free land. But the giving has been far from one-sided. Coming from 18 countries, with infinitely varied backgrounds, these exiles have brought to this land a phenomenally rich endowment of skill and talent. Adjusting themselves to American life with startling rapidity, they have contributed in a thousand ways to our culture, economy and national welfare.

In Berlin, huge ritual bonfires consumed the books of Europe's greatest writers. But here, such men as Nobel-laureate Thomas Mann, Ferenc Molnar, Erich Maria Remarque, Emil Ludwig and a host of others wrote again. In our theaters and on our screens, the great performers whom Hitler silenced once more found voice—among them Hedy Lamarr, Peter Lorre, Oscar Karlweiss and Oscar Homolka. Here too, producer Max Reinhardt, director Otto Preminger and hundreds of script writers, cameramen, scenic artists and other technicians, helped to blend European and American techniques into countless advances in theatrical and cinema production.

Among the 1500 musicians who settled here were such world-famed figures as the orchestral conductors Otto Klemperer and Bruno Walter; composers Kurt Weill, Paul Hindemith and Igor Stravinsky; pianist Artur Schnabel.

Under the Nazis, men who had brought Germany and Austria to world leadership in medicine found themselves barred from hospital and teaching posts, even from private practice. Here, fully 5000 of them were welcomed by their American colleagues who formed a National Committee for the Resettlement of Foreign Physicians. Many of the most renowned quickly won teaching posts in our leading medical schools. Many of these exiles could not practice or enter their patients in U.S. hospitals until they had acquired citizenship, a process that took at least five years. But despite language handicaps, over 90 percent became citizens and passed tough qualifying examinations before the sixth anniversary of their coming. Eventually, some 2500 held the coveted diplomas of medical specialty boards.

From Germany and the countries Hitler conquered, some 40,000 skilled workers and businessmen fled to America. With only their skills, inventiveness and courage, they started small workshops to produce precision tools, optical and surgical instruments, photographic supplies, leather goods, pharmaceuticals, ceramics and other products that America had once had to import. Far from taking jobs from Americans, many such firms created new jobs. In 1941 a survey revealed that 271 refugee enterprises provided work for 8620 employes. And, most important, 80 percent of the jobs were held by native Americans. Another survey showed that 50 refugee businesses had introduced products never previously manufactured here; 22 used fabricating processes new to this country; 13 trained American employes in skills new here.

More than 4000 of Europe's finest minds found freedom to teach and work again in American college classrooms and research laboratories. Among them were numerous exiled Nobel Prize-winners, including the most renowned of all scientists, Albert Einstein, and the physicist Enrico Fermi. The distinction of more than 300 others justified their prompt inclusion in *Who's Who* and *American Men of Science*. Hundreds more have since risen to leading positions.

These refugees have helped enrich every branch of scholarship in the United States. The Institute for Advanced Study at Princeton, N.J., became one of the world's leading centers of mathematical studies when such men as Hermann Weyl, Salomon Bochner, Reinhold Baer, Richard Brauer and Alfred Brauer came there to do research. Havard invited Walter Gropius—whose school had been closed by Hitler—to head its School of Architecture. There he inspired a generation of young American architects whose steel-and-glass skyscrapers transformed the appearance of our cities.

Shortly after Pearl Harbor outstanding refugee scientists were recruited for wartime research. At the University of Minnesota Professor Karl Sollner, a Viennese, helped develop a portable device for desalting sea water that saved the lives of thousands of shipwrecked sailors and stranded airmen. A Polish engineer, Thaddeus Janiszewski, invented a new type of portable bridge which became standard U.S. Army equipment. Dr. Ernst Berl, chief chemist for Austria-Hungary during World War I, devised new types of explosives for the Navy and the Chemical Warfare Service.

The Board of Economic Warfare benefited when F.P. Hellin, an Austrian refugee, mobilized a committee of 300 exiled businessmen and industrialists who revealed the location of hidden munition plants. One of these refugees, for instance, pinpointed the secret, camouflaged heavy-water plant operated by the Germans in conquered Norway, which was subsequently demolished by Allied bombers.

But it was in the race to unleash atomic energy that refugee scientists made their most far-reaching contribution. Germany had gained a tremendous advantage when early in 1939 the possibility of releasing energy by splitting the atom was experimentally confirmed at the Kaiser Wilhelm Institute in Berlin. The first in this country to realize its frightening military potential were the Italian refugee Enrico Fermi and the Hungarian exiles Leo Szilard, Edward Teller and Eugene Wigner. They induced Einstein to warn the President of this dangerous development and to urge immediate initiation of an American atomic program.

Fermi and Szilard designed and built at the University of Chicago the first all-essential atomic pile. At Los Alamos a number of other refugees played key roles in pushing the development of the bomb to its final, triumphant conclusion.

After the war, the refugee problem in Europe assumed new dimensions. Of the millions of displaced persons, hundreds of thousands became permanent exiles from their Communist-dominated homelands. Soon other thousands began to stream westward through the Iron Curtain. Many of these DPs have found a sympathetic welcome in the United States.

The contributions of these newcomers, though less conspicuous, have been no less valuable. Thousands of DP farmers today command the respect and admiration of their neighbors for the success which their diligence and care of the land has quickly won for them. Others have brought trade skills badly needed by our industries. Far from opposing this influx of new laborers, several unions waived initiation fees to permit them to start work immediately upon their arrival. Some unions, notably in the needle trades, joined with manufacturers in sending delegations to DP camps to seek out skilled craftsmen.

Once again, the well-educated and talented have formed an astoundingly large proportion of these new immigrants. The 30,000 who came here from little Lithuania, for example, have included no less than 500 architects and engineers, 400 school teachers, 300 lawyers, nearly 500 physicians and dentists.

A large proportion of earlier immigrants, dreaming of returning to their native villages, lived among us for years without applying for citizenship. But our newest immigrants have been eager to become citizens just as soon as our laws would allow.

With equal determination they have set about acquiring a command of our language, deliberately reading only English-language newspapers and avoiding use of their mother tongue at home. Nor have they crowded into the old "nationality" areas that once grew to such large proportions in our cities. Thousands have settled in rural communities or small towns where few other immigrants are to be found. They have joined churches, PTAs, service clubs and civic associations. Thus native Americans have come to know and respect them as interesting and vital individuals.

"I Give You Mr. Charley American!"

by Joe Vergara

DURING the 1930s, when my brothers and I were growing up, we had a secret goal. It had to do with our father. Pop had changed his first name from Rosario to Charley when he came to America from Italy, but that was about all he'd changed. As native-born citizens, Al, Wheezer and I wanted more than anything to make Pop an American, too. It was a battle we fought constantly, in what we regarded as crafty, subtle ways. The trouble was that our plans had a tendency to backfire.

Take the matter of card games. Pop was always playing the game of *scopa* with his Italian cronies. Simple—we'd teach him to play American poker instead. He listened amiably enough as we explained the rules. But when we reached the part about the value of the picture cards, he threw up his hands. "The queen-a is higher than the jack?" he demanded incredulously. In Italian cards there is no queen. If there were one, the jack would undoubtedly rank above it, as befits the masculine status. Pop throught the idea over. "Maybe next thing we have is lady President in White House," he said. "What's wrong with this country, eh?" With that, he reshuffled the cards and dealt them out. "Come, I teach-a my sons *scopa*."

Or we fought him with flattering words. "Charley, that's a swell name you picked," I told him one night, when he came back from his shoe-repair shop near our home on Long Island. "It sounds real American."

Pop shook his head. "Name don't make me American, Joe. I always be *italiano*. Some-a day I go back, like I promise my mother." Pop had left his mother behind in Calabria; they exchanged letters every week, and faithfully he sent her a monthly check. It was his intention to return to Calabria with Mom, after their family was grown. "It's where I belong," he would say.

"I Give You Mr. Charley American!" 197

We decided to get him to grow a lawn, thinking there was nothing more splendidly American than a nice green front lawn. Like many Italian immigrants, however, Pop despised lawns. To him, every inch of ground was precious for growing tomatoes, peppers, beans, grapes, the good things of life. His grape arbor and vegetable garden out back gave lavish testament to his creed. "Why you want good-for-nothing grass, eh?" he asked. "Maybe we gonna raise-a-sheep?"

"Pop, everbody in America has a lawn," I said. "Why can't we be like everyone else?"

After days of loud, emotional debate, Mom finally joined the offensive. Never, she swore, would she let the neighbors call us greenhorns who knew nothing about lawns. "Okay, okay," sighed Pop wearily, capitulating at last. But he made it clear that Al, Wheezer and I were to assume full charge of its care. The project began while Pop withdrew to the back yard, his little patch of Italy on Long Island. What we counted on was his love for helping things grow. As soon as we'd coaxed a smooth green carpet from the front yard, we reasoned, he would take it over.

The green blades began to poke up. As we toiled over them, Pop would sometimes throw taunts at us from the window: "Too bad I don't bring over my goat, Luisa. She do better job and give milk besides."

Then one afternoon, as we were coming home from school, Al grabbed my arm half a block from the house. There was Pop, kneeling on the lawn, busily at work. Victory! Eagerly we ran toward him. "You don't have to weed the lawn," Al said. "We'll do it."

Pop straightened up and looked at Al as though doubting his son's sanity. "This, you call-a weeds?" he said, holding aloft a handful of dandelions. "First-a time I see something good in lousy grass, and you call-a weeds. *Mamma mia*, what you learn in American *scuola*—nothing? Make-a best salad you ever taste."

And that night, sure enough, we had a dandelion salad. Mom fixed it with olive oil, vinegar, garlic and a leaf of basil. Italian-style.

The fact that Pop defeated our schemes without even trying didn't discourage us. As I moved through grade school, I longed to pass on to Pop all the wonderful knowledge I was acquiring about American history and geography, most of all, about its astounding know-how in business techniques.

Pop's own methods of conducting his shoe-repair business were childishly simple. His accounting system was based on a cigar box. As bills came in, he'd lay them face down in the box. Meanwhile, all cash receipts went into his pockets—paper money into the left pocket, coins into the right. When he felt that the wad in the left pocket had grown thick enough, he'd turn over the pile of bills and pay as many as he regarded expedient.

"Pop, mind if I ask a question?" I began, entering his shoe-repair shop one afternoon. (My brothers and I took turns helping him at the shop after school and on Saturdays.) He was taking nails rapidly from his mouth and hammering them down on a heel. "How can you tell if you're making money in this store?" I asked him.

He put down the hammer and stared at me. "How I know I make-a money?" he repeated. "You and your brothers don' get plenty food, warm bed to sleep in?"

"No, we live fine," I assured him. "I was just talking about how you run the business, Pop. You don't keep records, so how can you know how much you take in or pay out? The whole business is in your pockets."

"And what's-a wrong with 'at?" exploded Pop. "Look, how much you want—93 cents? Here." His right hand darted into his pocket and instantly came out with three quarters, one dime, one nickel and three pennies. "See? It's-all right."

Al, Wheezer and I held another secret meeting and agreed that Pop's most urgent, though unrecognized, need was for a cash register. We hoarded the tips we got from shining shoes and delivering newspapers. Finally we had enough to purchase a secondhand machine in time for his birthday.

We made quite a ceremony of presenting the machine to him. We even tied a bow on it. "Ah, you good boys," he murmured.

As far as we could make out, Pop was highly pleased with this revolution of his business methods. He patted the cash register affectionately. When Al, Wheezer or I worked at the store, he paraded over to the machine each time a customer paid a bill, and the bell rang merrily as the cash drawer opened.

One day, I happened to be at the counter when he pushed down the keys. "Is like-a-music, Joe," he said, as the cheerful

"I Give You Mr. Charley American!" 199

sound chimed out. Then I looked at the register closely.

Poor Pop. His instincts just naturally fought against the machine, I guess. Maybe he thought that it robbed him of the dignity and independence he'd crossed an ocean to find. He simply rang up "No Sale" on the register, while slipping the money as usual into his pockets.

The cash register didn't prove an entire failure, however. Pop used it as a convenient storehouse for the pins, tacks, can openers and other objects that formerly littered the shop. "Now we got everything nice and tidy," he explained.

It seemed that our campaign was hopeless. But there was a turning point. Letters to Pop from our grandmother in Italy arrived regularly once every week. She herself couldn't write, of course; the letters were penned, with many flowery phrases, by the village schoolmaster. Mom read the letters aloud to Pop and, with each sentence, the smile on his face would broaden.

Then one letter arrived which Mom didn't bring out until after supper. As her eyes ran over the first page, her lips trembled.

"What's wrong?" Pop asked, reaching for the letter. Mom held it away from him and all at once began to cry. "My mother," he said in Italian. "Is she dead?" The tears told Pop the truth. He took a few unsteady steps and lay down heavily on the couch, drained of all emotion.

No need now for Pop to send monthly checks. No need to talk anymore of going back to Italy. Pop's old dream was put away that night, like the keepsakes of his mother's, which he kept in a drawer.

We finished school, and then World War II broke out. Soon after the United States entered the war, Al's, Wheezer's and my mailing addresses changed to: care of Uncle Sam's training camps. I was the first son inducted, and the first to come home on furlough. I was naturally prepared for an emotional reception, but not for the particular welcome Pop had devised. This time he had turned the table on his sons and hatched a scheme of his own.

My homecoming combined the features of Christmas, New Year's and Easter, with overtones of Columbus Day and the Fourth of July. Flowers, streamers and tiny American flags festooned the house. For dinner, Mom outdid herself. Such light ravioli, such tender veal cutlets, chicken cacciatore, zucchini—after Army food, this was heaven indeed.

Pop was strangely quiet through the meal. Toward the end, Mom began to act bubbly, like a schoolgirl with a secret. Suddenly she sprang up from the table and in a minute was back, carrying a bottle of anisette in one hand and an official-looking paper in the other.

"A little drink to celebrate," Mom said, raising her glass in a toast. "On account of tonight we have big news!" She paused for effect and handed me the document. Citizenship papers! "Before you sits fellow you never know before," Mom announced. "I give you Mr. Charley American, citizen first-class!"

Then Pop sprang up and, with a grin as wide as all Calabria, he threw me a snappy salute, American-style. But it wasn't until later that night that the truth finally came to me. Lying in bed, I thought of the years gone by; of the spirit of independence that had brought him to this country; of his determination to provide advantages for his family, and—for his sons—an education which in another land might have been impossible. Suddenly, I understood what had-eluded me all those years.

Pop had been an American all along.

Fighting for Freedom

The British Are Coming!

by O.K. Armstrong

"THE regulars are marching! The regulars are marching!"

So called Paul Revere as he galloped through the night of April 18, 1775, from Charlestown, Mass., toward Lexington about 12 miles away. At every village and at many farmhouses, the Boston silversmith leaped from his horse and knocked on doors to rouse the inhabitants and muster the Minutemen.

Paul Revere belonged to the Committee of Safety, a group of patriots including Boston physician Joseph Warren, who kept watch on movements of British troops quartered in Boston under the command of Gen. Thomas Gage. Several days before that historic night, Warren and his patrol learned that Gage planned to seize the powder and arms hidden at Concord, 17 miles west of Boston. They also believed he was eager to arrest John Hancock and Samuel Adams, who had vigorously opposed "British tyranny," and who were staying at the home of the Rev. Jonas Clarke in Lexington.

There were ample signs before Revere's ride that General Gage would soon send out a military expedition: boats had been launched from transport ships, and grenadiers and light infantry removed from all duties on April 15; on the evening of the 18th, British officers were seen on the road to Lexington; and, that same evening, Redcoat troops began assembling at the foot of the Boston Common. Clearly, it was time to act. As Revere later wrote of his historic ride:

"About ten o'clock, Dr. Warren sent in great haste for me, and begged that I would immediately Set off for Lexington, where Messrs Hancock and Adams were....I went to the North part of Town, where I kept a Boat; two friends rowed me across Charles River."

After leaving Dr. Warren's house, Revere stopped just long enough to have signal lanterns hung in the steeple of the Old North Church in case the British prevented him from leaving Boston. When he reached Charlestown, watchers there told him they had seen his two signal lanterns ("one if by land, two if by sea") and, in fact, even as he began his ride, British troops were boarding boats to cross the river.

Dr. Warren had dispatched another rider, William Dawes, toward Concord. Near one o'clock, Revere and Dawes (who had taken a different road) met at Lexington. There they roused Capt. John Parker, commander of the local militia (called "Minutemen" because they had sworn to come together at a minute's notice to defend their farms and villages against attack).

As Parker sounded the alarm, clamor filled the night. The big bell on the Common rang out. The drum call was sounded. Muskets cracked. Soon, Minutemen were running toward the Lexington green, guns at the ready. For the most part they were family men. Some were youths in their late teens.

After alerting Hancock and Adams, Revere and Dawes set out for Concord and soon met another patriot, Dr. Samuel Prescott, who volunteered to join them. The three had not gone far when they were surprised by a British patrol. Prescott escaped by jumping his horse over a stone wall, and continued on to Concord to spread the alarm. Dawes also eluded capture and made his way back to Lexington on foot after losing his horse, but Revere was detained and forced to dismount—his famous ride ended.

Meanwhile, when an hour had passed and no British soldiers appeared, Captain Parker dismissed his men, ordered them to return to the green "at the drum call to arms."

It was well after one o'clock that same morning of April 19 before the British troops finally got under way. When the regulars reached the town of Menotomy (now Arlington), it was three o'clock. There they met an advance patrol and learned that the Minutemen were mobilizing at Lexington.

An hour and a half later, Minutemen scouts east of Lexington galloped back to inform Captain Parker that the British were only a mile and a half away. Again the drum rolled, and soon about 60 Minutemen had assembled on the Common. Parker drew up in two lines across the green. Dawn was breaking when they first saw the light infantrymen of Maj. John Pitcairn's command. "Stand fast, men! Don't fire unless fired upon!" Parker ordered.

The Minutemen stood motionless as the British front

The British Are Coming! 205

ranks approached. "Disperse and lay down your arms!" shouted Major Pitcairn. The British regulars rushed forward. Now Captain Parker decided that a formal battle against such a superior force would be hopeless. "Fall back! Let the troops pass!" he ordered.

In that brief moment, America's destiny hung in the balance. Then a shot rang out. No one knew then—or ever will know—who fired it. But, as though it were a signal, the British light infantrymen surged forward, shouting and firing at the rebels. The colonials scattered about the green, turning to fire, to retreat, to find shelter while they reloaded and fired again.

"Cease firing!" shouted Major Pitcairn. "Hold your fire!" After about 20 minutes Pitcairn brought his soldiers back into line, and most of the Minutemen dispersed, although a few stood their ground. Eight Americans lay dead upon the field, ten had been wounded. Only one or two of the British had been wounded and, after firing a traditional victory volley, their 700 regulars resumed the march to Concord.

In the meantime, Dr. Prescott had aroused Maj. John Buttrick and other Concord Minutemen. Several volunteers had set off to call out the companies in nearby villages including those at Westford, commanded by Lt. Col. John Robinson, and at Acton, headed by Capt. Isaac Davis. As he marched away, Davis turned to his wife. "Take good care of the children," he called. She waved back, tears in her eyes.

Convinced that they should go out and "meet the British," Major Buttrick led a combined forced of 250 Minutemen down the road toward Lexington. Soon they met the British, marching on the same road to Concord. Buttrick, realizing that he was outmatched, ordered his men to about-face and march back to Concord. The 700 British regulars followed, about a third of a mile behind—each side with fifes and drums playing.

Ahead, spanning the Concord River, lay the vital North Bridge with its east-west road. Major Buttrick marched his men across to the west side of the river, where they assembled with other units of Minutemen on Punkatasset Hill. As reinforcements arrived, the units moved to a lower elevation on the Buttrick farm, where they had a better view of the bridge. Meanwhile, the British ransacked Concord's Town House in search of military stores, then moved on to search private homes.

By nine o'clock, a force of some 400 Minutemen and

militia had assembled on the ridge above the North Bridge. They milled about uneasily while their officers and local citizens debated what to do. Finally, as smoke rose from the town, Joseph Hosmer, the Concord Adjutant, cried: "Will you let them burn the town down?" After a hurried conference, it was agreed that they should march back over the bridge, into the town, and put a stop to the burning.*

The Acton company, headed by Captain Davis, was given the honor of leading the American advance, stepping to their fifer's tune, "The White Cockade." With him were Major Buttrick and Colonel Robinson. As the Americans neared, the British, under the command of Capt. Walter Laurie, fired several warning shots, which fell into the river to the right of the marching men. The warning went unheeded. A single shot rang out and two Americans were wounded. Moments later, the Redcoats fired a full volley at the provincials, who were now less than 75 yards away. Captain Davis and a private fell dead. Major Buttrick leaped into the air. "Fire!" he shouted. "For God's sake, fire!"

The Minutemen responded with their first volley—the famous "shot heard round the world." The British companies reeled back in disorder, leaving at the bridge two dead, another mortally shot and nine wounded. The Minutemen held their fire and, after some indecision, the British began their retreat to Boston.

By the time the troops reached Meriam's Corner between Concord and Lexington, over a thousand Minutemen had assembled in the vicinity. As the British marched down the road, the rebels opened fire. Muskets blazed on both sides, and the Minutemen scattered behind stone fences, trees and buildings, continuing to fire. When the British troops reached Lexington, they were thoroughly demoralized and running out of ammunition. Only the timely arrival of 1000 reinforcements under Lord Percy kept them from defeat.

Nevertheless, the battle lasted throughout the day as the colonials kept up their attack all the way back to Charlestown. The Minutemen hid behind the many fences that lined the roads, standing only to fire, then hiding again. It was a new and baffling kind of guerrilla warfare for British soldiers,

---

*The provincials had no way of knowing it, but the fires came only from the burning of military stores, not houses.

trained to stand in close order in clear view of the enemy, both sides firing at each other like gentlemen engaged in a duel. Still, when the Redcoats spotted a target, they returned the rebel fire with precision. Probably the oldest to be killed was Josiah Haynes, who, standing to reload, was mortally wounded. The inscription on his gravestone in Sudbury reads: "In memory of Deacon Josiah Haynes, Who Died in Freedom's Cause the 19th of April, 1775, in the 79th Year of His Age."

It was well after seven o'clock when the weary British troops reached Charlestown. A total of 49 Americans "died in freedom's cause" that day; 46 more were wounded or missing. British casualties were 73 dead, 200 wounded or missing.

By fast riders, the news of Lexington and Concord was broadcast to every corner of the colonies. From New Hampshire to Georgia, the majority of the colonists, while deploring the outbreak of war, rallied to the support of the Minutemen, who had stood the first tests of battle. In his report of the events of April 18 and 19 to Lord Dartmouth and the London government, General Gage concluded with this unintended compliment to the vigor and determination of the Massachusetts Minutemen: "The whole country was assembled in arms, with surprising expedition, and several thousand are now assembled about this town."

The American forces indeed surrounded Boston and kept the seaport effectively under siege. In May 1775, a second Continental Congress convened in Philadelphia and formed a Continental Army to defend all the colonies. The Congress selected a calm Virginia planter, Col. George Washington, to be its commander-in-chief. And by the following spring, Washington and his soldiers had forced the British troops out of Boston.

What of the heroic horseman who aroused the Minutemen on that April night? Henry Wadsworth Longfellow lifted him from a footnote of history to a place in American poetic literature with a ballad that includes these words:

So through the night rode Paul Revere; ...
A cry of defiance and not of fear,
A voice in the darkness, a knock at the door,
And a word that shall echo forevermore!

All Quiet on the Western Front

by Jerry Klein

THE 11th hour of the 11th day of the 11th month. That used to mean something special in the days between the wars when I was growing up. Armistice Day was not so big as July 4th, but big. And at that hour—the moment the armistice ending the Great War had been signed—the bells would peal out from church steeples, factory whistles would blow, and there would come a moment of suspended stillness in tribute to all who died in that war.

Wars have come and gone since then, and Armistice Day has lost much of its meaning. But to anyone traveling through France today, World War I remains an inescapable reality. The fallen dead still lie here, in scores of neatly trimmed cemeteries with row on row of orderly white crosses.

There are 31,000 Americans here, many of them forgotten now. Another 4500 missing. One finds occasionally a wreath before one of the eloquent white crosses, but not often. The cemeteries are rather like quiet, ghostly parks, symmetrical and orderly and sadly desolate.

The American Cemetery at Belleau Wood is as neatly kept as a country club. The grass is thick and cushiony as a shag carpet. There are men here from New York, Arizona, Illinois, Ohio—2288 in all. Another 250 are unknown, and a thousand were never found. Most of them died during the final months of the war, when American strength helped turn back Ludendorff's last drive toward Paris.

Tourists used to come here in droves. Now the cemetery is often deserted. The battlefield is empty. There is a ring of artillery pieces, a 75, a howitzer, an American flag slowly unfurling in the breeze. The woods have grown over, hiding the scarred ground, but it remains hillocked and lumpy from shellfire.

And those who lie here are forever young. They never knew those glorious football weekends, those beery Legion conventions, their children crying in the night, winter vacations in Florida. They missed the Depression, house payments, the new cars with the shift levers on the steering columns.

The survivors are going now, too, scattered by wind and time into thousands of cemeteries. But many of them keep the same memories—of the sound of shells going over like express trains, of the dreadful chatter of machine guns, of men blown to pieces and of the way horses died, screaming, in the shellfire.

The French, the British, the Germans are here almost beyond number. On the first day of the Battle of the Somme, July 1, 1916, some 60,000 British troops were killed. They went walking across no man's land in neat rows, led by an officer kicking a soccer ball. And they died and are buried in the same neat rows.

At Verdun there is an ossuary—cool and silent as a church—that contains the bones of more than 130,000 men. Equal to the whole population of Peoria, Ill.

The scale is overpowering and poignant: vast fields of crosses and small memorials. Off one roadside, down a well-tramped path, are two graves and the sign, *Deux héros parmi tant d'autres* ("Two heroes among so many others"). There are faded flowers on the graves. Verdun. People cry even today when they leave here.

The poppies still grow in Flanders Field. In Belleau Wood the wind sighs softly through the rows of crosses. It is a gentle wind, these late autumn days along the road to Paris. For the guns that blazed across these scenic and wooded hills are stilled. Forever, we hope. As another Armistice Day comes, all is quiet on the western front.

"Not Far From God"

by George Kent

I HAVE just come back from the most moving journey a man could make—a tour of the American military cemeteries in Europe. But it was not a depressing experience. There is peace in these green and flowering acres, peace and beauty.

I remember especially St.-Laurent-sur-Mer in Normandy, high on a cliff overlooking Omaha Beach, with its statue of a youth reaching triumphantly for the sky, on the pedestal the words *Mine eyes have seen the glory of the coming of the Lord.* Roses bloom there all through the summer and, though people wander unwatched, no one has ever broken a stem or picked a flower.

It is not only our own people who mourn and revere these American dead. Of the million who come to the cemeteries each year, the greater number are Europeans. And in England and France, Belgium and Italy, Holland and Luxembourg—wherever our dead lie buried—the people of the area have made Memorial Day their day of mourning, in which they bow their heads and remember the sacrifice of these young men who came from far away.

Each cemetery has its tale of devotion to tell, but that of Margraten, where lie more than 8000 dead, is in many ways the most memorable. In this southernmost portion of the Netherlands our soldiers lived for weeks in the homes of the people, became for them sons and sweethearts and big brothers. And as the dead of these young men came back from the West German front in U.S. Army trucks, the Hollanders sorrowed for them as for their own.

More than 100 men of Margraten helped in digging graves. Others fashioned and painted the white wooden crosses. Then, as Memorial Day, 1945, drew near, men and women in 60 towns stripped their gardens and fields and canal banks of flowers, heaped them before their town halls to be carried by Army trucks to Margraten on May 29. There, 400 girls and young men separated the flowers into loose bouquets and laid them on each grave until the field of white crosses bloomed. It was midnight when they finished.

Next morning a crowd of 30,000 assembled at the cemetery. They came on foot, on bicycles without tires, in trucks and buses, on farm horses. A Catholic priest from the United States opened the ceremony; he was followed by a Protestant minister and a rabbi. A representative of the Queen spoke. The commander of the U.S. 9th Army laid a wreath. An infantry platoon fired a salute. And when taps died away, the sobbing of women was clearly audible.

That was the beginning of the Margraten story, not the end. Back in a small Alabama town in the summer of 1945 a girl sat in her kitchen crying. She was writing about her husband, killed in action six weeks after their marriage. "He was my whole life," she wrote. "I see on the map that Margraten Cemetery is close to your city. Would you please locate his grave, bring a few flowers, take a picture and write to me?" She addressed the letter to "Burgemeester, Maastricht, Holland" and mailed it.

In Maastricht, the *burgemeester,* Baron Michiels van Kessenich, read the letter and passed it to his wife without a word. She had just finished outlining to him a plan whereby she would adopt—that is, decorate and lovingly care for—the graves of the American soldiers buried at nearby Margraten. The *burgemeester* had vetoed it: she was too tired; she needed a rest. "Out of the question," he had added, "unless you get a sign from heaven."

If ever there was a sign from heaven, this was it. Next day, Baroness van Kessenich covered the grave of the boy from Alabama with iris. Then she photographed it so that the soldier's name on the cross was visible, and mailed the prints with a note which began, "With all my heart I will help to give your dear one's grave the care you would give it yourself."

The girl in Alabama read the letter again and again. Then, deciding that others ought to know of such kindness, she sent the picture to *Life,* which published it in its Letters department. As a result, letters from all over the United States poured into Maastricht—from mothers and fathers, from widows, sisters and brothers of the men lying in Margraten.

By coincidence, a priest of Margraten, Father Johannes Heuschen, had also had a letter, and he, too, had laid flowers on a grave. He in turn had received hundreds of letters. Now he asked the baroness to help him organize a committee to give expression to the passionate need of the people to do something for the men who had freed them from the Nazis and lived in their homes. And when the committee appealed for individuals to adopt a grave, there were sponsors for all, plus a waiting list of 3000.

Since then, the labors of the people of Maastricht and Margraten have gone on undiminished. In 1946 the baroness came to the United States to tell Americans what was being done. She remembers most vividly being approached in a Massachusetts town by a fireman. "My boy is buried in Margraten," he began, "and I got a letter from there which I read every day—from someone who puts flowers on the grave. Could you please tell her thanks, because I can't make out the signature." The baroness glanced at the letter. "It's me," she said with a smile. The man's eyes filled with tears. He could not speak. He put his arms about her.

I tell this story of Margraten because it is representative of all our cemeteries abroad. Approximately 360,000 American fighting men died during World War II. Almost three fifths were brought home by their relatives to resting places in the United States. When the transport was completed, the American Battle Monuments Commission engaged leading architects, landscape gardeners, sculptors and painters to create cemeteries of permanence and beauty for the 148,000 who remained abroad. Today there are 12 such cemeteries in Europe, one in Carthage, Tunisia, one in Manila, the Philippines. In addition, there are eight which date back to World War I.

Situated in unspoiled areas away from cities, on land given by the host country, the cemeteries blend beautifully with the landscape. Grass covers the burial area—grass so thick and luxuriant that many visitors touch it to make sure it is real. On the edges are roses and flowering shrubs; in the background, rhododendron and small forests of oaks, sycamores, maples, evergreens. The wooden crosses and Stars of David of the early interments have been replaced by similar white marble markers anchored in cement so that no wind can disturb them.

Each cemetery has its "Wall of the Missing," on which are chiseled the names of those whose bodies were never identified or never found. Their number varies from 293 at Draguignan, in southern France, to 36,279 in Manila. The total is 55,581 either missing in action or lost at sea.

In the great democracy of death, colonels lie beside corporals, generals beside privates. The only exception is Gen. George S. Patton. So many people sought his grave in Luxembourg that it was moved forward, but the headstone is no larger than any other.

Brothers are always interred side by side. There are 40 such pairs in the Margraten Cemetery. Perhaps the best-known brothers are Theodore and Quentin Roosevelt, buried in the St.-Laurent Cemetery. The former, a brigadier general, died after the D-Day landing in Normandy in 1944. The other, a young Air Corps lieutenant, was shot down during World War I.

Many years have gone by since World War II, and many fathers and mothers have died. A surprising number still come, however, to weep unashamedly at the graves. At the cemetery in Nettuno, Italy, Ralph Mancini—like all other superintendents, an American—told me of a lieutenant's mother who wept as much in relief as in sorrow. "I always reproached myself," she said, "that I did not bring my boy home. Now I am glad I left him here. It is so beautiful."

It is a feeling that other relatives have when they visit the cemeteries. All of them would agree with Monica, mother of St. Augustine, who when dying far from home said, "Bury my body where you want, for nowhere is far from God."

The Epic Story of Gettysburg

by Bruce Catton

As JUNE of 1863 came to an end, the governments in Washington and in Richmond, plain people North and South, found themselves watching a quiet little market town in Pennsylvania known as Gettysburg. Under sweltering heat and the heavy dust of torn roads, rival armies—without design, as if something in the place drew them irresistibly—were moving toward this dot on the map where all the roads crossed. What was about to happen amid these rolling Pennsylvania hills was destined to linger and shine in American memory forever.

The battle at Gettysburg was a three-day explosion of storm and flame and terror that would come to symbolize all the blunders and all the heroism of the war fought over the great question of Union. Yet it was the queer fate of the men who fought there that the significance of the battle would not be entirely comprehensible until after the fighting ended. Then it would come clear: that at Gettysburg the Confederacy had gambled heavily, at long odds, for its dream of independent existence. But in the final and most heartbreaking moments of the battle that dream was doomed. Gettysburg would be seen as the focus of the entire war, and American history would be different ever after.

For two years the fog of war had lain on the land. Opposing armies had fought many battles in many places, so that every peaceful village and every great city knew what names like Antietam and Bull Run meant. But by the spring of 1863, despite a dazzling victory over the Union Army of the Potomac at Chancellorsville, the doom of the Confederacy was beginning to take visible form in Mississippi and Tennessee.

On the Mississippi River, Gen. Ulysses S. Grant's Union army was besieging the city of Vicksburg, gateway to the South's rich trans-Mississippi empire. As long as Vicksburg held, the Confederacy controlled a 200-mile stretch of the river, from Vicksburg to Baton Rouge, across which it could ship invaluable supplies from the West: horses and cattle from Arkansas, munitions brought into Texas ports by ships which dared run the blockade with which the Union had sealed off Confederate seaports.

Within Grant's vast semicircle 31,000 Confederates were locked up, helpless, and outside an inadequate Confederate army tried in vain to find some way to crack the shell. Without reinforcements from the Army of Northern Virginia, Vicksburg was bound to fall, and when that happened the Confederacy would be cut in two, its life-giving supply line across the Mississippi forever severed. The river would become a Federal waterway, and an Illinois farmer could again send his wheat to the outside world as if the war had never happened.

In the North, the Chancellorsville defeat had humiliated the Union Army of the Potomac, but it had not crippled it. In a month or two the Federals would be ready to invade ravaged Virginia anew, and a Federal victory there would mean loss of Richmond, the Confederate Capital, and of essential munitions.

Gen. Robert E. Lee, commander of the Army of Northern Virginia, had the habit of success, and overpowering prestige. Now he pointed out that the fall of Richmond would mean speedy loss of the war itself, whereas the doom in the West would come more slowly. Instead of sending reinforcements to Vicksburg, he argued, better to defend Virginia by invading the North. A Confederate victory above the Potomac River might convince war-weary Northerners that the Confederacy could never be beaten. It might even bring recognition of the Confederacy by England and France. In short, it might be the deciding stroke of the war.

Lee was used to long odds, and he had commanded at Chancellorsville. The government in Richmond agreed to his proposal. The tragic, fated invasion of the North began.

The Union Army of the Potomac—about 95,000 men soon to come under the command of Gen. George Gordon Meade—was also on the move, marching for the Potomac crossings above Washington, circling warily to keep itself between the invader and the national capital. When Lee's army began scooping up supplies from the fat Pennsylvania farming country, Lee learned that the Army of the Potomac was looking for him. His troops, estimated at 75,000, were strung out now along 60 miles of highway, from Chambersburg in the west to the neighborhood of York and Harrisburg in the east.

At once Lee sent out couriers, to call the scattered divisions together. The Gettysburg area was the handiest place for them to meet, and so to Gettysburg they were coming.

At daylight on July 1 a Union cavalry division bivouacked on a low ridge just west of town saw the head of a Confederate infantry column advancing toward it. From that moment the two armies were committed to their most terrible fight.

It opened with a flourish and a snatch of song. The Federal I Army Corps, swinging up the Emmitsburg Road into action, took a short cut, cross-lots, and some impulse made the commander of this leading brigade shake out the battle flags and put the fife and drum corps at the head of the column. On they came, five regiments of lean Middle Westerners, roar of battle just ahead, shrill fifes playing "The Campbells Are Coming." They were giving a last salute to the fraudulent romance of war.

This day began well for the Federals but ended disastrously. The I Army Corps knocked the first Confederate attack back on its heels, but Confederate reinforcements were reaching Gettysburg faster than the Federals, and the battle lines grew until they formed a great semicircle west and north of the town. The Federals were outflanked, and the I Army Corps were cut to pieces, its commander killed. Another Yankee Corps, the XI, came up on the double and collided with Confederates, who crumpled them. By evening the Federals who were left (they had upward of 10,000 casualties) were reassembling on the high ground south and east of Gettysburg, grimly determined to hold on until the rest of the army came up, but not at all certain they could do it.

Perhaps Lee could have driven them off that evening and clinched the battle—the Federals were badly outnumbered. But by the time the Southern generals had conferred and considered and weighed risks, night had come and it was too late.

July 2 came in hot after a windless night. Meade was on the scene now, part of his army in hand and the rest coming up fast. He held good ground: the center of his line lay on Cemetery Hill, a massive height on the southern edge of town, with his right flank on wooded Culp's Hill half a mile to the east. The line continued south from Cemetery Hill along the crest of Cemetery Ridge to two rocky knolls a mile or more away, Little Round Top and Big Round Top—the left flank. On these heights the Army of the Potomac waited. Wherever the Confederates made their fight, they would have to come uphill.

One Confederate did not like the looks of it. Gen. James Longstreet felt that Gettysburg was not a fit place for the Confederates to fight—an opinion he clung to with massive stubbornness. But Lee looked at the ranks of waiting Federals and made the inescapable decision: the enemy is there, and there I will attack him.

The second day at Gettysburg was made up of many separate fights, each one a moment or an hour of concentrated fury. Sweating artillerymen rammed home charges, stood aside for a salvo, then ran in to lay hold of wheels and handspikes to make ready another blast. Ragged lines of infantry swayed in and out of the shifting veils of smoke. The ground was covered with dead and wounded.

Confederate Gen. Richard Ewell sent his men toward Culp's Hill, right flank of Meade's line. There they found the Federals posted in solid breastworks of earth and felled trees. The Confederates struggled up the hillside, stumbled back down, tried again, won a foothold that threatened the Union army with disaster—and could not quite make it.

South of Gettysburg, near the Emmitsburg Road, General Longstreet drove his army corps in toward the union's left flank. Here was a peach orchard, where men fought hand to hand with bayonets and musket butts. Here was a wheat field, grain trampled flat and strewn with dead bodies, where Northerners and Southerners knelt 30 paces apart and blazed away with unremitting fury.

Near the wheat field was a tangled area of boulders and stunted trees known as the Devil's Den. It earned its name that afternoon, while men fired from behind rocks and trees and wounded men dragged themselves into rocky crevices for shelter and Yankee batteries in the rear blasted the place indiscriminately.

East of Devil's Den was Little Round Top, defended by last-minute Federal reinforcements who ran panting along the uneven hillside to drive back the Confederates who had swept through Devil's Den. For a time there was a great gaping hole all along the left of Meade's line, but Little Round Top held, and a line of Federal guns was posted in a farmyard, where they held off Longstreet's men until Meade could get fresh infantry on the scene.

At one time a Confederate division charged all the way to the crest of Cemetery Ridge, and the Army of the Potomac was in danger of being broken in half. But the invaders could not stay; a series of disorganized but effective counter-charges drove them back. Over near Culp's Hill was a final flare-up as charging Southerners broke an infantry line and got in among the Yankee guns. But a union brigade ran in, fighting in pitch-darkness with only the spitting fire from gun muzzles to tell where the battle line was, and the Southerners drew off at last. As the second day at Gettysburg came to a close, the union continued to hold the high ground.

In the rear of the Union army, however, was a great confused huddle of bewildered fugitives, walking wounded, wrecked artillery units and panicky non-combat details. During the night and early morning the last of Meade's reinforcements came up through this backwash. A gunner in the VI Corps remembered how the stragglers and wounded men told doleful tales of defeat: "There was all kinds of stories flying around, some telling us that we were whipped to death and that any God's quantity of our artillery was captured." When the replacements got to the battle line, though, they found everybody confident.

Daylight that third morning brought a renewal of the Confederate attempt to seize Culp's Hill. The Federals beat off the attack with smooth competence. After this there was a lull, broken only by an occasional sputter of skirmish-line fire. The Confederate Army of Northern Virginia had enough strength left for one final assault; the Union Army of the Potomac was strong enough for one more desperate stand. Everybody knew it, and the armies waited, tense.

Meade had predicted the night before that if Lee attacked again he would hit the center of the Union line; he had tried both flanks and failed. Meade was right. While he waited, there was a stir along the Confederate line. Rank upon rank of artillery took position in the open; sunlight glinted off the rifle barrels of moving troops. Lee was massing strength for that one last blow.

At one o'clock the whole line of Confederate guns opened in a thunderous bombardment. Yankee infantry huddled behind low breastworks, dazed by the storm. The Confederate guns swept Cemetery Ridge with flame and fragments of flying metal, killing men and animals, breaking gun carriages to fragments, exploding caissons. But the great assault, when it came, would go about as it would have gone if there had been no bombardment. The supreme moment lay just ahead.

To look at that hour is to see it through the eyes of the sweating Federals who crouched on Cemetery Ridge and squinted west toward the afternoon sun. What they saw was an army of 15,000 men with banners, moving out from the woods into the open field, rank upon endless rank drawn up with parade-ground precision, battle flags tipped forward. These were Gen. George Pickett's 5000 Virginians, plus 10,000 men from other commands—men appointed to try the impossible.

It takes time to get 15,000 men into line, and these Southerners were deliberate about it, perhaps out of defiance, perhaps out of pride. When at last they moved forward, all the guns opened again, and a great cloud of smoke filled the hollow plain.

Some of Meade's batteries which had been silenced because they had run out of long-range ammunition now opened fire on their attackers at close range. The crash of battle rose higher and higher as the men came to grips with each other on Cemetery Ridge, Federals from right and left swarming over to join the center. Then suddenly the fight was finished. The charging column had been broken to bits. Survivors were going back to the Confederate lines, the smoke cloud was lifting, and the battle of Gettysburg was ended. Between them the two armies had paid 50,000 casualties.

And far down in Mississippi a white flag was coming out of Vicksburg, and General Grant was being asked what terms he would give to a surrendering army.

Lee would withdraw his army from Gettysburg, sullenly, and the war would continue until Palm Sunday, 1865, when Lee and Grant, sitting down together in the front parlor of a modest house at Appomattox Court House in Virginia, would bring the fighting to an end. But after the battle of Gettysburg the Confederacy would be a cut flower in a vase, seeming to live for a time but cut off forever from the possibility of independent nationhood.

On a day in November 1863, President Lincoln would come to Gettysburg to dedicate a national cemetery and speak a few sentences. Then the deep meaning of the fight would at last begin to clear. Gettysburg would reveal itself as a great height from which men could glimpse a vista extending far into the future: one nation, running from ocean to ocean.

"I Died a Soldier"

Reprinted from Army Times

A 20-year-old soldier killed in action in Vietnam on February 1, 1966, has been honored posthumously with the top 1966 Freedoms Foundation award, for a "last letter" to his parents. The foundation's George Washington Award, which carries a $5000 honorarium, was presented to Mr. and Mrs. Donald A. Strickland of Graham, N.C., in the name of their son, Pfc. Hiram D. Strickland. Private Strickland's letter was found among his personal effects after his death.

DEAR FOLKS,

I'm writing this letter as my last one. You've probably already received word that I'm dead and that the government wishes to express its deepest regret.

Believe me, I didn't want to die, but I knew it was part of my job. I want my Country to live for billions and billions of years to come.

I want it to stand as a light to all people oppressed and guide them to the same freedom we know. If we can stand and fight for freedom, then I think we have done the job God set down for us.

It's up to every American to fight for the freedom we hold so dear. If we don't, the smell of free air could become dark and damp as in a prison cell. We won't be able to look at ourselves in a mirror, much less at our sons and daughters, because we know we have failed our God, Country and our future generations.

I can hold my head high because I fought, whether it be in heaven or hell. Besides, the saying goes, "One more GI from Vietnam, St. Peter. I've served my time in hell."

I fought for Sandy, Nell, Gale [his sisters], Mom and Dad. But when the twins and Sandy's kids get old enough, they'll probably have to fight, too. Tell them to go proudly and without fear of death because it is worth keeping the land free.

I remember a story from Mr. Williams' [Thomas Williams, a teacher at Strickland's high school] English classes, when I was a freshman that said, "Cowards die a thousand times. The brave die but once."

Don't mourn me, Mother, for I'm happy I died fighting my Country's enemies, and I will live forever in people's minds. I've done what I've always dreamed of. Don't mourn me, for I died a soldier of the United States of America.

God bless you all and take care. I'll be seeing you in heaven.

Your loving son and brother,
Butch

American Voices

Listen to the Sound of America!

by Jean Bell Mosley

AMERICA has a flag, a bird, a song, a pledge, all deliberately chosen. Does she have a sound? One that we cannot choose, but nevertheless is ours, made up of notes past and present and tangled into a single tone?

Sometimes I think I hear it, faint and far off, a high murmurous wind passing over, a wind that has known the Rockies, played hide-and-seek in the Grand Canyon, whispered in prairie grass, bent willows along some bayou, sifted snow in Montana and transferred Oklahoma dust to Kansas—a tumbleweed wind, stirring, roaring, sighing.

At my club's meeting there is the fall of the opening gavel. Not a very loud sound and, as it fades away, I fancy I can hear its little echoing overtones joining somewhere out there the raps of thousands of other gavels, thousands of other mallet strokes, thousands of other hammers. Hammers building houses, bridges, chicken coops. Hammers crushing rocks, cracking walnuts, soling shoes, driving railroad spikes, chiseling stone faces, nailing up signs of WANTED FOR MURDER, PUPPIES FOR SALE, FRESH EGGS. Momentarily my mind's ear and my physical ear seem tuned to the same frequency, and I hear a unison "beat, beat, beat." Or is it only my own heart, excited with the thought and the wondering?

Soon the gavel raps again. We have voted to plant a red maple in the town park. It was a close vote between the maple and the golden-chain tree, and there were many words—businesslike, oratorical, humorous—words to be caught up and snatched away to mingle with other words from other times, weaving in and out with curious equal stature.

"The red maple is more colorful—give me liberty or give me death—ask not what America can do for you—the golden-chain tree is unusual—liberty and union, now and forever—all in favor—one giant step for mankind—does it require a special soil—I pledge allegiance."

Words lifted in song will be there in that elusive cosmic note. Sweet benedictions and whispered prayers will move in and out of America's sound like bright shuttles weaving it together. Alas, there will be lying words, raucous, argumentative uproars, curses and threats, for sounds made cannot be recalled.

There will be wheels, too. In the early morning hours I awake and hear singing tires on the highway to the west, distant clacking of train wheels to the east—wheels and tires that are moving jobs and lead, cabbages, cotton and cows, transporting restless mortals here and there. Screeching, droning, these wheels and tires are yet strangely haunting as they pluck their strings of steel and concrete, speaking dimly now of ancestral covered wagons and wooden farm carts.

While I am trying to encompass the sum of America's multiple turning wheels, spinning gravel in a nearby driveway speaks of my neighbor backing out his car to go to work. It is as if the uncountable instruments in a great orchestra have paused to let me hear in detail the resonance and syncopation of a single one.

At the supermarket a pyramid of oranges comes tumbling down, sending out rolling rays in all directions. There is a brief silence—then rippling laughter from a young throat, a sound more golden than the fruit. This fragment of mirth from the girl now gaily picking up the oranges is so temporary, so swift to depart. But depart it does, to mingle with all laughter from all children playing ring-around-a-rosy, watching monkeys, circus clowns, doodlebugs, big-eyed frogs. Laughter from old throats, too, seasoned by the predicament of man. Rich notes these laughs, flaring up like torches of freedom to lead us through the fog and dark.

And I hear marching feet. Like drumbeats as they tramp to their cause—war, protests, work, play, fitness, justice, truth. Eager, high-stepping feet parading in high-school bands. Old, stumbling feet marching to some remembered inspiration. I seem to hear, faint and distant, echoes of other footfalls—through Argonne's forest and up Suribachi, through strife-torn Georgia, along the dusty Chisholm Trail, a road to Selma.

Engines everywhere! Pulsating, humming and drumming. Grinding meal, moving wheels, mowing fields. Sawing logs, separating molecules. Sowing and raking bread from Dakota's fields, clothes from Mississippi's. Are engines the theme that holds our tumbleweed tones together?

Walking in old fence rows, I hear meadowlarks lacing the fields with song, speaking of little secret things. There is cricket song from the timothy, call notes of the cardinal, a cowbell on the mountainside.

Listening, I am of two minds, wanting these Eden-sweet sounds to stay, hover close, to blot out pistol shots in the night, groans of the dying, slamming of windows to silence cries for help, sounds of cataclysmic sirens.

Put them all together: wind, hammers, words, wheels, laughter, marching feet. What is the ultimate song? My mind goes round and round with the question. Then I recall the friend who on occasion goes to clean out a clogged spring. He kneels on the moss and lichen-covered rocks and pulls out great handfuls of accumulated leaves and twigs, muttering, "Ought to run free." He tosses the debris aside with a vengeance as if he were getting rid of the troubles that choke the world.

Soon water is splashing at over-hanging ferns, slapping smartly against the bordering stones, and I, watching, let my "ear" run away with the bubbling stream to hear other waters. Ocean battering at Plymouth's rocks. Niagara, Mississippi. Water rushing, rising, turning wheels, making lights, floating homes away, splitting to oars, foaming and churning behind majestic *Robert E. Lees*. Raindrops renewing dry places, pattering on old weathered kitchen roofs, keeping time with simmering stews and steaming kettles.

Somehow, sitting there by running water, everything seems clear. The mind wanders in its own green meadows, and the sounds that I now hear in fragments fuse mystically together in what surely may be called the heartbeat of America.

Even my own heartbeat is a part of the whole, caught up into the overall to beat in immortality alongside the call note of a long-ago bobwhite or some future hammer nailing up heaven-knows-what. My feeling is strong that, despite discords, the sound of America will keep on making the bowed head lift and sing, the timid brave, the weak to rise. Ever— and at the same time—a tender wood-thrush note and a trumpet call, proud, clear and compelling.

A Walk With Robert Frost

ROBERT FROST, four times a Pulitzer Prize winner, was for most of his long life a practicing poet. His poems, writes critic Mark Van Doren, "are the work of a man who never stopped exploring himself—or, if you like, America, or, better yet, the world." Americans, in taking Frost to their hearts, have proved that he does speak for them. The following thoughts are quoted from his conversation, lectures and poems:

Courage is the human virtue that counts most—courage to act on limited knowledge and insufficient evidence. That's all any of us have, so we must have the courage to go ahead and act on a hunch. It's the best we can do.

•

The people I want to hear about are the people who take risks.

•

I'll discuss anything. I like to go perhaps-ing around on all subjects.

•

People have got to think. Thinking isn't to agree or disagree—that's voting.

•

Education is turning things over in the mind.

•

What is required is sight and insight—then you might add one more: excite.

•

On the United States and its young people: We're like

A Walk With Robert Frost

a rich father who wishes he knew how to give his sons the hardships that made him rich.

•

You can be a rank insider as well as a rank outsider.

•

I own I never really warmed
To the reformer or reformed.

•

There's doing good—that's sociology. There's also doing well—that's art. It's the doing well that's important. My little granddaughter said, "I think I would like to do good well." I let her have that one.

•

As for rhyme and meter in poetry, I'd as soon write free verse as play tennis with the net down.

•

The greatest thing in family life is to take a hint when a hint is intended—and not to take a hint when a hint isn't intended.

•

If one by one we counted people out
For the least sin, it wouldn't take us long
To get so we had no one left to live with.
For to be social is to be forgiving.

•

Poets like Shakespeare knew more about psychiatry than any 25-dollar-an-hour man.

•

They cannot scare me with their empty spaces
Between stars—on stars where no human race is.
I have it in me so much nearer home
To scare myself with my own desert places.

•

People keep saying it's not good to learn things by heart, but if you don't have things by heart, what are you going to have to think about when you lie awake and can't sleep at night? Pretty things that are well said—it's nice to have them in your head.

•

Love is an irresistible desire to be irresistibly desired.

•

A lot of people are being scared by the Russians into hardening up our education or speeding it up. I am interested in *toning* it up.

•

There cannot be much to fear in a country where there are so many right faces going by.

•

Don't be an agnostic. Be *something*.

•

I'm like a modern car in religious matters. I may look convertible, but I'm a hardtop.

•

One year, a Robert Frost Christmas card to his friends was a six-stanza verse with these closing lines:

> And I may return
> If dissatisfied
> With what I learn
> From having died.

•

All the fun's in how you say a thing.

Walt Whitman's Song of Democracy

by Max Eastman

EVERY GREAT people has its poet. Shakespeare, Goethe, Pushkin, Dante, Hugo, Li Po—these names float over their countries almost like the national flag. In America—there is little doubt left now—it is Walt Whitman who will occupy this unique place. A popular anthology gives him 74 pages to 27 for Edgar Allan Poe, seven for Longfellow, six for Whittier.

To me there is drama in this, for within my lifetime Walt Whitman died in a shabby little house in Camden, New Jersey, hardly known to the reading public at all and where known regarded for the most part as a disreputable and rather unclean character.

Whitman was, in fact, immaculately clean—so much so that all his friends mentioned it. He was, moreover, by comparison with most poets, a model of Christian virtue. He had no vices or bad habits. He never swore or smoked or gambled; he seldom took a drink. His chief dissipation was to ride on Broadway horse cars.

He was born in 1819 near Huntington, Long Island, in a small gray-shingled cabin, but most of his boyhood was passed in Brooklyn, where his father built houses. By the time he was 20, he had learned the printer's trade, taught school and started a newspaper—writing and printing it himself and delivering it on horseback. For the next nine years he worked in the print shop, newsroom or editorial office of different New York and Long Island papers. During the last two of these years he was editor of the Brooklyn *Eagle*.

While working on these papers he wrote one or two sentimental verses. But until he was 29 the idea never occurred to him, and certainly never to anybody else, that he might be a great poet.

Everybody around town knew Walter Whitman, and everybody liked him. He was big and strong, had a perfect build, and his face and head were as fine as nature ever produced. But the one thing he was famous for was a magnificently casual attitude toward work. Any afternoon he didn't knock off and go swimming, it was because he had spent the morning riding back and forth on Fulton Ferry, or up and down Manhattan on the Broadway car. One of his first employers remarked that "if the boy came down with fever and the ague, he would be too lazy to shake," and that reputation grew up with him.

There is a fog around the question of why Whitman left the *Eagle*, and you can see his character looming pretty clearly through the fog. He was a Free-Soil Democrat; that is, he wanted slavery excluded from the new states. The owners of the paper wanted the states to decide.

Less than a month after Whitman left the *Eagle*, he had a contract to edit the New Orleans *Crescent*. His trip to New Orleans was the dividing event in his life. It woke the emotional and imaginative giant slumbering within him. I think there are three reasons for this.

First, the journey over the Alleghenies and down America's great rivers astounded his eyes. He saw spread before him the vastness and incredible richness of the young republic. He fell in love with America. Second, he cast loose a little, in the freely languorous French atmosphere of New Orleans, from the stern mood of the reformer.

Most important, he fell in love with a girl whom he could not, or would not, marry. Nothing is known of that love beyond the girl's heart-melting picture pasted in one of his notebooks, for Walt's reticence about the whole incident was made of Egyptian stone. But there is little doubt—in my mind at least—that her touch was what finally broke open the fountains of immortal song that this strange, indolent, ardent, majestic and yet callow youth contained.

Walt came home from New Orleans, like Saul from the road to Damascus, a changed and consecrated man. He had seen a vision—a vision of the American republic, casting off the last shred of the stale trappings of feudal Europe and leading mankind into a new era of fearlessly free and equal, boldly scientific and yet richly poetic, joyfully expanding physical and spiritual life. He came back the poet and prophet of that sublime event.

Like Saul he made a slight change in his name: he would be what his good friends called him—Walt. And he made a big change in his apparel. As the poet of democracy he peeled off his bow tie, unbuttoned his shirt to where the undershirt showed, and put on for good and all the everyday clothes of the ordinary workman or mechanic. The change was not quite so artificial as it sounds, for he was working now as a carpenter for his father, and that was the costume in which he worked. But it was deeply meaningful to him.

He believed he was making a corresponding change in poetry. Instead of turning pretty verses in imitation of England's poets, he would say what he had to say straight out, the way American workmen do and the Bible does, and let the words sing their own song.

It was not his way of singing, however, that made Walt Whitman great. The greatness lay in the things he sang. A Song of Myself—a declaration of the divine and sovereign importance of the individual man, not to be found elsewhere in literature. A Song of Sympathy—a larger giving of the self than had ever been sung before. A song of religion transcending the church; of democracy transcending the boundaries of nations; of love breaking free from the prison of silence in which a false shame and a false, puritanical piety had confined it.

It was this last song that gained Whitman an unsavory reputation. In these days when any college girl can buy books on married love at the nearest drugstore, Walt's famous frankness about sex seems almost shy and amateurish. It was in fact prophetic. His was the first book in the world, outside the medical library, to speak of sex relations candidly and yet without comic or erotic emotion. He spoke with intensely reverent emotion—a sense of the sacredness of all being, every least atom, and of himself as part of it. This new serious candor was one of the most momentous changes in the history of human culture.

Walt worked six years on his exalted book of verse, jotting down the lines on ferryboats, along the wharves, on buses, or lying on the lonely beach at Coney Island. He brought them home to the house on Myrtle Avenue, and worked them up on a pine table in a little upstairs room with a single window, a narrow bed and a washstand. To signify democracy and the sacred worth of small and simple things, he called his book *Leaves of Grass*.

When Walt spoke of himself in the book he spoke *for* the everyday working American. He made some prodigiously insolent claims for himself, but what he was trying to say was: "This is the way the American common man should talk. This is how he should stand."

> And I or you, pocketless of a dime, may
> purchase the pick of the earth,
> And to glance with an eye, or show a
> bean in its pod, confounds the learn-
> ing of all times,
> And there is no trade or employment
> but the young man following it may
> become a hero,
> And there is no object so soft but it
> makes a hub for the wheel'd
> universe,
> And I say to any man or woman, Let
> your soul stand cool and composed
> before a million universes.

Walt printed 800 copies of his book in a little print shop, seeing them through the press himself. Then he inserted an ad in the New York *Tribune*, sent review copies to critics and editors, and gift copies to a number of eminent Americans. To the bookstores in New York and Brooklyn he peddled them himself in a big canvas bag.

Not a copy so far as history records, was sold. A friend on the *Tribune* wrote a mildly favorable hack review. The rest of the critics either ignored him or burned him up:

"A heterogeneous mass of bombast, vulgarity and nonsense."..."He is as unacquainted with art as a hog with mathematics."..."We can conceive of no better reward than the lash."

The verdict of the eminent Americans was little better. Wendell Phillips remarked that he found all kinds of leaves there except the fig. John Greenleaf Whittier threw the book out of the window.

Such was America's reception of her national poet. And then out of the clear sky, out of New England's icy silence, came a letter—a letter that is almost as famous now as the poems:

"Dear sir, I am not blind to the wonderful worth of

Leaves of Grass. I find it the most extraordinary piece of wit and wisdom that America has yet contributed. I greet you at the beginning of a great career." It was signed with the one pre-eminent name of those times—Ralph Waldo Emerson.

Walt never doubted his own greatness from that day on. But his rise to the heights of fame was slower than an ocean tide. The average American for whom he sang preferred the jingly tinkle of Poe's *The Bells* or *The Raven* to Walt's full-throated song.

The Civil War slowed Walt Whitman's climb to glory. Walt was no soldier. He had a mother's gift for sympathy. As he moved through the world, he loved it all, the good and the bad, instinctively. It is hard for those with a genius for love to take sides in a fight. Moreover Walt had dedicated himself to be the poet of the whole nation.

He solved the conflict in his heart in a way that has given him a place in the history not only of poetry but of love. He moved to Washington, where the great military hospitals were, abandoned his writing, and gave himself to the task of tending the wounded soldiers. Earning a meager livelihood in a paymaster's office, living in a small top-floor room, he visited the hospitals each day from noon to four o'clock and again from six to nine. He carried a big bag full of gifts for the soldiers—tobacco, paper and envelopes, oranges, gingersnaps. But his greatest gift to them was a mother's tenderness in the robust and powerful figure of a man.

Before each visit he walked a while in the sun and wind, or under the stars. He drank only water and milk, avoided "fats and late suppers," in order to assure himself of a "pure, perfect, sweet, clean-blooded robust body," through which the healing powers of nature could flow to the suffering soldiers.

He was not obeying the dictates of any creed or faith. He was following the inmost impulse of his own nature, which he believed to be prophetic of what the world, when democracy fully unfolds itself, is destined to become.

Walt gave his prodigious health in that service. He was himself like a wounded soldier when the war was done. He was at home in Brooklyn with his mother, recuperating a second time from "hospital malaria," when the news came of Lincoln's assassination.

It was spring and the lilacs were in bloom in the yard

of the little house where they lived. Brooklyn in those days was little more than a rural village, and he did not have to walk far to hear a hermit thrush singing as the evening star peered out in the twilight. He composed his noblest poem there, twining the lilac, the star, the song of the bird and his grief into as sublime a tribute to a hero—and to life and death—as has ever been spoken. Swinburne described his poem *When Lilacs Last in the Door-Yard Bloom'd* as "the most sweet and sonorous nocturne ever chanted in the church of the world." More perhaps than any of his other works, this sublime requiem has given Walt Whitman by gradual universal consent the name of America's poet.

After the war Walt got a clerical job in the Indian Bureau. He was working on a new edition of *Leaves of Grass*, and kept the scribbled proof sheets in his desk. Secretary of the Interior Harlan, a preacher-politician from Iowa City, got an itch of curiosity one night and sneaked in and took a look at the book. It gave him a terrible shock there in the lamplight, and he won himself a place in history as a snooping prude by firing his immortal employe. Walt's Irish friend William O'Connor wrote a sizzling pamphlet about the incident, under the title of *The Good Gray Poet*, giving Whitman an inadequate sobriquet that has clung to him ever since.

In 1873 Walt's glorious physique gave out. He woke up one night and found he could not move his left arm or leg. He went calmly to sleep again and the next day waited quietly for his friends to come. Throughout the 20 years of decline and increasing confinement that followed, he never lost that calm. He never lost his patient, friendly humor. He met the inevitable narrowing of his selfhood with a fortitude equal to the arrogance with which he had announced its expansion.

Friends and admirers, a tiny but increasing company, sent funds to help him. He followed the slowly growing fame of his book with anxious joy, as a mother follows the career of her well-trained child. Tributes came, once in a while—and visits—from those eminent enough to encourage his belief that his book would live.

Walt would have been proudly delighted—and yet also, in his still depths, unsurprised—to know that 50 years after his death a British prime minister, reporting a great military victory to the House of Commons, would quote, like a text from the Bible, his noble admonition:

"Now understand me well—It is provided in the essence of things that from any fruition of success, no matter what, shall come forth something to make a greater struggle necessary."

The Wizard Who Created Oz

by Daniel P. Mannix

AT THE TURN of the century, a man who had failed at almost everything he had attempted wrote to his sister: "When I was young I longed to write a great novel that should win me fame. Now that I am getting old my first book is written to amuse children. For, aside from my evident inability to do anything 'great,' I have learned that to please a child is a sweet and lovely thing that warms one's heart."

The man was Lyman Frank Baum, and his best-known book began to take form when a group of children, led by his own four boys, waylaid him one evening in his modest Chicago home, demanding a story. Baum told them about a little Kansas farm girl named Dorothy, who was carried by a cyclone to a strange land where she met a live scarecrow, a man made of tin and a cowardly lion.

One of the children asked, "What was the name of this land?" Stumped, Baum looked around for inspiration. In the corner of the room were filing cabinets, and one bore the letters O-Z. "The land of Oz!" he exclaimed, unaware that he had added a new word to the English language.

Baum seldom wrote down the stories he liked to tell his children, but he was strangely attracted to this one. Jotting it down on a handful of scrap paper, he took it to William W. Denslow, a well-known illustrator. Denslow outlined an ambitious book—24 Denslow drawings as full-page illustrations in a six-color printing scheme and innumerable sketches tinted in various tones to be superimposed on the text. Baum eagerly agreed.

Publishers did not. The two men were turned down by nearly every house in Chicago. Baum's conception of an "American fairy story" was too radical a departure from traditional juvenile literature, and Denslow's elaborate illustrations would price the book off the market. But at last George Hill agreed to publish the book, provided Baum and Denslow pay all printing expenses. He thought the new book might sell as many as 5000 copies.

The Wonderful Wizard of Oz was published on August 1, 1900. By October, 25,000 more copies had to be printed, and 30,000 more in November. Today, over five million copies have been published, making it one of the best-sellers of all time. It has been made into musical comedies, movies, puppet shows, radio shows and LP records. The 1939 movie musical with Judy Garland, shown on television every year, has become an American tradition. The book has been translated into more than a dozen languages and in Russia is being used to teach English to school-children.

Frank Baum was born in Chittenango, N.Y., in 1856, the seventh of nine children of a prosperous oilman. A sickly child, he spent much of his time acting out fantasies with a host of imaginary playmates. When he was 12, his parents sent him to Peekskill Military Academy to shake him out of his dream world. From then on he was always to dislike the military. A favorite theme in the Oz books is the overstaffed army, composed of hordes of generals, colonels, majors and captains commanding one browbeaten private who is expected to do all the fighting. But Baum was never capable of malice: even the officers are affectionately described. A general's explanation for his abject cowardice is the reasonable statement that "fighting is unkind and liable to be injurious to others."

For a time Baum was enamored of the stage and, aided by his father, started a Shakespearean troupe. By his own admission, the most memorable performance occurred when the ghost of Hamlet's father fell through a hole in the stage. The audience of oil workers was delighted.

About this time, Baum fell in love with 20-year-old Maud Gage, daughter of a militant suffragette. The mother regarded Baum as hopelessly impractical and violently opposed a marriage. But in her resolute daughter the strong-minded woman met her match. The couple were married in 1882.

Baum worked for a while in his family's petroleum-products business; but after his father died the business failed. He opened a store, Baum's Bazaar, in Aberdeen, S.D. The store went bankrupt. He then took over a newspaper called *The Aberdeen Saturday Pioneer*, setting the type himself and doing most of the writing, including a special column called "Our Landlady." One of his columns described a community where people rode in "horseless carriages" (the first American automobile had not yet gone on sale) or flying machines, used mechanical dishwashers and slept under electric blankets.

In 1891 the *Pioneer* failed; as Baum put it, "The sheriff wanted the paper more than I did." The family left for Chicago, where Baum worked as a reporter for $20 a week, then as a crockery salesman. He now had four sons. Maud gave embroidery lessons at ten cents each. About the only recreation the children had was to listen to their father's stories—his escape from his miserable existence.

Mrs. Gage, Maud's mother, was a regular winter visitor. She, too, listened to his stories. One day she said, "You should try to have those published." Baum laughed at the idea, but his wife said firmly, "Mother is nearly always right about things." So, urged by the two women, Baum submitted a collection of stories suggested by the Mother Goose rhymes, which was published in 1897 under the title *Mother Goose in Prose*. The illustrator was an unknown young artist named Maxfield Parrish. It was a "first" for both of them. The book did well, and Baum followed it with *Father Goose, His Book*, illustrated by Denslow. Then came the miraculous success of the *Wizard*.

When Baum was possessed by his fantasies, he wandered around in a trance. His characters were intensely real to him. Once, when he had not written for several weeks, his wife asked him what was the matter. "My characters won't do what I want them to," replied Baum irritably. A few days later he was back at work. He had solved the problem. By letting them do what *they* wanted to do, he explained.

The format of the *Wizard* is simple. As Baum says in his introduction, he intended to eliminate "all the horrible and bloodcurdling incidents" of the old-time fairy tales. He also hoped to eliminate the "stereotyped genie, dwarf and fairy." He was remarkably successful. Like all his characters, the Scarecrow, the Tin Woodman and the Cowardly Lion are distinct personalities.

Dorothy was, perhaps, Baum's most successful creation. Unlike the immortal Alice, who wanders politely through Wonderland without trying to influence events, Dorothy—although always gentle and innocent—is a quietly determined little girl. She intends to get back to her aunt and uncle. She

The Wizard Who Created Oz

is the leader of the little group of adventurers; though she turns to the Woodman for comfort, the Scarecrow for advice and the Lion for protection, they would obviously be lost without her. Dorothy is the descendent of the pioneer woman who crossed the plains, and the grandmother of every soap-opera heroine who ever faced life. She is as American as Alice is Victorian British.

Delighted as he was by the success of the *Wizard*, Baum had no intention of writing another Oz book. He wrote books that were not about Oz. But, to children, Oz was a real place, and Baum himself felt attracted to it. So in 1904 he wrote *The Marvelous Land of Oz*. It was nearly as successful as the *Wizard*.

Baum again did other books. He wrote *Queen Zixi of Ix*, a beautifully plotted fairy tale, and three adult novels. The novels were unsuccessful. In 1907, he returned to his kingdom with *Ozma of Oz*. It was a great success. Baum followed it with several more Oz books and again made a determined effort to end the series. The last book ended with a letter from Dorothy, "You will never hear anything more about Oz because we are now cut off forever from all the rest of the world." The panic that struck juvenile circles can only be compared to the consternation that hit London when Conan Doyle threw Sherlock Holmes off a cliff. For thousands of American youngsters, finding a new Oz book under the tree had become part of Christmas.

Though Baum wrote other books and tried other ventures, it was no good. The children wanted Oz, and Baum had no choice. He wrote eight more Oz books, beginning with *The Patchwork Girl of Oz* in 1913, and turned out at least one a year thereafter, although his heart, never strong and now worse, caused him constant trouble. He named his house, now in Los Angeles, Ozcot. Here he lived quietly, raising flowers, and feeding the birds in his giant aviary. To the many children who came to see the "Royal Historian of Oz" and listen to his stories, the house was a shrine. On May 5, 1919, his heart finally gave up. He lapsed into unconsciousness and died the next day.

Children could not believe he was dead. Even today his publishers get letters addressed to him. There is also a growing Oz cult among grownups. The Oz books continue year after year to outsell almost all other juveniles. It is an extraordinary tribute to the dreamer who found that to please a child is a sweet and lovely thing.

America Celebrates

An Old-Time Iowa Christmas

by Paul Engle

EVERY Christmas should begin with the sound of bells, and when I was a boy in Cedar Rapids, Iowa, mine always did. They were the sleigh bells on my father's team of horses, as he drove up to our hitching post with the sleigh that would take us to celebrate Christmas on the family farm ten miles out in the country.

There are no such departures any more: the whole family piling into the sleigh with a foot of golden oat straw to lie in and heavy buffalo robes to lie under; the horses stamping the soft snow, and at their every motion the bells jingling, jingling.

There are no streets like those any more: the snow sensibly left on for the sake of sleighs and easy travel. Along the way we met other horses so that we moved from one set of jangling bells to another. There would be an occasional brass-mounted automobile laboring on its narrow tires and as often as not pulled up the slippery hills by a horse, and we would pass it with a triumphant shout.

But the great moment was when we left the country road and turned up the long lane on the farm. My father would stand up, flourish his whip and, with a final burst of speed, bring the sleigh right up to the farmhouse door.

There are no such arrivals any more: the harness bells ringing and clashing; our horses whinnying at the horses in the barn and receiving a great, trumpeting whinny in reply; the dogs leaping up; a yelling of "Whoa, whoa!" at the excited horses; boy and girl cousins howling around the sleigh; and our descent into the snow with the Christmas basket carried by my mother.

While my mother and sisters went into the house, the team was unhitched and taken to the barn. A stable with cattle and horses is the place to begin Christmas. After all, that's where the original event happened, and the smell of the stable was in the first air the Christ child breathed.

The winter odor of a barn is wonderfully complex, rich and warm with the body heat of many animals; the tangy smell of oats, hay and straw; the manure steaming; the sharp odor of leather harness rubbed with neat's-foot oil; the molasses-sweet odor of ensilage in the silo. It is a smell from strong and living things, and my father always said it was the secret of health, that it scoured out a man's lungs. He would stand there breathing deeply, one hand on a horse's rump, watching the steam come out from under the blankets as the team cooled down. It gave him a better appetite, he argued, than plain fresh air, which was thin and had no body to it.

By the time we reached the house my mother and sisters were wearing aprons and busying in the big kitchen, as red-faced as the women who had been there all morning. The kitchen was the biggest room in the house and all family life save sleeping went on there. The kitchen range, a tremendous black and gleaming monster called the Smoke Eater, had pans bubbling on top and a reservoir of hot water at the side. My job was to go to the woodpile out back and split the chunks of oak and hickory to keep the fire burning.

It was a handmade Christmas. The tree came from down in the grove and on it were many paper ornaments made by my cousins, as well as beautiful ones brought from the Black Forest in southern Germany, where the family had originally lived. There were apples, popcorn balls, paper horns full of homemade candy. The gifts tended to be hand-knit socks, or wool ties, or tatted collars for blouses, or doilies with fancy flower patterns. There would usually be a cornhusk doll.

There are no dinners like that any more: every item from the farm itself. As we ate the apple, mince and pumpkin pies we could look out the window and see the cornfield where the pumpkins grew, the trees from which the apples were picked. As my aunt hurried by I could smell in her apron that freshest of all odors with which the human nose is honored—bread straight from the oven, baked that morning. There would be every form of preserve: wild grape from the vines in the grove, crab-apple jelly, wild blackberry, strawberry from the bed in the garden, pickles from the rind of the watermelon we had cooled in the milkhouse tank and eaten on a hot September afternoon. The carrots, turnips, cabbages, potatoes and squash came from the vegetable cellar cut into the hill behind the house, the sauerkraut from a ten-gallon crock in the basement.

An Old-Time Iowa Christmas

All the meat was from the home place, too. Most useful of all, the goose. Here was the universal bird of an older Christmas. Its down was plucked and washed to be put into pillows; its awkward body was roasted until the skin was crisp as paper; and the grease from its carcass was melted down, a little camphor added, and rubbed on the chests of coughing children. We ate, slept on and wore that goose.

To eat in the same room where food is cooked—that is the way to thank the Lord for His abundance. The long table, with its different levels where additions had been made for the small fry, ran the length of the kitchen. The last deed before we ate was grinding the coffee beans in the little mill, adding that exotic odor to the native ones of goose and pumpkin pie. Then all would sit at the table and my uncle would ask the grace:

Come, Lord Jesus, be our guest,
Share this food that You have blessed.

All through dinner my aunt kept a turmoil of food circulating and to refuse any of it was somehow to violate the elevated nature of the day. To consume the length and breadth of that meal was to suffer! But we faced the ordeal with courage. Uncle Ben would let out his belt with a snap and a sigh. The women managed better by getting up and trotting to the kitchen sink or the Smoke Eater or outdoors for some item left in the cold. The men sat there grimly enduring the glory of their appetites.

After dinner, late in the afternoon, the women would make despairing gestures toward the dirty dishes and scoop hot water from the reservoir at the side of the range. The men would go and look after the livestock. Bones would be thrown to the dogs, a saucer of milk set out for the cats, crumbs scattered on a bird feeder and suet tied in the oak trees for the juncos and chickadees. Sleds would be dragged out and we would slide in a long snake, feet hooked into the sled behind, down the hill and across the sloping fields into the sunset. Then we would go back to the house for a final warming-up before leaving for home.

There was usually a song around the tree before we were all bundled up, and many thanks all around for the gifts. My father and uncle would have brought up the team and hooked them to the sleigh, and we would all go out into the freezing air of early evening.

We would dig down in the straw and pull the buffalo robes up to our chins. As the horses settled into a steady trot, the bells gently chiming in their rhythmical beat, we would fall half asleep, the hiss of the runners comforting. As we looked up at the night sky through half-closed eyes, the constant bounce and swerve of the runners seemed to shake the little stars as if they would fall into our laps. But that one great star in the East never wavered. Nothing could shake it from the sky as we drifted home on Christmas.

Small-Town Parade, Decoration Day

by Phyllis McGinley

Below the lawns and picket fences,
  Just past the firehouse, half a block,
Sharp at eleven-five commences
  This ardent and memorial walk
  (Announced, last night, for ten o'clock).

Solemn, beneath the elmy arches,
  Neighbor and next-door neighbor meet.
For half the village forward marches
  To the school band's uncertain beat,
  And half is lined along the street.

O the brave show! O twirling baton!
  O drummer stepping smartly out!
O mayor, perspiring, with no hat on!
  O nurses' aid! O martial rout
  Of Bluebird, Brownie, Eagle Scout!

And at the rear, aloof and splendid,
  Lugging the lanterns of their pride,
O the red firemen, well attended
  By boys on bicycles who ride
  With envious reverences at their side!

The morning smells of buds and grasses.
  Birds twitter louder than the flute.
And wives, as the procession passes,
  Wave plodding husbands wild salute
  From porches handy to the route.

Flags snap. And children, vaguely greeted,
   Wander into the ranks awhile.
The band, bemused but undefeated,
   Plays Sousa, pedagogic style,
     Clean to the Square—a measured mile.

Until at last by streets grown stony,
   To the gray monument they bring
The wreath which is less testimony
   To Death than Life, continuing
     Through this and every other spring.

American October

by Thomas Wolfe

Now October has come again which in our land is different from October in other lands. In Maine, the frost comes sharp and quick as driven nails, just for a week or so the woods, all of the bright and bitter leaves, flare up: the maples turn a blazing red, and other leaves turned yellow like a living light, falling about you as you walk the woods, falling about you like small pieces of the sun so that you cannot say where sunlight shakes and flutters on the ground, and where the leaves.

The season swings along the nation, and a little later in the South dense woodings on the hill begin to glow and soften, and when they smell the burning wood-smoke in Ohio children say: "I'll bet that there's a forest fire in Michigan."

October is the richest of the seasons: the fields are cut, the granaries are full, the bins are loaded to the brim with fatness, and from the cider-press the rich brown oozings of the York Imperials run. The corn is shocked: it sticks out in hard yellow rows upon dried ears, fit now for great red barns in Pennsylvania, and the big stained teeth of crunching horses. The barn is sweet with hay and leather, wood and apples. The late pears mellow on a sunny shelf; smoked hams hang to the warped barn rafters; pantry shelves are loaded with jars of fruit.

There is a smell of burning in small towns in afternoon, and men are raking leaves in yards. The oak leaves, big and brown, are bedded deep in yard and gutter: they make deep wadings to the knee for children in the streets. The fire will snap and crackle like a whip, sharp acrid smoke will sting the eyes, in mown fields the little vipers of the flame eat past the black coarse edges of burned stubble like a line of locusts.

The bladed grass, a forest of small spears of ice, is thawed by noon: summer is over but the sun is warm again, and there are days throughout the land of gold and russet. The sun flames red and bloody as it sets, there are old red glintings on the battered pails, the great barn gets the ancient light as the boy slops homeward with warm foaming milk. Great shadows lengthen in the fields, the old red light dies swiftly, and the sunset barking of the hounds is faint and far and full of frost: there are shrewd whistles to the dogs, and frost and silence. Wind stirs and scuffs and rattles up the old brown leaves, and through the night the great oak leaves keep falling.

Trains cross the continent in a swirl of dust and thunder, the leaves fly down the tracks behind them: the great trains cleave through gulch and gulley, they rumble with spoked thunder on the bridges over the powerful brown wash of mighty rivers, they toil through hills, they skift the rough brown stubble of shorn fields, they whip past empty stations in the little towns and their great stride pounds its even pulse across America. Field and hill and lift and gulch and hollow, mountain and plain and river, a wilderness with fallen trees across it, a thicket of bedded brown and twisted undergrowth, a plain, a desert, and a plantation, a mighty landscape with no fenced niceness, an immensity of fold and convolution that can never be remembered, that can never be forgotten, that has never been described—weary with harvest, potent with every fruit and ore, the immeasurable richness embrowned with autumn, everlasting and magnificent—American earth in old October.

Thanksgiving, U.S.A.—The Privilege

by Janina Atkins

I CAME to this country with $2.60 in my purse, some clothes, a few books and a beautiful china tea set for 12—a going-away gift from my friends. I was an immigrant girl from Poland hoping for a new life in a strange new country.

About ten years later I celebrated Thanksgiving Day as an American citizen and, as for millions of Americans before me, it was a day of gratitude.

Mine is not a spectacular success story, nor is that of my husband. We both left the "old country" in 1964. We did not know each other at that time, but when we met in New York City we had to face the same problems. We had language difficulties, no steady jobs, no family, few friends. It was easy to be despondent.

But, slowly, times changed. There is something in the air of America that filled my soul with a feeling of independence, and independence begot strength. There is no one here to lead you by the hand, but also no one to order you about. Once you land in America you are left to yourself, to shape your own future, to test yourself. This, I suppose is what living in freedom means.

Working by day—I as a secretary, my husband as a clerk—and studying by night, we took the old route so many Americans have taken. Whatever we earned went for rent, food, tuition. We believed in the future. And the future did not disappoint us.

Today we work as librarians. My husband is studying for his doctorate. We live in a comfortable apartment in Manhattan. Weekends we drive to the country, and every year we travel to some faraway place. All this, we know, we owe to ourselves. And to the most hospitable and beautiful country in the world.

Among some of our American-born friends it is not fashionable to be enthusiastic about America. There are drugs, urban and racial conflicts, poverty, inflation, the Watergate affair. Undoubtedly this country faces serious problems. But what we, the newcomers, see are not only the problems but also democratic solutions being sought and applied. On Thanksgiving Day we might well remember that there is much in America to be grateful for.

I love America because people accept me for what I am. They do not question my ancestry, my accent, my faith, my political beliefs. I love this country because when I want to move from one place to another I do not have to ask permission—I just go. I love America because I do not have to stand in line for hours to buy a piece of tough, fat meat. I love America because America trusts me. When I go into a shop to buy a pair of shoes, I am not asked to produce my identity card. My mail is not censored. My conversation with friends is not reported to the secret police.

Sometimes, when I walk with my husband through the streets of New York, all of a sudden we stop, look at each other and smile and kiss. People think we are in love—and it is true. But we are also in love with America. Standing in the street, amid the noise and pollution, we suddenly realize what luck and what joy it is to live in a free country.

New York Snowstorm Reverie

by Ben Hecht

A SNOWSTORM came to town the other day and shouldered its way onto the front pages. This snowstorm was no blizzard; it froze nobody, wrecked nothing. Yet it was news.

But though the editors gave it space, they were too shy to tell the truth about it. They would have blushed to report what readers were thinking: that everybody was looking at the falling snow full of a sense that something beautiful was happening.

You can't blame the press for this. As well expect the British Admiralty to describe a sunrise over Valona as to expect a story of our snowstorm to begin:

> The soul of New York was thrilled today by a lovely and capering snowfall that painted ghostly summer on the trees of Central Park and brought to the harried citizens of the town a few hours of esthetic exaltation superior to anything the stage or screen has offered this season.

Yet this is why the snow was news. The town looked up and saw Pavlova in the air, saw Cellini at work, and consorted with seraphs. But journalistic tradition kept reporters from stating the truth of what they had seen and experienced—the white capes on the electric signs, the white-haloed lampposts, the shrubbery looking like lace fountains; the busy snow-covered streets suddenly haunted with long-ago village memories, the familiar and the commonplace taking on rakish fairy-tale contours. The buildings swayed behind white veils like ballet dancers; there were Moorish rooftops where only factory chimneys had been, and muted avenues that seemed to be sleepwalking and full of dreams.

People on the street had the look of those jerky figures in the old silent films, and seemed launched on equally dramatic errands. The poor looked full of a poetry usually missing from their poverty, and the rich acquired a carnival air that seldom attaches to mink coats.

Yet it was only a sonnet of a snowfall. I am sure most of us hoped for more, and dreamed of impassable roads, of gas buggies reduced to impotence, of inaccessible offices, of an hour of childhood the storm would bring them if it lasted long enough to blot out the face of the boss and the world crises.

Perhaps the memories were the real news. For of all pleasant events of the past, a snowstorm is about the only thing that hasn't changed. No new meanings have come into the flakes. They have not been harnessed for progress or conquest. They have remained an unaltered souvenir of happier days. And so when the snow came down, people drifted with it into the past, smelled again the freshness of young and untroubled times.

When Summer Bursts

by Joan Mills

IN THE upward drift of spring, I accumulate a longing for the ultimate confrontation with blaze and brilliance—summer; the sun and the year at their zenith. Daily, as earth turns, a fragile thread of tension pulls ever more taut in me. I begin to ask: "Is it now?"

In our garden, bees thrum over a multitude of blossoms and spiral exultantly into the sky—but the sky is not yet the blue of summer. A baby, last year a-drowse with newness on his mother's shoulder, this year makes his first barefoot tracks in dew-tipped grass. Still, summer has not come—quite.

Girls in pretty dresses are faintly gilded; soft shadows shorten at noon; boys strip for a first swing off a rope into a country pond, and surface in a thrash of shivering surprise—how can water be so chill when the calendar now says summer? When, *when*, will the sun be hot enough to brown the girls, bedazzle every noontide, and warm the water for adventuring boys?

At last, on the fourth morning of July, the fine thread of tension snaps: a boy wakes, blinks happily at sight of a glory day, and at once reaches under his pillow for a finger-length of forbidden firecracker. He lights it with a match and hurls it out his window. Thus summer begins with a bang; and from one end of the country to the other, 20 million kids are tossed from their beds by that joyful noise.

I wake and listen. With an inward thump of pleasure, I too salute the Fourth. "Hurrah for the splendid racket of liberty!" I think. "Hurrah for summer begun!"

For it is summer indeed. On this morning, who can doubt it? Lofty at the peak of poles, sun-bright, spangled banners lift on the shimmering air. Fresh breezes enter summer rooms and blow away a wintering of secret scents—mice, must, mothballs and memories. The ocean glints silvery and restless, sifting pebbles, patterning the sand. In clear lakes, fish sink into cooler waters, while just-christened motorboats putt past above. Today the grass grows, and tomorrow will be mowed. Today the sun is hot; ice cream is cold. Father scrubs rust from the charcoal grill, and small stomachs cramp with sudden hunger for food that is burnt and leaks catsup.

Every firecracker that bangs announces it: Summer! Listening, I am half in the moment, half in the past. Firecrackers are so rare now; each makes a solitary clap of sound. But when I was a child...

When *I* was a child, I squandered six months' allowance to celebrate a fitting Fourth. Two dollars went for firecrackers (as if ten cents' worth wasn't enough to deafen); 50 cents for cherry bombs (figuring one dud for every detonation); $3.50 for rockets, pinwheels and things to go "Pffft!" in the night. I bought seashells that opened under water, releasing tiny flags. Sparklers I loved. And punk.

Punk smelled like incense, oriental and mysterious. It mingled with salt wind from the sea; with the warm tarry smell of asphalt and the sweet smell of grass. It was the authentic fragrance of summer begun.

With punk for a smoldering scepter, we children ruled the day. Our allowances went up in smoke, making happy sounds. (Cats perched in treetops, glowery as owls; dogs flattened themselves under porches and rolled their eyes.) We pelted roofs with tin cans blasted by giant salutes, and alarmed our mothers by exploding devilish devices in kitchen ovens.

We were foolish—but on the Fourth, foolishness was a freedom we could claim. It was a gift of our parents, and of the season. We were free of shoes and rules; free to make collective uproar, or be loud alone. We were the kings and citizens of summer, and we hailed the flags that flew over our domain.

Now children fill the Fourth with lesser clamor, but they are also free. My boys swing out over the water and drop with great shouts; my daughter browns in the sun, dialing up transistorized hullabaloo. They are happy; so are we all. Each of us has a special summer freedom to savor.

The dusk that follows this good day is popcorn-scented, aflutter with moths, gentled by a lingering touch of sun. Now, and in my recollection, the Fourth seems most glorious at night.

Where I grew up, a parade still precedes darkness into town. It is led by the flag aloft, paced by drums and the proud, sour notes of young buglers. Kids in costume pass in review: George Washington, bewigged in cotton batting; clowns dour with embarrassment; a terrible cardboard dragon; Betsy Ross on a bicycle. Bands tune up by towering bonfires. Children run in circles as their elders dance in squares, and night slowly surrounds.

The very best is last—full dark, when the fireworks begin. The child in me stirs with suspense; I am ancient with nostalgia. Ever and ever it is the same—an intake of breath as the first rocket jets to heaven; the burst and spread of stars; the whole town saying, "Ahhh!"

Always at this moment I remember a night when, to my eye, the scene turned upside down. In the valley of the sky, the stars were as steady as streetlights; but earth's deep dark was populous with hurtling comets and meteors expiring in celestial sparks.

Always, too, as in my childhood, I feel a minor ache of melancholy when the life melts out of each starburst—but every next flight of rockets creates new stars. Aerial bombs wake echoes 12 months unheard. Pinwheels whirl dervishly, and Roman candles pop pink fireballs.

Light and noise fragment the sky; it is almost too much of much—and never quite enough. Even the grand finale fails to finish it. Children past their bedtime wave sparklers. "Look at me!" they cry, swirling traceries of white on the surface of the dark. "Look at *me!*"

I do look. I see the child I was, chasing the shadows of the children that are mine—through summer days as fine and free as this one and summer nights sky-streaked with falling stars. Memory, the moment, the season's promise now are joined. Summer is in my heart and everywhere about.

*Informative...Entertaining...Essential Books
From America's Most Trusted Magazine*
READER'S DIGEST

THE AMERICAN SPIRIT 05016-5/$2.50_____
is a fascinating collection of articles and stories that express the unique spirit of freedom called "American."

KEEPING FIT 05017-3/$2.50_____
tells you the vital secrets of good health: what to eat, how to exercise, for a longer, healthier life.

LOVE AND MARRIAGE 05014-9/$2.50_____
contains provocative, informative articles and stories about every aspect of life's most intimate adventure.

RAISING KIDS 05015-7/$2.50_____
offers practical advice on health, manners, dealing with adolescents—a must for everyone who wants to appreciate the joys of raising kids.

Berkley/Reader's Digest Books

Available at your local bookstore or return this form to:
Berkley Book Mailing Service
P.O. Box 690
Rockville Centre, NY 11570

Please send me the above titles. I am enclosing $_____
(Please add 50¢ per copy to cover postage and handling). Send check or money order—no cash or C.O.D.'s. Allow six weeks for delivery.

NAME_____
ADDRESS_____
CITY_____STATE/ZIP_____ 90

Four Entertaining, Informative Books From America's Most Trusted Magazine
READER'S DIGEST

DRAMA IN REAL LIFE 04723-7/$2.50 _____
contains stories of endurance, ingenuity and incredible bravery that take place among real people in unexpected situations.

THE LIVING WORLD OF NATURE 04720-2/$2.50 _____
explores the marvels and mysteries of earth, sea and sky in a collection of distinguished essays by nature specialists.

UNFORGETTABLE CHARACTERS 04722-9/$2.50 _____
is drawn from the highly popular "The Most Unforgettable Character I Ever Met" series, featuring short, amusing tales of both the famous and the obscure.

WORD POWER 04721-0/$2.50 _____
is a fascinating anthology of tests from "It Pays to Enrich Your Word Power," with articles by such language experts as Clifton Fadiman, Edwin Newman and Vance Packard.   *Berkley/Reader's Digest Books*

Available at your local bookstore or return this form to:
Berkley Book Mailing Service
P.O. Box 690
Rockville Centre. NY 11570

Please send me the above titles. I am enclosing $_____
(Please add 75¢ per copy to cover postage and handling). Send check or money order—no cash or C.O.D.'s. Allow six weeks for delivery.

NAME_____
ADDRESS_____
CITY_____ STATE/ZIP_____ 82